WEB DESIGN

INTRODUCTORY

WEB DESIGN

6th Edition

INTRODUCTORY

JENNIFER T. CAMPBELL

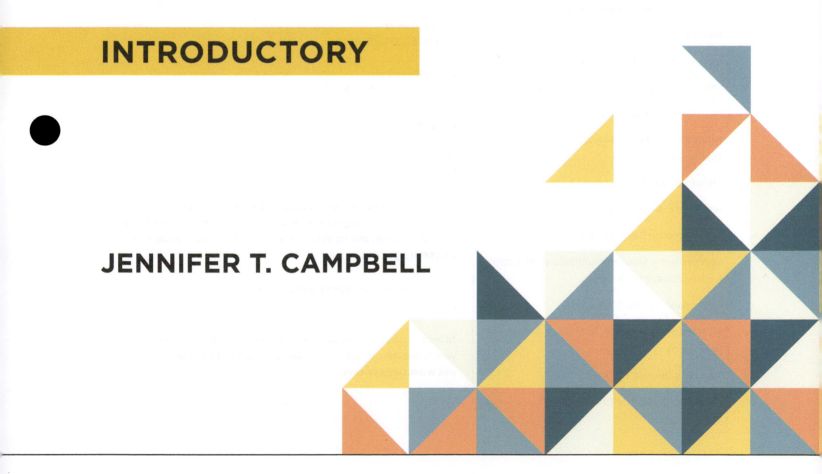

CENGAGE

Shelly Cashman Series

Australia • Brazil • Mexico • Singapore • United Kingdom • United States

Web Design: Introductory, **Sixth Edition**
Jennifer T. Campbell

SVP, GM Science, Technology & Math:
Balraj Kalsi

Senior Product Director: Kathleen McMahon

Product Team Manager: Kristin McNary

Associate Product Manager: Kate Mason

Executive Director of Development:
Julia Caballero

Senior Content Development Manager:
Leigh Hefferon

Associate Content Developer: Maria Garguilo

Development Editor: Karen Porter

Product Assistant: Jake Toth

Manuscript Quality Assurance: John Freitas

Senior Production Director: Wendy Troeger

Production Director: Patty Stephan

Senior Content Project Manager:
Jennifer Feltri-George

Manufacturing Planner: Julio Esperas

Art Director: Diana Graham

Cover Template Designer: Diana Graham

Cover image(s): Mrs. Opossum/Shutterstock.com;
karawan/Shutterstock.com

Compositor: Lumina Datamatics

VP, Marketing for Science, Technology, & Math:
Jason Sakos

Marketing Director: Michele McTighe

Marketing Manager: Jeff Tousignant

For product information and technology assistance, contact us at
**Cengage Customer & Sales Support, 1-800-354-9706
or support.cengage.com.**

For permission to use material from this text or product, submit all requests online at **www.cengage.com/permissions.**

Library of Congress Control Number: 2017932190

Student Edition:
ISBN: 978-1-337-27793-8

Loose-leaf Edition:
ISBN: 978-1-337-68572-6

Cengage
20 Channel Street
Boston, MA 02210
USA

Cengage is a leading provider of customized learning solutions with employees residing in nearly 40 different countries and sales in more than 125 countries around the world. Find your local representative at:
www.cengage.com.

Cengage products are represented in Canada by
Nelson Education, Ltd.

To learn more about Cengage platforms and services, register or access your online learning solution, or purchase materials for your course, visit **www.cengage.com.**

Printed at CLDPC, USA, 10-20

Contents

Chapter 4

Chapter 5

Chapter 6

Preface

In this Shelly Cashman Series® *Web Design: Introductory, Sixth Edition* book, you will find an educationally sound and easy-to-follow pedagogy that artfully combines screen shots, marginal elements, and text with full color to produce a visually appealing and easy-to-understand presentation of web design. This textbook conveys useful design concepts and techniques necessary to start a career in web design. It explains the connections between a detailed design plan that considers audience needs, design trends and considerations, and technical requirements. Students learn the principles that go into creating a successful, responsive website.

The book's seven chapters emphasize key concepts and principles with numerous Design Tips boxed throughout the text. A variety of challenging research-based and hands-on activities, both within and at the conclusion of each chapter test comprehension, build web research skills and design awareness and encourage critical thinking about current issues in web design.

Objectives of This Textbook

Web Design: Introductory, Sixth Edition is intended for a one-unit introductory web design course or a web authoring course that teaches web design techniques and also covers HTML, creating device- and platform-independent websites using responsive web design techniques, CSS, and SEO. The objectives of this book are to:

- Present a practical approach to web design using a blend of traditional development guidelines with current technologies and trends, including responsive web design

- Give students an in-depth understanding of web design concepts and techniques that are essential to planning, designing, creating, testing, publishing, and maintaining websites

- Define and describe in detail the six steps in developing a solid web design plan: identify the website's purpose and target audience; determine the website's general content; select the website's structure; specify the website's navigation system; design the look and feel of the website; and test, publish, and maintain the website

- Encourage critical thinking through the extensive end-of-chapter exercises and the Your Turn exercises within each chapter

- Provide students with Toolkit marginal elements that indicate related content available in the appendices

- Direct students to the web to do additional research, and allow them to evaluate and assess the design techniques and technologies discussed in the book by providing them with search terms in the Q&A marginal elements, Your Turn exercises, and end-of-chapter exercises

- Provide an ongoing case study and assignments that promote student participation in learning about web design

Distinguishing Features

The distinguishing features of *Web Design: Introductory, Sixth Edition* include the following:

Responsive Web Design

This text focuses on the basic concepts of responsive web design that teach considerations for creating websites that are device- and platform-independent.

A Blend of Traditional Development with Current Technologies

This book goes beyond a theoretical view of web design; every effort has been made to use procedures, tools, and solutions that parallel those used by web designers in today's business world.

Realistic examples support definitions, concepts, and techniques, enabling students to learn in the context of solving realistic problems, much like the ones they will encounter while working in the web design field. In this textbook, students learn to apply best practices while avoiding common pitfalls. In addition, the numerous Design Tips summarize and highlight important topics.

Visually Appealing

The design of this textbook combines screen shots, drawings, marginal elements, boxes, tables, and text into a visually appealing and easy-to-read book. The screen shots and figures in the book reinforce important points and show screen shots that reflect the web design topics being discussed. The marginal elements and boxes highlight features such as exploratory exercises, design topics, common questions and answers, and search terms for students to do additional research on the web.

Introductory Presentation of Web Design

No previous web design experience is assumed, and no prior programming experience is required. This book is written specifically for students for whom continuity, simplicity, and practicality are essential.

> More than 80 Design Tips are boxed throughout the book. The purpose of the Design Tips is to reinforce the surrounding content by summarizing the web design topic being discussed.

Toolkit Feature

The Toolkit elements in the margins indicate relevant, additional coverage in one of the appendices: HTML5, CSS, Responsive Web Design, and SEO. The appendices explore these topics in more technical detail.

Your Turn Exercises

Multiple Your Turn exercises within each chapter provide hands-on activities that allow students to put concepts and skills learned in the chapter to practical, real-world use. Your Turn exercises call for critical thinking and often require online research.

Q&A Boxes

These marginal annotations provide answers to common questions that complement the topics covered, adding depth and perspective to the learning process.

Organization of This Textbook

Web Design: Introductory, Sixth Edition provides basic instruction on how to plan and design a successful website that achieves the website's intended purpose. The material comprises seven chapters, four appendices, and a glossary/index.

CHAPTER 1 — THE ENVIRONMENT AND THE TOOLS   In Chapter 1, students are introduced to the Internet, World Wide Web, websites, and web pages. Topics include domain names; how the Internet and the web influence society; methods and devices users use to connect to the Internet and the web; types of websites; tools for creating websites; and web design roles.

CHAPTER 2 — WEB PUBLISHING FUNDAMENTALS   In Chapter 2, students are introduced to the advantages of web publishing, basic design principles, and writing techniques for the web. Topics include publishing advantages related to connectivity, timeliness, interactivity, reduced production costs, and economical, rapid distribution; responsive web design issues; balance and proximity; contrast and focus; unity; scannable text; using color as a design tool; and technical, privacy, accessibility, and usability issues.

CHAPTER 3 — PLANNING A SUCCESSFUL WEBSITE: PART 1   In Chapter 3, students are introduced to the initial three steps in the six-step planning process for developing a solid website design plan: (1) identify the website's purpose and target audience; (2) determine the website's general content; and (3) select the website's structure. Topics include identifying a specific topic for a website; defining target audience wants, needs, and expectations; choosing content; adding value-added content; and using an outline, storyboard, or flowchart to plan the site's structure.

CHAPTER 4 — PLANNING A SUCCESSFUL WEBSITE: PART 2   In Chapter 4, students are introduced to the remaining three steps in the planning process for developing a design plan: (4) specify the website's structure; (5) design the look of the website; and (6) test, publish, and maintain the website. Topics include the relationship between page length, content placement, and usability; maintaining visual consistency across all pages at the site using color and page layout; and creating both a user-based and a user-controlled navigation and search system that works with touch screens and all device types. A final design plan checklist is provided.

CHAPTER 5 — TYPOGRAPHY AND IMAGES   In Chapter 5, students are introduced to typography and images for the web environment. Topics include typographic principles, guidelines, and tips; web image file formats and sources; and optimization techniques for creating web-ready images.

CHAPTER 6 — MULTIMEDIA AND INTERACTIVITY   In Chapter 6, students are introduced to the basics of multimedia and interactivity and methods to add these elements to web pages. Topics include guidelines and sources for using multimedia; types of web page animation; adding and editing web page audio and video; and web-based forms, avatars, live chat, and other interactive web page elements.

CHAPTER 7 — PROMOTING AND MAINTAINING A WEBSITE   In Chapter 7, students learn how to implement a plan to test, publish, promote, and maintain a website successfully. Topics include beta testing of webpages; acquiring server space and uploading a website's files to a server; promoting a published website using search tools, social media, and online advertising networks; the importance of regular website maintenance; and using web analytics to evaluate website performance.

APPENDIX A — HTML5   This Appendix is a reference for HTML, a markup language used to create webpages. A fundamental knowledge of HTML5 tools helps interpret the source code of features and functions found on other websites that students might want to include on their own websites.

APPENDIX B — CASCADING STYLE SHEETS (CSS)   The CSS Appendix is a brief introduction to Cascading Style Sheets in support of the discussion of CSS in various chapters in this book.

APPENDIX C — RESPONSIVE WEB DESIGN   This Appendix provides a brief introduction to the decision-making process and the technologies and considerations involved when creating a site for multiple devices, platforms, and screen sizes.

APPENDIX D — SEARCH ENGINE OPTIMIZATION (SEO)   This Appendix introduces students to how search engines rank and evaluate websites to include in search results as well as techniques for and careers in SEO.

End-of-Chapter Student Activities

A notable strength of the Shelly Cashman Series textbooks is the extensive student activities at the end of each chapter. Well-structured student activities can make the difference between students merely participating in a class and students retaining the information they learn. The activities in this book include the following:

- **CHAPTER REVIEW**   A review of chapter highlights is presented at the end of each chapter.

- **TERMS TO KNOW**   This list of key terms found in the chapter together with the page numbers on which the terms are defined helps students master the chapter material.

- **TEST YOUR KNOWLEDGE**   Two pencil-and-paper activities are designed to test students' understanding of the material in the chapter: matching terms and short-answer questions.

- **TRENDS**   The Trends exercises encourage students to explore the latest developments in the web design technologies and concepts introduced in the chapter.

- **@ISSUE** Web design is not without its controversial issues. At the end of each chapter, two topics are presented that challenge students to examine critically their perspective of web design concepts and technologies.

- **HANDS ON** To complete their introduction to web design, these exercises require that students use the web to gather and evaluate additional information about the concepts and techniques discussed in the chapter.

- **TEAM APPROACH** Two Team Approach assignments engage students, getting them to work collaboratively to reinforce the concepts in the chapter.

- **CASE STUDY** The Case Study is an ongoing development process in web design using the concepts, techniques, and Design Tips presented in each section. The Case Study requires students to apply their knowledge starting in Chapter 1 and continuing through Chapter 7 as they prepare, plan, create, and then publish their own websites.

Instructor Resources

The Instructor Resources include both teaching and testing aids and can be accessed online at www.cengage.com/login.

- **INSTRUCTOR'S MANUAL** Includes lecture notes summarizing the chapter sections, figures and boxed elements found in every chapter, teacher tips, classroom activities, lab activities, and quick quizzes in Microsoft Word files.

- **SYLLABUS** Contains easily customizable sample syllabi that cover policies, assignments, exams, and other course information.

- **FIGURE FILES** Illustrations for every figure in the textbook are available in electronic form. Figures are provided both with and without callouts.

- **POWERPOINT PRESENTATIONS** A one-click-per-slide presentation system provides PowerPoint slides for every subject in each chapter. Presentations are based on chapter objectives.

- **TEST BANK AND TEST ENGINE** Test Banks include questions for every chapter, feature objective-based and critical-thinking question types, and include page number references and figure references, when appropriate.

- **ADDITIONAL ACTIVITIES FOR STUDENTS** Consists of Chapter Reinforcement Exercises, which are true/false, multiple-choice, and short-answer questions that help students gain confidence in the material learned.

1 | The Environment and the Tools

© 2016 Microsoft

© 2016 Facebook

© 2013 Condé Nast

Introduction

Using new and developing technologies, even beginner web developers can create professional-looking websites that include multimedia, social media, and dynamic content viewable on various devices and screen sizes. Applying web technologies is only one part of what is required to produce a successful website: a website that effectively communicates, educates, entertains, or provides a venue for conducting business transactions also requires good web design. This book explains the basic elements of good web design and shows you how to develop compelling websites and webpages for specific purposes or audiences. This chapter begins the process by describing the Internet and the World Wide Web. Next, you learn about the various ways users connect to the Internet. The chapter then describes different types of websites and the tools for creating them. Finally, the chapter discusses the various roles, responsibilities, and skills essential to successful web design.

Objectives

After completing this chapter, you will be able to:

1. Describe the Internet and the World Wide Web
2. Discuss ways to access the Internet and the web
3. Categorize types of websites
4. Identify web design tools
5. Explain web design principles, roles, and required skills

The Internet and the World Wide Web

A computer **network** consists of connected computers, mobile devices, printers, and data storage devices that share computing resources and data. Computer networks are everywhere—in home offices, in student computer labs, in public places such as coffee shops and libraries, and in the offices of organizations and businesses around the world. The **Internet** is a worldwide public network (Figure 1-1) that connects millions of these private networks. For example, on a college campus, the student lab network, the faculty computer network, and the administration network all can connect to the Internet.

Figure 1-1 The Internet is a worldwide public network that connects private networks.

© Mmaxer/Shutterstock.com; © Alfonso de Tomas/Shutterstock.com; © SSSCCC/Shutterstock. com; © iStockphoto.com/Petar Chernaev/Pixelfit; © amfoto/Shutterstock.com; © iStockphoto.com/scanrail; ©iStockphoto.com/scanrail; © iStockphoto.com/sweetym; Source: Microsoft; © Oleksiy Mark/Shutterstock.com; Source: © iStockphoto.com/SKrow; © iStockphoto.com/skodonnell; Source: Apple Inc; © iStockphoto.com/skodonnell; Source: Nutrition Blog Network; © iStockphoto.com/arattansi; Source: Microsoft; © Oleksiy Mark/Shutterstock.com; Source: Microsoft

Q&A

Are the Internet and the web the same thing?

Although some use the terms *Internet* and *web* interchangeably, the Internet and the web are not one and the same. The Internet is a worldwide public network that links private networks and gives users access to a variety of resources for communication, research, file sharing, and commerce. The web, a subset of the Internet, is just one of those resources.

Q&A

What is a landing page?

A **landing page** is the page on a website that a visitor sees when he or she clicks a link from an ad, search engine result, or social media promotion. The copy on a landing page is specific to the method by which the user arrived at the page and often is a marketing tool. A landing page can be, but is not always, a website's home page.

World Wide Web

The **World Wide Web (web)** is a part of the Internet that consists of connected computers called **web servers** that store electronic documents called webpages. A **webpage** is a specially formatted document that can contain images, text, interactive elements, and hyperlinks. A **hyperlink**, or simply a **link**, is a word, phrase, or image that connects webpages. A **website** is a group of related webpages. A website's primary page, or **home page**, typically provides information about the website's purpose and content. Figure 1-2 shows the home page of Jive Software. Jive's home page includes standard home page elements, including a company logo, navigation elements, a search feature, and links to additional content.

As previously stated, a link provides access to other webpages. Figure 1-3 shows the Gourmet.com home page and the webpage that appears when you click a link on the home page. You often can identify a text link by its appearance. Text links usually are bold, underlined, or differ in color from the rest of the text. An image link might be more difficult to identify visually; however, if you are using a desktop or laptop computer, pointing to either a text or image link with the mouse pointer changes the pointer from

Figure 1-2 A website's primary page is its home page.

Figure 1-3 Webpages at the same website or across different websites are connected by links.

an arrow to a hand pointer. When you click a link, you might view a picture or video, listen to a song, jump to a different webpage at the same website, or move to a webpage at a different website. **Browsing** or **surfing the web** is exploring the web by moving from one webpage to another. To visually indicate that you have previously clicked a text link, the color of the text link might change. You can see this change in color when you return to the webpage containing the clicked link.

Q&A

Who originally created the World Wide Web?
Historians credit Tim Berners-Lee, a programmer at CERN in Switzerland, with the early vision and technological developments that led to today's World Wide Web.

Whether you choose to indicate hyperlinks in text by color, bold, or underline, be consistent throughout your website.

DESIGN TIP

Influence on Society

The Internet and the web have influenced the way the world communicates, educates, entertains, and conducts business significantly. Friends, families, and business colleagues electronically exchange messages, documents, and information using texting, email, collaborative workspaces, and chat programs. Students use the web for research, to access podcasts or transcripts of lectures, or to collaborate on a group project. Individuals access the Internet and the web for entertainment using gaming, music, video, and other apps on their computers or mobile devices. Consumers who shop online save time, gas, and sometimes money by taking advantage of online shopping websites and websites that offer reviews and pricing comparisons. Businesses use Internet and web technologies to interact with their suppliers and customers for increased productivity and profitability. Businesses also can use tools such as videoconferencing to reduce costs associated with business travel or to allow employees to telecommute.

COMMUNICATION   Individuals and organizations of all types use websites to communicate ideas and information. By effectively designing webpages and selectively choosing content, you can ensure that your website's webpages deliver the website's message successfully and persuasively. When a webpage's design is consistent, balanced, and focused, and the content communicates trustworthiness, timeliness, and value, such as the MSN home page shown in Figure 1-4, you are more likely to spend time on it and even return to it. You can save a link to the webpage, called a **bookmark** or **favorite**, create a **shortcut** to it on your desktop or mobile device's home screen, or access the company or organization's social media profiles. On the other hand, you quickly will move on from a poorly designed website or if the content appears unreliable, outdated, or trivial. You will learn more about design values in Chapter 2.

Other communication options that rely on Internet and web technologies include email, blogging, social networking, social bookmarking, chat, instant messaging, virtual meetings and collaborative workspaces, video sharing, VoIP, interactive gaming, and 3D virtual worlds.

Q&A

Is the Internet's societal influence all good?
Being constantly connected has its price. In the past, employees' workdays were done when they physically left the office. Now employees might feel pressure to keep on top of work-related communication during what used to be personal, family, or leisure time. The need to constantly check social media, sports scores, or text messages can have a negative effect on human relationships. To learn more, use a search engine to search for *the Internet's negative effects*.

Figure 1-4 The MSN home page communicates up-to-date, accurate information.

Businesses and individuals heavily rely on electronic messages called **email**. Popular email software, such as Mozilla® Thunderbird®, Microsoft Outlook®, or Google Gmail™, allows users to attach graphics, video, sound, and other computer files to email messages. Email is a fast, inexpensive, and widely used online communication tool.

Internet Relay Chat (IRC) and **web chat** are communication technologies that provide a venue, such as a group chat or discussion forum, where a group of users can exchange text, video, files, or multimedia messages in real time. **Instant messaging**, also called **IM chat**, and **group messaging apps** are another popular way individuals can exchange messages in real time using a chat window that is only visible to those participating in the chat. Examples of IM chat programs are AOL's AIM®, Yahoo! Messenger, and Trillian™. IRC chats are public exchanges between two or more people in a chat room, who may or may not know each other or share a connection in social media. With an IM or group messaging program, you privately chat with people with whom you have opted to connect using the group messaging platform or social media. Social networking platforms such as Facebook (Figure 1-5) and Twitter include IM technology.

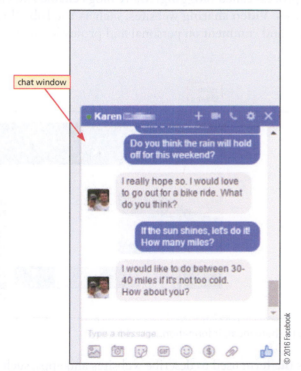

chat window

Figure 1-5 IM chat programs allow users to exchange private messages in real time.

Group conferencing software, such as Skype for Business, WebEx, and GoToMeeting (Figure 1-6), provides access to **collaborative workspaces** or **virtual meeting spaces**, which are websites that allow users to communicate with each other using text, audio, video, whiteboard, and shared files without leaving their own desks. Businesses that use collaborative workspaces and virtual meeting spaces can improve employee productivity and reduce expenses.

Q&A

What is cloud computing?
The term **cloud computing** refers to an environment where files and software are stored and shared online. For example, Google Drive™ provides a suite of online software, file storage, and collaboration tools. You can edit, save, and share documents without downloading either the software or the files to your computer.

Q&A

What is an app?
An **app** (short for **application**) is a software program. The term *app* typically refers to programs that run on mobile devices (*mobile apps*) or the web (*web apps*). Apps are an integral part of Internet technology. This book focuses on general web design principles rather than app development, design, and integration.

Q&A

What is text speak?
Text speak describes abbreviations and shortcuts for phrases commonly used by text and chat users, such as LOL (laugh out loud) or gr8 (great). For more information, use a search engine to search for *text speak*.

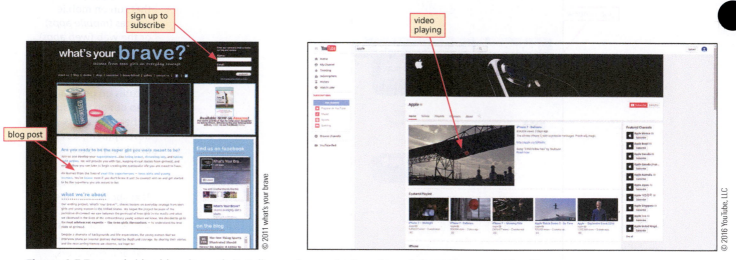

Figure 1-6 Collaborative workspaces support teamwork from remote locations.

A **blog** (short for *weblog*), such as What's Your Brave? (Figure 1-7), is an online journal or diary. Millions of people go online to share ideas and information by hosting and participating in blogs—a process called **blogging**. Many blogs enable and encourage users to add comments to posts. **Video sharing** websites, such as YouTube (Figure 1-7) and Vimeo, allow users to share and comment on personal and professional videos and also feature video blogs (vlogs).

Figure 1-7 Text and video blogging websites allow web users to share ideas, information, and video files.

Social networking is the term used to describe websites and apps, such as Twitter, Instagram, Facebook, and LinkedIn (Figure 1-8), that allow participants to create a personal network of friends or business contacts. Users then use communication tools provided by the website or app to interact with those in their personal network by sharing text, comments, pictures, articles, videos, contacts, and more. **Social bookmarking**, provided by websites such as Delicious, Pinterest, and Digg (Figure 1-8), allows users to share their webpage favorites, news articles, bookmarks, and **tags**—keywords that reference specific images or documents—with others.

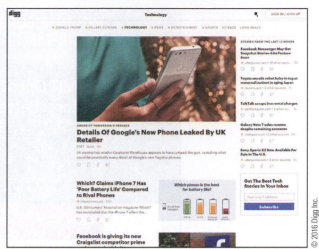

Figure 1-8 Social networking and social bookmarking websites allow users to share information with one another.

Gamers by the millions interact with each other by playing **massively multiplayer online games (MMOGs)**, such as Minecraft™ and World of Warcraft®. Others create alternative personas that live exclusively online in **3D virtual worlds**, such as Second Life® or Entropia Universe®.

A **wiki** is a group of related webpages to which users add, edit, or delete content. A well-known example of a wiki is Wikipedia, an online encyclopedia. Figure 1-9 shows a Wikipedia webpage that displays information about Wi-Fi.

Figure 1-9 Wikipedia and other wiki websites enable users to catalog and manage content collaboratively.

EDUCATION There are very few topics you cannot learn about on the web. You can take an online course from an academic institution to earn a degree or certificate, or watch a video or read a blog post by amateurs or experts. Many universities and academic institutions, such as MIT (Figure 1-10), publish some or all of their educational materials online, including homework and video lectures, so that they are free and open to everyone. A **Massive Open Online Course (MOOC)** is an online course delivered over the web, often for free. Many MOOCs are self-guided, but others offer interactive user forums and provide virtual assistance and other resources.

Figure 1-10 The web offers formal and informal teaching and learning opportunities.

Q&A

Are online classes real time or any time?
Some online classes are synchronous, or real time, requiring students to be online to listen or participate in lessons and lectures at a certain time. Others are any time, or asynchronous, meaning that students can download lectures as podcasts or transcripts and add comments or answer questions at the student's convenience.

Instructors often use the web to publish podcasts or videos of lectures, webpage links for research, syllabi and grades, and more for their students. A **learning management system (LMS)** is a program or app that provides a scheduling, communication, and document sharing platform for students and teachers. Many LMS apps, such as Blackboard®, Moodle™ (Figure 1-11), or SkillSoft®, offer additional learning and testing resources.

moodle   About ▾   Solutions ▾   MoodleCloud ▾   News   Stories   Contact

Wish all your learners were on the same page?

Moodle is the open source platform that lets you build the perfect education solution for your needs.

LEARN MORE

Your wish is our command. Powerful and Free solutions from Moodle.

You can download Moodle software from our community site and install it on your own servers. However, if you need more, you've come to the right place!

moodle
CERTIFIED SERVICES
partner

Figure 1-11 An LMS enables communication and file sharing among teachers and students.

Any formal or informal educational website should contain content that is timely, accurate, and appealing. Such websites also should include elements to provide feedback, maintain records, and assess learning. In addition, educational websites should supply information about the authority or experience of the website's content providers.

DESIGN TIP

ENTERTAINMENT AND NEWS   Interactive multimedia experiences and continually updated content lure millions of people to the web for entertainment and news. Popular entertainment websites offer music, videos, sports, games, and more. For example, you can use the web to watch last night's episode of your favorite television program, check out entertainment news at IMDb (Figure 1-12), or play fantasy baseball at mlb.com. At sophisticated entertainment and news websites such as NBCNews.com (Figure 1-12), you can read news stories or watch video clips from programs or live broadcasts of event coverage. Additionally, the NBC News website provides interactive elements, such as immersive 360 videos of news events or the ability to share an article on your social media profile.

Figure 1-12 Entertainment and news websites provide continually updated multimedia content.

Include methods to share your website's content by providing links to allow users to send content using email, or post to a Facebook page, RSS feed, or account on Pinterest or Twitter. Also provide links to related content that your users would find interesting and relevant.

DESIGN TIP

E-COMMERCE   Electronic commerce or e-commerce encompasses a wide variety of online business activities, including consumer shopping and investing and the exchange of business data and transactions within a company or among multiple companies (Figure 1-13). For example, a pet groomer might offer his or her services using an e-commerce website where a pet owner could find valuable information, such as the groomer's telephone number, location, list of services, and rates charged; the pet owner then could schedule an appointment online. At the other end of the e-commerce spectrum, a large manufacturing company could use the Internet and the web to communicate policies and procedures to its employees, exchange business information with its vendors and other business partners, process sales transactions, and provide online support to its customers.

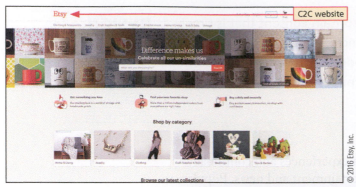

Figure 1-13 E-commerce involves all business transactions that use the Internet.

E-commerce websites can be categorized by the participants involved in the transactions (Figure 1-14), such as businesses and consumers.

E-Commerce Transaction Types

Category	Description
Business-to-consumer (B2C) e-commerce	B2C e-commerce involves the sale of an endless assortment of products and services directly to consumers. Transactions take place between an online business and an individual consumer.
Business-to-business (B2B) e-commerce	B2B e-commerce involves the sale of products and services and the exchange of data between businesses, and accounts for the majority of e-commerce transactions in the corporate world.
Consumer-to-consumer (C2C) e-commerce	In C2C e-commerce, business transactions occur between consumers. Examples of C2C e-commerce include online auctions and person-to-person classified ads.

Figure 1-14 B2C, B2B, and C2C are types of e-commerce transactions.

DESIGN TIP To develop an e-commerce website, you must determine the potential customers for your products or services. If appropriate to do so, associate your e-commerce website with a database that supplies up-to-date product information such as available inventory, sizes, colors, and more. Provide a search feature so that customers can easily find what they need, as well as electronic payment services, such as direct purchase or a third-party payment service such as PayPal.

Ways to Access the Internet and the Web

Users access the Internet and web using a variety of means. In the earliest days of the web, the most common way to access the Internet was using a telephone line.

The speed at which data travels from one device to another is the **transfer rate**. Transfer rates measure the number of bits the line can transmit in one second (expressed as *bits per second*, or *bps*). Transfer rates range from thousands of bits per second (called *kilobits per second* or **kbps**) to millions of bits per second (called *megabits per second* or **Mbps**). A faster transfer rate translates into more expensive Internet access. Higher-quality connections are better suited for viewing or listening to **streaming media**—video or sound that downloads to a computer continuously to be watched or listened to in real time, such as watching TV programs, web conferencing, and gaming. Transfer rate has a direct impact on the user's experience with a website; Chapter 2 discusses the effect of Internet access speeds on web design considerations.

Broadband Connections

Today, most individuals and businesses are able to access the Internet and web over a broadband connection. The term **broadband** defines high-speed data transmissions over a communication channel that can transmit multiple signals at one time. Types of broadband connections available include:

- **Digital subscriber line (DSL)**: A **digital subscriber line (DSL)** is a dedicated digital line that transmits at fast speeds on existing standard copper telephone wiring. An **asymmetrical digital subscriber line (ADSL)** is a type of DSL that supports faster transmissions when receiving data than when sending data.
- **Cable television (CATV) line**: Data can travel very rapidly through a cable modem connected to a **cable television (CATV) line**, enabling home or business users to connect to the Internet over the same coaxial cable that delivers television transmissions. Using a splitter, the line from the cable company connects to both the television and computer.
- **FTTP: Fiber to the Premises (FTTP)** uses fiber-optic cable to provide high-speed Internet access to homes and businesses. FTTP requires a permanent physical location for the network and router; costs for FTTP are decreasing steadily.
- **Satellite:** Using a satellite dish that communicates with a satellite modem, this method provides high-speed wireless Internet connections.

Connecting to the Internet and the Web

Most homes and businesses today use the aforementioned wireless and wired methods to connect a network to the Internet and web; users then connect to the network typically using wireless methods. People not physically connected to a network can use their computer or mobile device to access the Internet and web using **mobile wireless** technologies, which include radio signals, **wireless fidelity (Wi-Fi)** technologies, cellular telephones, and wireless providers' broadband networks. Wi-Fi provides wireless connectivity to devices within a certain range. A Wi-Fi network may be password-protected or open to the public.

Q&A **What is fixed wireless connectivity?**
Fixed wireless is an Internet connectivity service that uses satellite technology to connect stationary objects. Radio signals transferred between a transmitting tower and an antenna on a house or business provide a high-speed connection.

Q&A **Are there risks to using Wi-Fi?**
Security experts recommend that when using a public or municipal Wi-Fi network, avoid accessing personal information, such as financial transactions. If you have a Wi-Fi network in your home or business, use passwords and encryption to avoid unauthorized and potentially damaging access by others. For more information, use a search engine to search for *public and municipal Wi-Fi safety tips*.

Q&A **What is Bluetooth?**
Bluetooth is a popular, short-range wireless connection that uses a radio frequency to transmit data between two electronic devices, such as a smartphone and an earpiece.

Q&A

What is 5G and when can I expect it?
5G systems will continue to provide increased transfer speeds, as well as widen coverage areas. Experts expect 5G systems to make an impact in 2020.

Mobile Internet Access

Generations classify standards for mobile communications, including voice, mobile Internet access, video calls, and mobile TV. **3G**, the third generation, provides mobile broadband access to devices such as laptop computers and smartphones. 3G devices support speech and data services, as well as data rates of at least 200 kbps. **4G** systems improve on 3G standards by supporting services such as gaming apps and streaming media.

Mobile devices that provide Internet access include smartphones, tablets, ebook readers, laptop computers, and other handheld and mobile devices. These devices use an internal antenna or wireless card to connect to the Internet either at a **hot spot**, a location that provides public Internet access, or directly to a wireless provider's network. Some mobile devices enable you to set them up as a mobile hot spot. You can pay for mobile access on a per-kb basis, or buy a flat-rate monthly plan with unlimited text and data usage.

DESIGN TIP Although large images and multimedia elements on webpages can degrade the audience's viewing experiences at slower Internet access speeds, most websites now assume that users have broadband connectivity.

Q&A

Should I use Wi-Fi with my mobile devices?
You should check your mobile provider's recommendations and your data plan to decide which method is best for you. Typically, mobile devices use significantly less cellular data when you are connected to Wi-Fi than when you are using cellular service. Many mobile plans promise limited high-speed data transfer rates per month; once a user reaches the limit of high-speed data transfer, data transfer drops to a lower rate.

Internet Service Providers

An **Internet service provider (ISP)** is a business that has a permanent Internet connection and provides temporary Internet connections to individuals and companies. ISPs are either regional or national. A **regional ISP** provides Internet access for customers (individuals or businesses) in a specific geographic area. A **national ISP** provides Internet access in most major cities and towns nationwide. National ISPs may offer more services and generally have larger technical support staffs than regional ISPs. A cable company, such as Verizon (Figure 1-15), can be an ISP as well as provide cable television and telephone access. Negotiating one price for all of those services can save you money and hassle, but it also may limit your options. If you are tied into one provider for all three services, you can choose only from within the plans offered by that provider for each service.

Q&A

How can I keep safe while using the Internet?
Using the Internet is not without risks, including exposure to computer viruses, accidentally sharing personal information, and more. Be aware that others could share anything you type and any video or photo you post, even if you consider the exchange to be private. For more information, use a search engine to search for *Internet safety tips.*

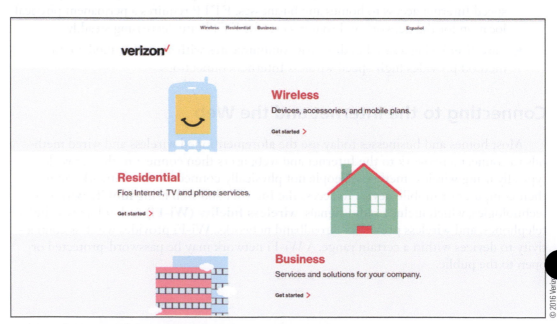

Figure 1-15 ISPs provide Internet access to homes and businesses.

Web Browsers

To view webpages, you need a **web browser**, also called a **browser**, which is a program or app that requests, downloads, and displays webpages stored on a web server. Most browsers share common features, such as an Address bar, a Favorites list, a History list, tabs that open multiple pages in one browser window, and Back and Forward buttons for navigating. The Google Chrome browser (Figure 1-16) is the most widely used browser software on desktop and laptop computers. Microsoft Edge (which replaces Internet Explorer) (Figure 1-16) and Mozilla Firefox make up a majority of the rest of the browser market, along with Opera and Safari.

Figure 1-16 Google Chrome and Microsoft Edge are examples of web browsers.

The size of a smartphone or tablet screen is much smaller than that of a desktop or laptop computer. Browsers for mobile devices take into consideration the size of your screen when displaying webpage content. Most mobile devices also include a touch screen, which enables you to interact with the device by tapping, dragging, and other touch gestures. Mobile web browsers are capable of resizing and reordering the content and navigation on a webpage to make browsing easier for mobile users. Some companies create mobile versions of their websites. Increasingly, web designers use a design strategy called **responsive web design (RWD)**. The goal of RWD is to create websites that adjust layout, and in some cases, content, to the device and screen displaying the webpages. You will learn more about RWD in later chapters. Mobile web browsers exist for tablets, smartphones, ebook readers, and other devices. Some mobile web browsers are scaled-down versions of browsers used for desktop or laptop computers. Others, such as Android, are device-specific. The website for Slate uses RWD; Figure 1-17 shows how the Slate home page appears when viewed on a desktop or laptop (left) and using a smartphone (right).

Figure 1-17 Responsive web design adjusts content and layout to fit different screen sizes.

You can access a webpage by entering its unique address, called the **Uniform Resource Locator (URL)**, in a browser's Address bar (Figure 1-18). At a minimum, a URL consists of a domain name and a top-level domain designation. Many URLs also include folder and file designations indicating the path to a specific webpage. If a URL includes folder and file names, a forward slash character follows the top-level domain designation. Other URLs specify a website category before the domain.

Figure 1-18 A URL identifies a webpage or other resource on the Internet.

Q&A

Who controls the registration of domain names?
ICANN controls the Domain Name System (DNS) and the registration of domain names through its accredited registrars, such as GoDaddy.

An **IP address** is the numeric address for a computer connected to the Internet. Every device in a computer network has an IP address. The Internet Corporation for Assigned Names and Numbers (ICANN) works with regional and local entities to assign IP addresses. A **domain name** is the text version of a computer's numeric IP address. Companies known as domain name registrars are responsible for assigning domain names. A **top-level domain (TLD)** designation (Figure 1-19) indicates the type of organization or general domain—commercial, nonprofit, network, military,

Top-Level Domains

Top-Level Domain	Domain Type	Top-Level Domain	Domain Type
.aero	Air-transportation industry	.jobs	Human resources managers
.asia	Asia Pacific community	.mil	U.S. military
.biz	Businesses	.mobi	Consumers and providers of mobile products and services
.cat	Catalan linguistic community	.museum	Museums
.com	Commercial, personal	.name	Individuals
.coop	Cooperative associations	.net	Network providers
.edu	Postsecondary institutions	.org	Noncommercial community
.gov	U.S. government	.pro	Credentialed professionals
.info	General information	.tel	Business and individual contact data
.int	International treaty organization	.travel	Travel industry

Figure 1-19 Top-level domains identify the type of organization or general domain for a registered domain name.

and so forth—of the domain name. Some countries have their own TLDs, such as Australia (.au), France (.fr), and Canada (.ca).

In a URL, a **protocol**, or rule, precedes the domain name and top-level domain designation. The protocol specifies the format used for transmitting data. For webpages, that protocol is the **Hypertext Transfer Protocol (HTTP)**, which is the communications standard for transmitting webpages over the Internet. It generally is not necessary to type the protocol when you enter the webpage domain name and top-level domain designation in the browser's Address bar.

Select a short, easy-to-remember domain name that ties directly to a website's purpose or publisher's name. Examples of effective domain names include *business.com* (business-oriented search directory) and *ask.com* (search tool).   **DESIGN TIP**

Exploring Domain Name Registration

YOUR TURN

1. Identify three to five possible domain names for a computer repair business.
2. Use a search engine to search for domain registry services.
3. Click one of the domain registry services to open it in your browser.
4. Follow the steps on the domain registry website to search existing domain names and determine whether your possible domain names are available. Locate pricing information, as well as available alternate names and TLDs.
5. Rank the options, taking both price and effectiveness into account. Which would you choose, and why?
6. Submit the results of your domain name search in the format requested by your instructor.

Types of Websites

Types of websites include personal, organizational/topical, and commercial. A website's type differs from its purpose. The type, determined by the company or individual responsible for the website's creation, is the category of website. The purpose of a website is its reason for existence—to sell products, share information, collect feedback, and so on. Chapter 3 provides detailed discussion about defining purpose. An overview of personal, organizational/topical, and commercial websites follows, along with the individual design challenges they present.

Personal Websites

Individuals create their own **personal websites** for a range of communication purposes. You might use a personal website to promote your employment credentials, share news and photos with friends and family, or share a common interest or hobby with fellow enthusiasts. Depending on your website's purpose, you might include your résumé, blog, photo gallery, biography, email address, or a description of whatever you are passionate about—from Thai food to NASCAR® racing.

Creating a personal website generally is less complex than creating other types of websites, and designers typically have fewer resources available than when creating a commercial website. Working independently, however, means you must assume all the roles

Q&A

Should I reserve a personal domain? Even if you have no current need for creating a personal website, many experts recommend reserving a personal domain name for yourself. For more information, use a search engine to search for *reserving a personal domain*.

necessary to build the website. Web roles are discussed later in this chapter. Despite these challenges, you can publish a successful website to promote yourself and your services. You also can use a content management system, discussed later in the chapter, to allow you to focus on the content of your website and not its structure. The web offers a range of tools for creating personal websites. For free alternatives to creating a personal website to communicate and share information with your friends and acquaintances, you can turn to blogging or social networking tools, such as Facebook. Rather than create a website to provide your résumé, references, and business connections to potential employers, LinkedIn provides a platform for showcasing your experience, education, and skills and also enables you to network with colleagues and others in your industry.

DESIGN TIP

Be careful what you put online, whether it is on a personal website or a social networking website. Employers and college recruiters can find information, posts, or photos quite easily, even with privacy settings enabled. Unscrupulous users scan the web for personal information, which they use for malicious purposes, such as identity theft. Assume that anything you put online has the potential to stay there forever, even if you attempt to delete or hide it.

Organizational and Topical Websites

How can I evaluate web content? As you browse the web, you will find that some organizational and topical websites lack accurate, timely, objective, and authoritative content. You must always carefully evaluate a website's content for these four elements. For more information, use a search engine to search for *critical evaluation of webpage content*.

A website owned by a group, association, or organization, whether it is a professional or amateur group, is an **organizational website**. A **topical website** focuses on a specific subject. For example, if you belong to a national photography association, you might volunteer to create an organizational website to promote member accomplishments or to encourage support and participation. Conversely, as a photographer, you might choose to design a website devoted to black-and-white photography to share your knowledge with others, including tips for amateurs, photo galleries, and online resources. The purpose of both types of websites is to provide a resource about a subject.

Professional, nonprofit, international, social, volunteer, and various other types of organizations abound on the web. Figure 1-20 shows the World Health Organization's

Figure 1-20 Organizational websites are owned by a group, association, or organization.

organizational website. An organization that lacks funding might encounter the same challenges creating its website as an individual creating a website—specifically, limited resources, including people to create and maintain the website.

Take care to ensure that your webpages contain accurate, current, objective, and authoritative content.

Commercial Websites

The goal of many **commercial websites** is to promote and sell the products or services of a business, from the smallest home-based business to the largest international enterprise. The design and content of a large enterprise's website might be much more sophisticated and complex than that of a small business's website. Figure 1-21 contrasts the home page for a large B2B enterprise, SAP, which sells and supports software, with that of a small B2C business, Constructure, which is a construction and design firm.

© 2016 SAP SE or an SAP affiliate company

© 2016 Constructure Inc.

Figure 1-21 Commercial websites promote and sell products and services.

In addition to websites that promote and sell products or services, commercial websites also include websites that generate their revenue largely from online services such as advertising—search tool websites and portal websites.

SEARCH TOOLS Search tools are websites that locate specific information on the web based on a user's search requirements. Such tools include search engines, metasearch engines, and search directories.

Q&A

Should I create an account on a website?
Many websites offer customized news, information, and experiences to users who register for an account. Registration enables a website to track content preferences to provide a custom experience. Before creating a website account, ensure that your security will be maintained by reviewing the website's privacy policies and researching user reviews.

A **search engine** is a web-based search tool that locates a webpage using a word or phrase found in the page. To find webpages on particular topics using a popular search engine, such as Google, Bing, or ask.com, you enter terms or phrases, called **keywords**, in the search engine's text box and click a button usually labeled *Search* or *Go*. The search engine compares your search keywords or phrases with the contents of its database of webpages and then displays a list of relevant pages. A **hit** is a match between a keyword search and the resulting occurrence.

A search engine might use a variety of methods to create its website database, called its **index**. For example, most search engines use **web crawlers** or **spiders**, which are programs that browse the web for new pages and then add the webpages' URLs and other information to their indexes. Some search engines might also use meta tags to build their indexes. **Meta tags**, which are special codes added to webpages, contain information such as keywords and descriptive data regarding a webpage. Other search engines might also use the information in a webpage title—the text that appears in the browser title bar when a webpage downloads—or keywords in the page text to index a webpage.

A **metasearch engine** is a search engine, such as Yippy, Info.com, or Dogpile, that performs a keyword search using multiple search engines' indexes. Figure 1-22 shows an example of a keyword search *SEO techniques* using the popular search engine Google. Figure 1-23 illustrates the same keyword search using the Info.com metasearch engine.

TOOLKIT

SEO Tools
To learn more about meta tags and other SEO tools, see Appendix D.

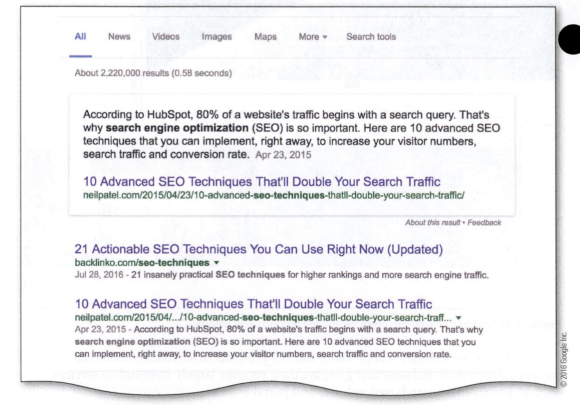

Figure 1-22 A keyword search using a search engine returns a list of webpages related to the keyword or phrase.

Figure 1-23 A metasearch engine searches the indexes of multiple search engines.

Search engine optimization (SEO) is the process of designing a webpage to increase the likelihood that the webpage will appear high in a search engine's search results list and to increase the likelihood of the webpage being visited. Search engine optimization tools include meta tags, descriptive page titles, relevant inbound links from other websites, and clearly written text.

Q&A

What is spamdexing?
Spamdexing is an example of SEO abuse, where a website uses repeated phrases, unrelated tags, and misleading headers to attempt to manipulate search results to gain a higher ranking.

DESIGN TIP

Adding meta tags to your webpages and carefully wording each webpage title can increase the probability that your webpages will be included in many search engines' indexes and that your pages will appear in search results lists for important keywords and phrases. Only include meta tags that directly relate to your website content and purpose.

In addition to designing and writing your content for SEO, you can include paid or sponsored placements in your website marketing plan. In a paid or sponsored placement, the website publisher pays the search engine a fee to list their webpages at or near the top of the search results list when a visitor uses specific keywords. Figure 1-23 illustrates an Info.com search results list for the phrase *SEO techniques*; paid placements are sponsored search results and appear prominently above the list. You will learn more about using paid or sponsored placement as a marketing tool in Chapter 7.

Unlike a search engine, a **search directory** builds its webpage index using human interaction. Website owners can submit website information to a search directory.

Q&A

When should I use a search directory or search engine?
Humans review and categorize the entries in a search directory, so if you are looking for information on a specific topic, a directory is a good place to start. Search engines will return a wider array of results, but might not be as accurate.

The search directory's editors review webpages they find or that are submitted to them, classifying them into categories such as arts and entertainment, jobs, health and fitness, travel, and news. The search directory's own webpages present a hierarchy of links—from the most general to the most specific—allowing users to target information in an organized fashion. Website directories can be general or cover only specific topics. Website directories also can include paid links within their results.

To use a search directory, such as DMOZ (Figure 1-24), you can click category and subcategory links to work your way down from the top of the hierarchy to eventually find webpages with useful information about a specific topic. For example, clicking the Food link in the search directory's general Recreation category link leads to a webpage with additional links to Food subcategories, such as Spicy. Within the Spicy subcategory, you will find links on topics ranging from Cooking to Science to Shopping, which you can click to see further categories and more specific results.

Figure 1-24 A search directory provides a hierarchy of linked categories and subcategories.

YOUR TURN

Conducting a Search Using a Search Engine

1. Use a web browser to locate the Google.com website.
2. Use the search box to search for spamdexing.
3. Click the first link and then follow additional links as necessary to locate information about spamdexing and other SEO abuse tactics.
4. Find known examples of SEO abuse and how search engines addressed them. How would you as a web designer ensure that your website followed approved SEO tactics?
5. Submit your plan in the format requested by your instructor.

Today, many popular search tools are hybrids that combine a search engine with a search directory. Additionally, some search tools actually provide the webpage indexes used by other search tools. Because search tools' webpage indexes are created in a variety of ways, the indexes can vary substantially from search tool to search tool. For best results, you should become comfortable searching the web for specific information using more than one search tool.

PORTALS **Portals**—websites that offer a starting point for accessing information—can be general consumer portals, personal portals, vertical or industry portals, or corporate portals.

- A **general consumer portal** website offers a variety of features, including search services, email, chat rooms, news and sports, maps, and online shopping. Many web users begin their web-based activities, including searching for specific information, from a portal, often setting a portal as a personal home page. Two early ISPs—AOL and MSN—and some of the web's original search tools, such as Excite and Yahoo!, have evolved into general consumer portals.
- A **personal portal** is a version of a general consumer portal, such as MyYahoo!, which a user can customize for personal preferences.
- A **vertical portal**, such as usa.gov (Figure 1-25), provides a starting point for finding information about specific areas of interest—in this example, U.S. government agency websites.
- A **corporate portal**, run on a company's intranet, provides an entry point for a company's employees and business partners into its private network.

Figure 1-25 Portals offer a variety of services, links, media, and information.

YOUR TURN

Exploring Consumer Portals

1. Use multiple tabs in a search engine to search for Excite, AOL, and MSN. Open each portal website in a different browser tab.
2. In each tab, click the portal in the search results to display the portal page.
3. Review the features offered by each of the portals. Identify the five features you believe are common to most portals.
4. Consider how analyzing the features of existing portal websites can help you plan the content for a new consumer portal website.
5. Determine how you might design a vertical portal for an area of interest. Include details such as the intended audience (for example, music fans, foodies, or outdoor enthusiasts) and sample content.
6. Submit your findings in the format requested by your instructor.

Other Types of Websites

Many other types of websites exist (Figure 1-26). Users visit travel and mapping websites to book flights or rent automobiles, get driving directions to a restaurant, or plan a bike ride. Financial websites enable users to pay bills, transfer funds between bank accounts, and make investments. Career websites provide searchable job databases, online resumes, and networking opportunities. Almost anything you would like to learn about can be found on the web: recipes, language translations, home décor, pet care, and much, much more.

Types of Websites

Category	Purpose	Examples
Travel	Book a flight or hotel	Travelocity, Expedia
Mapping	Get driving directions or plan a bike ride or run	Mapquest, MapMyRun
Financial	Pay bills, transfer funds between bank accounts, and make investments	Citizens Bank, E*Trade
Career	Search job databases, post online resumes, and network	Monster, LinkedIn, CareerBuilder
Web publishing	Publish web content in a blog or website	WordPress, Joomla!

Figure 1-26 Diverse websites exist for a variety of purposes.

Web Design Tools

Web technology is constantly changing—a new browser feature, touch screen technology, scripting language, or mobile platform seemingly revolutionizes the way the world accesses the Internet. As soon as these new technologies surface, some web designers charge ahead to implement these latest advances on their websites. Websites undoubtedly should implement web technology that represents true improvement; however, it is important first to determine the merit of new technologies. As a web designer, you should ask the following questions:

- Does the new technology meet currently accepted standards for web development and design?
- What specifically can the new technology do to further the purpose of my website?
- How will implementation of the new technology affect my website's visual appeal, accessibility, and usability?
- What impact will adding this technology have on security and other website elements?
- What are the direct and indirect costs of implementing the new technology?
- How soon will I see a return on investing in this new technology?

After evaluating the impact a new technology will have on your website, you can then make an informed decision about implementing the technology.

Make sure to integrate any new technologies with the design, features, and content of your website. Only add the new technology if it will enhance the experience for website visitors.

DESIGN TIP

Various tools exist to help you to create webpages and add dynamic content, animation, and interactivity. Successfully using these tools requires varying levels of skill and knowledge. Webpage creation tools include markup languages, Cascading Style Sheets (CSS), scripting languages, text editors, HTML editors, web development tools, web templates, and content management systems (CMS).

Markup Languages

A **markup language** is a coding system that uses tags to provide instructions about the appearance, structure, and formatting of a document. The markup languages used to create webpages are HTML, XML, and XHTML.

HTML   The **Hypertext Markup Language (HTML)** is a markup language used to create webpages. The HTML markup language uses predefined codes called **HTML tags** to define the format and organization of webpage elements. HTML tags must be in lowercase, surrounded by brackets, and inserted in pairs to define the beginning and the end of the target of the tag. For example, the *<form>....</form>* HTML tag pair indicates the beginning and the end of a webpage form, respectively. An attribute may be added to a tag to define an aspect of the target, such as the number of rows and columns in a text area. Attributes are used in the tag pair *<textarea rows="3" cols="60">....</textarea>*, for example, to specify that an area displaying text is 3 rows of text, 60 columns wide.

When a webpage downloads into a browser, the browser reads and interprets the HTML tags to display the webpage with organized and formatted text, images, and links. Figure 1-27 shows the home page of a baker, Bisousweet, and the underlying HTML code for the page.

TOOLKIT

HTML Tags
See Appendix A for more information on HTML tags and tag modifiers, called **attributes**, and how they are used.

Figure 1-27 HTML tags define webpage elements.

The most current HTML standard is HTML5, which includes tags for creating webpage sections and easily adding video and audio. HTML5 also incorporates standards and protocols that enable RWD and other adaptive features that incorporate adjustments for mobile browsers. Technology standards for the web are set by the World Wide Web Consortium (W3C). The W3C, through an HTML working group, continues to pursue advancements in the HTML standard.

DESIGN TIP Even if you are designing a website using a CMS or web development tool (both described later in this chapter) that does not require the use of markup codes, it is important to understand the basic principles of markup languages to understand how webpages are coded.

Q&A

What Is Wireless Markup Language? The **Wireless Markup Language (WML)** is an XML-based markup language intended for use in designing webpages specifically for mobile browsers.

XML **Extensible Markup Language (XML)** is a markup language that uses both predefined and customized tags to facilitate the consistent sharing of information, especially within large groups. Whereas HTML defines the appearance and organization of webpage content, XML defines the content itself. For example, using XML, a programmer can define the custom tag *<serialnum>* to indicate that the information following the tag is a product serial number.

YOUR TURN

Exploring a Webpage's Underlying Markup Language

1. Start your browser and type the URL of the webpage of your choice in the Address bar.
2. View the webpage's underlying markup tags in a new window. (*Hint*: if you are using a desktop or laptop, right-click or CTRL+ click the webpage, then click View Source or View Page Source or press F12. If you are using a mobile browser, you might not be able to view the HTML code, or you might need to install an app to do so.)
3. Scroll the window to view the markup tags.
4. Identify several of the markup tags and their purpose.
5. Submit your findings in the format requested by your instructor.

Cascading Style Sheets

A **Cascading Style Sheet (CSS)** is a document that uses rules to standardize the appearance of webpage content by defining styles for elements such as font, margins, positioning, background colors, and more. Web designers store CSS specifications for a website in a separate document, called a **style sheet**. A web designer can attach the style sheet to multiple website pages; any changes made to the style sheet automatically apply to the associated webpages. For example, changing a heading font in the CSS automatically will update that heading font in all webpages associated with the CSS. Cascading refers to the order in which the different styles are applied. Chapter 4 discusses CSS in greater detail.

TOOLKIT **CSS Benefits** See Appendix B for the benefits and guidelines for using CSS.

Apply Cascading Style Sheets (CSS) to all pages in a website to ensure that all the pages have the same look.

Scripting Languages

Scripting languages are programming languages used to write short programs, called scripts, that execute in real time at the server or in the web browser when a webpage downloads. **Scripts** make webpages dynamic and interactive by adding features such as multimedia, animation, and forms or by connecting webpages to underlying databases. JavaScript, PHP: Hypertext Preprocessor (commonly abbreviated as PHP), and CoffeeScript are examples of scripting languages.

A web designer might choose to purchase ready-made scripts to perform routine or common functions, such as e-commerce shopping carts, FAQ (frequently asked questions) lists, and banner ad management.

Active content is webpage content created using a scripting language such as JavaScript and PHP. Examples of active content include polls, streaming video, maps, embedded objects, and animated images. Most webpages today include some active content to enhance the user's experience and keep content dynamic and current.

Text and HTML Editors

You can create a simple webpage by typing HTML tags and related text into a document created in a plain text editor, such as Notepad (Figure 1-28), the text editor available with the Windows operating system. A **text editor** is software used to create plain (ASCII) text files. Some web designers or programmers prefer to use an HTML editor to create webpages. An **HTML editor** is a text editor enhanced with special features that easily insert HTML tags and their attributes. HTML-Kit, CoffeeCup HTML Editor, BBEdit, and NoteTab are examples of HTML editors.

Q&A **Are there risks to active content?** Unfortunately, hackers can use active content to transmit malware. **Malware** is malicious software, including computer viruses and Internet worms, which can infect a single computer or an entire network. Some visitors' browsers might block active content by default, requiring visitors to instruct their browsers to display the content.

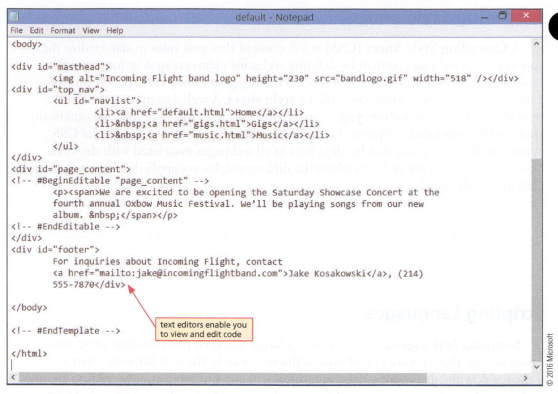

Figure 1-28 Web designers can use text editors such as Notepad to create webpages.

Web Development Tools

Many web designers use **web development tools**, such as Adobe® Dreamweaver® CC (Figure 1-29) or InnovaStudio® ContentBuilder.js, to create webpages. Another term for web development tools is **WYSIWYG editor** (WYSIWYG stands for "what you see is what you get"). Inserting and formatting text and inserting images or links in a webpage using a web development tool are similar to creating a document in a word processor, such

Figure 1-29 Web designers use web development tools to create and manage complex, interactive websites.

as Microsoft Word. Additionally, using a web development tool to create webpages eliminates the need to learn a markup language, which can involve complex coding procedures, because the web development tool automatically generates the underlying markup language tags as you insert and format text, images, and links. Most web development tools also allow you to view and manipulate the underlying HTML code, if desired. Additional benefits of using web development tools include the capability to create webpages rapidly.

If you are looking for a professional-strength web development tool to create and manage complex, interactive, and animated webpages, an **integrated development environment (IDE)**, such as Microsoft® Visual Studio Community, WebStorm, or Eclipse offers sophisticated website design, publishing, and management capabilities. Software vendors who create web development tools often provide additional support and resources at their websites, such as clip art and multimedia, training seminars, user forums, and newsletter subscriptions.

Using a web development tool presents some challenges:

- Although most web development tools have a preview option to simulate how a webpage looks in a browser, in fact, the webpage might look quite different when viewed with various versions of different browsers. Proprietary, nonstandard code generated by some web development tools contributes to the inconsistent display. Some critics claim that WYSIWYG editors are really WYSINWYG editors— "what you see is *not* what you get."

- A second challenge is that some web development tools insert unnecessary code, creating larger, slower-loading webpages.

- Finally, some web development tools—especially older versions—might not adhere to the latest markup language standards.

Chapter 2 discusses inconsistent display between web browsers and browser versions in more detail. Even if your web development tool includes features for previewing, accessibility checking, and compatibility checking, you still should perform additional testing using multiple browsers and devices before publishing your website.

Web Templates and Content Management Systems

With little or no knowledge of HTML or other web design tools, users quickly can create a website and its webpages using a web template or a CMS.

A **web template** or **theme** is a predesigned model webpage that you can customize for fast website or webpage creation and updating. Some web hosting websites, such as Wix, Squarespace, and Homestead, provide web templates (in addition to hosting services) that make it quick and easy for a small business owner to create his or her e-commerce website, focusing on the webpage's content rather than on the design details.

Other websites, such as DreamTemplate, Theme Circle, and TemplateMonster (Figure 1-30), sell an enormous variety of predesigned web templates for creating personal, organizational/topical, and commercial websites. Additionally, a number of websites, such as PixelMill or Expression Graphics, sell web templates for a specific web development tool. Finally, many web development tools also provide web templates for fast website and webpage creation.

Q&A

What is Bootstrap?
Bootstrap is a web design framework that supports HTML and CSS. Bootstrap includes templates and tools that help you incorporate RWD into your website.

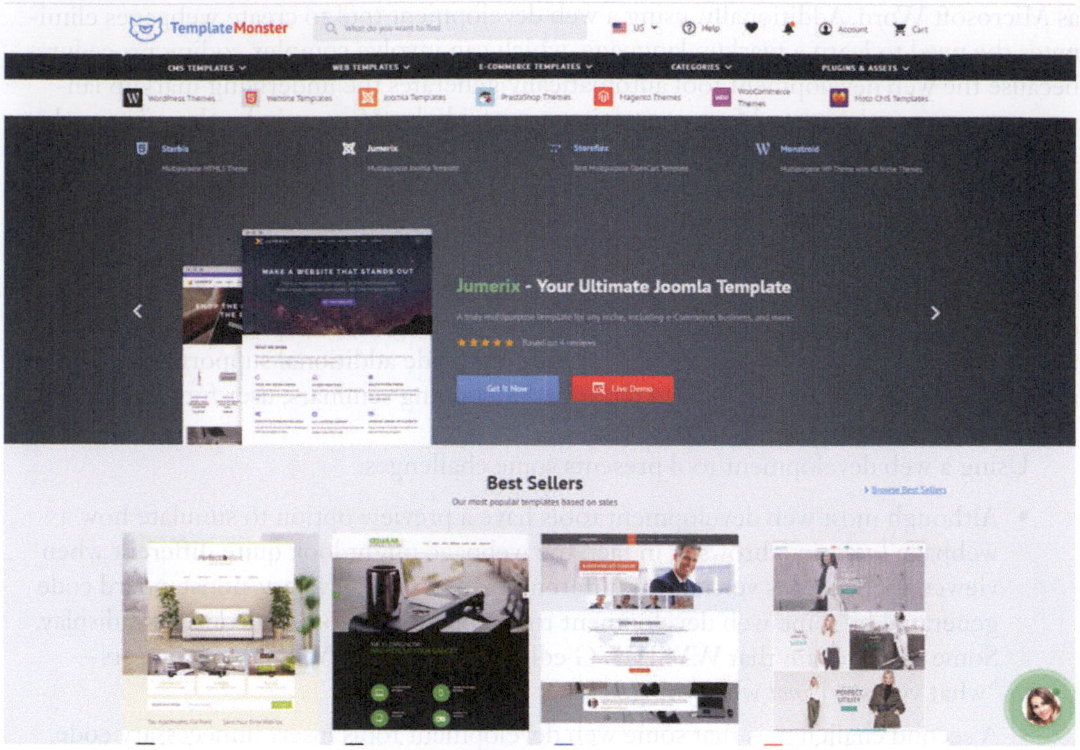

Figure 1-30 Web templates are customizable model webpages.

Q&A

What is a software development kit?
A **software development kit (SDK)**, sometimes called a *devkit,* contains the technology and tools needed to create apps or software to be used on a certain platform or device. SDKs often contain guidelines and rules about the type and format of programs; developers must license the SDK and abide by all guidelines.

A **content management system (CMS)** is software that provides website creation and administrative tools that enable the management of web content development, including authoring, reviewing, editing, and publishing. Content providers working within a CMS use web templates, style sheets, and other administrative tools to efficiently create, manage, update, and upload webpage content. The templates, style sheets, and other frequently used content elements, such as a logo graphic, are stored in a database called a **content repository**. Drupal, WordPress, and Joomla are examples of robust CMS software applications.

In addition to creating public webpages with templates or a CMS, website designers can use these technologies to control the look and function of all the internal website pages on a company's intranet. An **intranet** is a private network within a large organization or commercial entity that uses Internet and web technologies to share information among its members, employees, or business partners. Employees who have no web design experience or programming expertise can add webpages or update content on existing webpages on the intranet.

Web Design Roles

People plan and develop websites of all sizes working independently, in small groups, or as part of a large team. Ongoing communication between web development team members is crucial to the success of any website design project that involves multiple participants.

The following are responsibilities that can be an individual's only role or can be considered just one part of a job's skill set. Depending on the circumstances and the complexity of the web development project, you might take on one or more of the following web design roles. Regardless of your individual responsibilities, you should be familiar with both creative and technical aspects of website creation.

Creative Roles

If you assume a creative role, your focus primarily will be on how the website looks and its content. Jobs or skills in the creative role category include content writer/editor, SEO expert, web designer, user interface or user experience manager, artist/graphic designer, and multimedia producer.

As a **content writer/editor** or **SEO expert**, you create and revise the text that visitors read when they visit a website, and choose the links, images, video, or other media that enhance your text content. To achieve your website's purpose, you must write specifically for the web environment and a targeted web audience and take into consideration current SEO practices. An employer frequently looks for a highly creative applicant with demonstrated print and Internet writing experience, including SEO and social media.

As a **web designer**, your responsibilities might include graphic design as well as website setup and maintenance. To be a marketable webpage designer, you must communicate effectively, have a thorough knowledge of webpage design technologies, be familiar with RWD and other techniques for designing for multiple devices, have graphic design talent, understand your audience's needs, and possess some programming skills.

User interface (UI) or **user experience (UX) managers** focus on the experience of a user when viewing and interacting with a website. The goal of UI and UX is to create a website that not only is enjoyable to visit, but also enables the user to locate, use, and purchase the features and products promoted by the website.

The role of a **web artist/graphic designer** is to create original art such as logos, stylized typefaces, and avatars or props for 3D virtual worlds. This highly creative role demands experience with high-end illustration and image-editing software, such as Adobe Creative Cloud, as well as digital image capturing and editing devices and programs.

As a **multimedia producer**, you design and produce animation, digital video and audio, 2D and 3D models, and other media elements to include in a website. This role demands experience with sophisticated hardware and software, as well as familiarity with art theory and graphic design principles.

Technical Roles

If you play a technical role, your focus will be primarily on a website's technology, functionality, and security. Jobs or skills in the technical role category include webpage programming, security, and database development and maintenance.

A **web programmer** or **web developer** must be highly skilled in languages, such as JavaScript, PHP: Hypertext Preprocessor, and ASP.NET Core. Programmers use these languages to create interactive and dynamic webpages. Scripted webpages also handle data from web-based forms, such as those you complete when registering for an account on a website.

Q&A

How can I find a career in web design?
Many entry-level positions exist for web designers who have basic skills or interests. Certifications in web design show potential employers you possess some knowledge about web design. For more information about certifications that can help you train for a career in web design, use a search engine to search for *web design certifications*.

TOOLKIT

Careers in SEO
For more information about SEO careers, see Appendix D.

Frequently, web development roles are specialized and fall into one of two categories: front end or back end. A **front-end web developer** focuses on aspects that are visible to the website visitor, such as design, multimedia, and interactivity, creating webpages that combine text, images, and links. They must be able to use tools such as markup languages; CSS; and text, HTML, and web development tools. A **back-end web developer** is responsible for behind-the-scenes web technologies, such as databases, programming, and security. A web developer with both front- and back-end responsibilities is a **full-stack web developer**.

A **database developer** must possess the technical skills to plan, create, secure, and maintain databases of varying complexity. A large percentage of website content derives from databases, including storage of customer data and products on e-commerce websites. Database developers need to know how to integrate databases successfully with webpages and to protect the data from unauthorized access.

A **web server administrator** ensures the day-to-day functionality of the network and protects it from internal and external threats. Duties and responsibilities include ongoing network inspection, maintenance, and upgrades. An administrator must be aware of security alerts and advisories, protect the network with intrusion-detection software, and have a fully developed plan of action if the security of the network is compromised.

Oversight Roles

If you assume an oversight role, your focus is either on managerial and administrative issues or marketing/customer service. Examples of types of jobs in the oversight role category include web administrator, system architect, tester, and social media expert.

The responsibilities of **web administrator** vary. If he or she is working alone, the web administrator is responsible for creative, technical, and oversight roles. In an organizational or business setting, the web administrator might oversee a web development team that includes creative and technical roles. A web administrator must have familiarity with databases, markup and scripting languages, content development, creative design, marketing, and hardware.

Sometimes the web administrator takes on the role of the system architect. A **system architect** determines the structure and technical needs required to build, maintain, and expand the website.

All websites need to go through a testing process. **Testers** examine the website for usability and performance across different browsers and devices.

A **social media expert** determines the social media platforms to support, how the website shares content using social media, and methods for users to share content using social media.

Other Web Roles

As technology changes and develops, new roles are created to incorporate these trends. Some jobs that have emerged in recent years include e-commerce director, cloud architect, mobile app developer, and mobile strategy expert.

Exploring Web Design Roles

1. Use a search engine to identify job search websites, such as monster.com.
2. Click one of the job search websites to open it in your browser.
3. Follow the steps on the job search website to search for jobs related to three of the web design roles discussed in this chapter, including one of the newer roles.
4. Summarize your research by listing the job description, skill requirements, salary information, and job location for at least two job postings for each of the three web design roles you would be interested in.
5. Compare the skills needed for the job with your own skill set; what additional training will you need?
6. Submit the results of your job research in the format requested by your instructor.

Chapter Review

The Internet is a worldwide public network that links millions of private networks. The highly visual, dynamic, and interactive World Wide Web is a subset of the Internet. The Internet and the web have dramatically changed the communication, education, entertainment, and business practices of millions of people worldwide.

Users can access the Internet and the web over wired and wireless methods. Transfer rates determine the speed at which data moves between a server and a computer or device. Internet service providers (ISPs) provide Internet connections to individuals, businesses, and other organizations.

A browser is a software program or app that requests, downloads, and displays webpages. To view a webpage, enter its unique address, called a Uniform Resource Locator (URL), in the browser's Address bar. Three popular web browsers are Google Chrome, Mozilla Firefox, and Microsoft Edge.

Websites can be categorized as personal, organizational/topical, or commercial. Commercial websites include B2C, B2B, and C2C e-commerce; search tools; and portal websites.

Web design technologies include markup languages, Cascading Style Sheets (CSS), scripting languages, text and HTML editors, web development tools, and predesigned web templates and content management systems. Responsive web design techniques enable websites to adapt layout and content for different screen sizes and resolutions.

Depending on resources, developing a website might be the job of an individual person, two or three people, or a large web development team. Although actual titles vary and responsibilities can overlap, web design roles include creative, technical, and oversight, as well as those dealing with new technologies and strategies.

TERMS TO KNOW

After reading the chapter, you should know each of these key terms.

3D virtual world (7)
3G (12)
4G (12)
5G (12)
active content (25)
app (5)
application (5)
asymmetrical digital subscriber line
  (ADSL) (11)
attributes (23)
back-end web developer (31)
blog (6)
blogging (6)
Bluetooth (11)
bookmark (4)
broadband (11)
browser (13)
browsing the web (3)
business-to-business (B2B) e-commerce (10)
business-to-consumer (B2C) e-commerce (10)
cable television (CATV) line (11)
Cascading Style Sheet (CSS) (25)
cloud computing (5)
collaborative workspace (5)
commercial website (17)
consumer-to-consumer (C2C) e-commerce (10)
content management system (CMS) (28)
content repository (28)
content writer/editor (29)
corporate portal (21)
database developer (30)
digital subscriber line (DSL) (11)
domain name (14)
e-commerce (9)
electronic commerce (9)
email (5)
Extensible Markup Language (XML) (24)
favorite (4)
Fiber to the Premises (FTTP) (11)
fixed wireless (11)
front-end web developer (30)
full-stack web developer (30)
general consumer portal (21)
group messaging app (5)
hashtag (7)
hit (18)
home page (2)
hot spot (12)
HTML editor (25)
HTML tag (23)
hyperlink (2)
Hypertext Markup Language (HTML) (24)
Hypertext Transfer Protocol (HTTP) (15)
IM chat (5)

index (18)
instant messaging (5)
integrated development environment (IDE)
  (27)
Internet (2)
Internet Relay Chat (IRC) (5)
Internet service provider (ISP) (12)
intranet (28)
IP address (14)
kbps (11)
keyword (18)
landing page (2)
learning management system (LMS) (8)
link (2)
malware (25)
markup language (23)
Massive Open Online Course (MOOC) (7)
massively multiplayer online game (MMOG)
  (7)
Mbps (11)
meta tag (18)
metasearch engine (18)
mobile wireless (11)
multimedia producer (29)
national ISP (12)
network (2)
organizational website (29)
personal portal (21)
personal website (15)
portal (21)
protocol (15)
regional ISP (12)
responsive web design (RWD) (13)
script (25)
scripting languages (25)
search directory (19)
search engine (18)
search engine optimization (SEO) (19)
SEO expert (29)
shortcut (4)
social bookmarking (6)
social media expert (30)
social networking (6)
software development kit (SDK) (28)
spamdexing (19)
spider (18)
streaming media (11)
style sheet (25)
surfing the web (3)
system architect (30)
tag (6)
tester (30)
text editor (25)
text speak (5)

theme (27)
topical website (16)
top-level domain (TLD) (14)
transfer rate (11)
Uniform Resource Locator (URL) (14)
user experience (UX) manager (29)
user interface (UI) manager (29)
vertical portal (21)
video sharing (6)
virtual meeting space (5)
web administrator (31)
web artist/graphic designer (29)
web chat (5)
web browser (13)
web crawler (18)

web designer (29)
web developer (29)
web development tool (26)
web programmer (29)
web server (2)
web server administrator (30)
web template (27)
webpage (2)
website (2)
wiki (7)
wireless fidelity (Wi-Fi) (11)
Wireless Markup Language (WML) (24)
World Wide Web (web) (2)
WYSIWYG editor (26)
XML (24)

Complete the Test Your Knowledge exercises to solidify what you have learned in the chapter.

Matching Terms

Match each term with the best description.

_____ 1. app
_____ 2. blog
_____ 3. browser
_____ 4. hyperlink
_____ 5. ISP
_____ 6. LMS
_____ 7. MOOC
_____ 8. SEO
_____ 9. web crawler
_____ 10. style sheet
_____ 11. URL
_____ 12. webpage

a. A program or app that provides a scheduling, communication, and document sharing platform for students and teachers.

b. A webpage's unique text address.

c. A software program.

d. A business that has a permanent Internet connection and provides temporary Internet connections to individuals and companies for a fee.

e. A web content design technique that includes using meta tags, descriptive page titles, relevant inbound links from other websites, and clearly written text to increase the likelihood that the webpage will appear high in a search engine's search results list.

f. A specially formatted electronic document that contains text, graphics, and other information and is linked to similar, related documents.

g. A document that a web designer can attach to multiple website pages to ensure design continuity.

h. A word, phrase, or graphical image that connects pages at the same website or pages across different websites.

i. An online journal or diary.

j. A software program used to request, download, and display webpages.

k. An online course delivered over the web, often for free.

l. A program that browses the web for new pages and then adds the webpages' URLs and other information to its index.

Short Answer Questions

Write a brief answer to each question.

1. Differentiate between the Internet and the World Wide Web.
2. Describe the difference between a search engine and a search directory.
3. List and describe four broadband methods for accessing the Internet and web.
4. Differentiate between commercial and organizational websites.
5. List and explain SEO techniques and tools.
6. Differentiate between front-end, back-end, and full-stack web developer roles.
7. Identify the primary responsibilities associated with each of the following web design roles: content writer/editor, artist/graphic designer, UI/UX manager, web designer, web programmer/developer, social media expert, and web administrator.
8. Define the following terms: instant messaging (IM chat), cloud computing, social bookmarking, wiki, and collaborative workspace.

TRENDS

Investigate current web design developments with the Trends exercises.

Write a brief essay about each of the following trends, using the web as your research tool. For each trend, identify at least one webpage URL used as a research source. Be prepared to discuss your findings in class.

1 | Responsive Web Design

Responsive web design (RWD) strategies optimize websites for viewing on multiple device types and screen sizes. Research guidelines and techniques for responsive web design. Submit your findings in the format requested by your instructor.

2 | Web Conferencing

How do businesses use web conferencing to conduct meetings? Visit at least one web conferencing website to see what benefits for businesses and business users are listed. Find reviews of web conferencing software and apps. Besides providing two-way video, what other services can users take advantage of during a web conference? Search the web for tips and techniques for participating in a professional web conference, such as attire, background, preparation, and etiquette. As a web designer, how might you use web conferencing to work with your clients and business partners?

Challenge your perspective of the web and web design technology with the @Issue exercises.

Write a brief essay in response to the following issues, using the web as your research tool. For each issue, identify at least one webpage URL used as a research source. Be prepared to discuss your findings in class.

1 | Impact on Lifestyle

With developments in technology such as smartphones, people are able to stay connected constantly. Whether by phone calls, text messages, alerts from websites about new content, or social networking websites such as Facebook and Twitter, technology provides many distractions. How do these developments enhance daily life? How have they changed daily life from five or ten years ago? What is a negative impact? Discuss the impact of technology on your lifestyle and that of those around you.

2 | Meta Tag Abuse

Web designers use meta tags to enable search engines to easily categorize webpage content. Some web designers use meta tags that reflect popular search trends, but have nothing to do with their webpage content. Use a search engine to search for meta tag abuse. Is including unrelated meta tags unethical? How should search engines deal with websites that misuse meta tags? If possible, find examples of commonly misused meta tags. Discuss your conclusions regarding the ethical use of meta tags.

Use the World Wide Web to obtain more information about the concepts in the chapter with the Hands On exercises.

1 | Explore and Evaluate: An E-commerce Website

Browse the web to locate an e-commerce website. Follow links from the home page to view at least three related pages at the website. Then answer the following questions; be prepared to discuss your answers in class.

a. Who owns the website and what is its URL?

b. What is the focus of the products or services on the website?

c. Were the home page and related pages visually appealing? If yes, why? If no, why not?

d. What social media does the website incorporate? How are they used?

e. How easy was it to navigate to related pages using the home page links?

f. Conduct a search for a specific product or product type. Were the search results relevant to your search?

g. Were you able to identify any advertisements or paid promotional placements?

h. How long did it take for you to find useful information at the website?

2 | Search and Discover: Mobile Web Browsers

Using a search engine, perform a keyword search to identify popular types of mobile browsers. Read industry expert and user reviews of one mobile browser. Answer the following questions and submit your answers in the format requested by your instructor.

a. Which device(s) can use the mobile browser?

b. Are the reviews positive? What features do the experts and users like or dislike?

c. Are there any typical browser features that are missing? If so, what are they?

d. Does the browser come embedded on a device or can users download it? If it is available for download, is it free?

e. Is the browser's interface visually appealing? Why or why not?

f. Are there any identified security risks to the browser?

g. Do you have any experience using this browser? If so, describe your experience.

h. Would you use or recommend this mobile browser? Why or why not?

TEAM APPROACH

Work collaboratively to reinforce the concepts in the chapter with the Team Approach exercises.

1 | Compare Content Management Systems

Pair up with one or more classmates and work as a team to research and compare content management systems. As a team, determine which systems you will research. Assign one CMS to each team member.

a. Using a search engine, find at least three sources listing advantages or disadvantages of your chosen CMS.

b. Answer the following questions:

- What qualifications are necessary to use the CMS?

- What are the two main advantages to using the CMS?

- What are two disadvantages to using the CMS?

c. Find three examples of websites created using the CMS.

d. Present your findings to your other team member(s). As a group, determine which you would choose.

e. Submit your findings in the format requested by your instructor.

2 | Team and Client Communication Challenges

Join with four or five classmates to establish a mock web development team. Assume the web development team has been hired by a client to plan and create a B2B e-commerce website. Each team member should choose one or more of the creative, technical, or oversight roles discussed in this chapter. Then use the web to research current challenges that individuals in each role might face, and identify potential resolutions to those challenges. Next, as a team, brainstorm communication issues that might arise among team members and between the team members and the client. Identify ways to resolve any potential communication issues. Finally, prepare a detailed report describing potential design and communication challenges and the team's approach to handling them. Submit the report to your instructor and be prepared to present your report to the class.

Apply the chapter concepts to the ongoing development process in web design with the Case Study.

The Case Study is an ongoing development process using the concepts, techniques, and Design Tips presented in each chapter.

Background Information

You now will begin the process of designing your own personal, organizational/topical, or commercial website. As you progress through the chapters in this book, you will learn how to use design as a tool to create effective webpages and websites. At each chapter's conclusion, you will receive instructions for completing another segment of the ongoing design process.

The following are suggestions for website topics. Choose one of these topics or determine your own. Select a topic that you find interesting, feel knowledgeable about, or are excited about researching.

1. Personal website

   - Share a hobby or special interest: music, remote control cars, mountain biking, fantasy sports, or other

2. Organizational/topical website

   - Increase support and membership for: Habitat for Humanity, Red Cross, or a campus organization

   - Promote awareness of: health and fitness, endangered species, or financial assistance for college

3. Commercial website

   - Start a new business: childcare or dog walking, or expand an existing business with a web presence

   - Sell a service: tutoring, web design, graphic design, or home maintenance

   - Sell a product: laptop stickers, workout programs or gear, or beauty/boutique products

The evaluation of your completed website, which will consist of 5 to 10 webpages, will be based primarily on the application of good web design concepts.

Chapter 1 Assignment

Follow Steps 1–6 to complete a plan for developing your website.

1. Identify which type of website you will design—personal, organizational/topical, or commercial. Write a brief paragraph describing the website's overall purpose and its targeted audience. Create a name for your website.

2. List at least three general goals for your website. You will fine-tune these goals into a mission statement in a subsequent chapter.

3. List elements in addition to text—photos, music, animation, and so forth—that you could include on your website to support your general goals.

4. Identify the design tools you expect to use to develop your website.

5. Identify an available domain name and URL for your website. Research to make sure it is available.

6. Submit your findings in the format requested by your instructor. Be prepared to discuss your plan with the class.

2 | Web Publishing Fundamentals

Introduction

Chapter 1 introduced you to the Internet and the web and design tools used to create webpages. In this chapter, you learn about the advantages of web publishing and discover the basic design principles behind publishing a successful website. The chapter discusses responsive web design, adding interactivity to your website, writing for the web, and effective uses of color and layout. Finally, you learn about the technical, legal, privacy, accessibility, and usability issues surrounding web publishing.

Objectives

After completing this chapter, you will be able to:

1. Describe the advantages of web publishing

2. Discuss basic web design principles

3. Define the requirements for writing for the web

4. Explain the use of color as a web design tool

5. Identify web publishing issues

Advantages of Web Publishing

At one time, web publishing was an afterthought to print publishing. For many years now, content publishers have considered web and other electronic forms of publishing to be a primary (i.e., electronic only) or secondary (in conjunction with print) source of content publication. With the prevalence of ebook readers, tablets, and smartphones, web designers must embrace responsive web design to make content accessible on multiple device types and screen sizes. Print publishing has its benefits, namely, enabling you to share and distribute publications without relying on access to technology. Web publishing has many advantages over print including currency, connectivity, interactivity, cost, and delivery.

The Currency Advantage

Whether you are logged into your school's learning management system to access your grades and class schedule from your laptop, researching movie times and locations using a tablet, or checking the weather from your smartphone, you expect that the web content you are accessing is current. A print publication cannot reflect more current information without being reprinted and distributed, whereas web publishers can update content instantaneously and continually.

The web's **currency advantage** lies in the ability to update webpages quickly and inexpensively. For example, suppose you are a web administrator. The chief executive officer (CEO) of your company suddenly leaves the company. The board of directors wants to assure customers of a smooth transition to new management. In just a few minutes and at a very low cost, you can update or create a new webpage that includes a press release explaining the change in management, along with a photograph and biography of the new CEO. You then can publish or republish the webpage to the company's website, and submit the content through its Twitter feed, Facebook page, RSS (Really Simple Syndication), or other apps or services, where it appears in users' inboxes or news feeds. Using the company's website and connectivity tools, your company can communicate with customers instantly. **Connectivity tools** include social media sharing tools that enable instant publication of website content in the form of social media posts across a variety of platforms. By initiating the exchange of information and controlling the message of the content, your company increases its reputation for trustworthiness.

Many websites provide updates on an hourly or daily basis. News websites and blogs post updates on a real-time basis as stories develop. For example, a news website may have several reporters using web tools to post updates, stories, videos, photos, or interviews of a swiftly unfolding news event. As noted in Chapter 1, news organizations exploit the web's currency advantage by hosting popular, high-traffic websites, such as washingtonpost.com or USATODAY.com (Figure 2-1), to provide continually updated weather, stock market quotes, and stories about newsworthy events—seconds after the events occur.

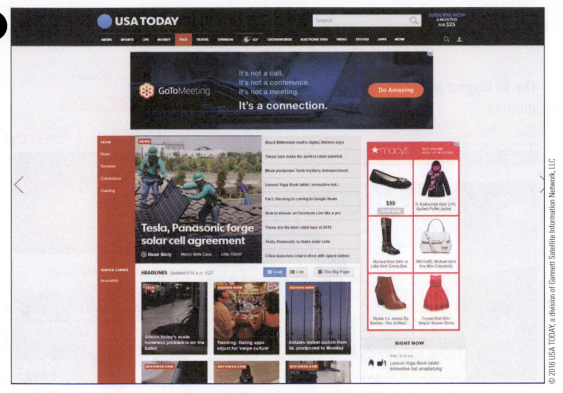

Figure 2-1 High-traffic news websites exploit the web's currency advantage.

Website visitors expect that websites providing sports, news, and weather information or e-commerce opportunities offer timely content presented in a fresh, appealing manner. If visitors do not find timely content at these types of websites, they are likely to leave, perhaps finding what they need on a competitor's website. Since these websites rely on high traffic to sell advertisements or the company's products, currency is one of the more important goals of web publishing.

The Connectivity Advantage

Sharing a story, press release, article, or blog post from a website is an instantaneous process. Using content **aggregators** that display preferred content from several sources such as RSS feeds, social networking tools such as Facebook pages and Twitter feeds, and social news websites such as Digg or StumbleUpon, a website's administrators instantly can alert followers to new content. In addition, the same connectivity tools can allow those users to share links to the content with their friends and followers, spreading the news quickly, as the sharing tools from Career Addict shown in Figure 2-2 illustrates. Unlike photocopying a news article or book content, sharing a link to the original source does not infringe copyright laws. Web publishers encourage shares of content and track these as a measure of the success of the publication. The web's **connectivity advantage** is the ability to instantaneously distribute and share content widely.

Q&A

Do all websites contain continually updated content? No. Some websites focus on content that might not change over time, for example, academic or historical websites that publish biographies or content based on research papers. The primary concerns of visitors to these types of websites are author credibility and content accuracy.

Figure 2-2 Web articles can include tools for sharing the content and links to supplemental information.

© 2016 Delta Quest Media Holding ApS

> **DESIGN TIP**
>
> Although your website might not need as frequent updating as a news-oriented or B2C website, you still must take care to keep the website's content up to date, and take advantage of connectivity tools to communicate and interact with website visitors.

Q&A

Are connectivity and convergence the same?
No. Connectivity refers to connections between content, such as links and shares. **Convergence** is the trend of connecting information and accounting between devices. For example, convergence means that you can access your social media accounts on multiple devices without separate log-ins.

The connectivity advantage also can streamline the writing process. A web article can include links directly in the content to additional resources or background. This enables the author to keep articles short, which helps to make them more attractive to read, while still providing the content necessary to convey the information or tell the story. In addition, many articles contain a list of related links to other stories or articles about the same or related topics.

The Interactivity Advantage

In Chapter 1, you learned that the Internet is a worldwide public network that connects smaller private networks for the purpose of sharing data and other resources. The web's **interactivity advantage** allows for data and resource sharing that enables, for example, communication with a website's Customer Service or Sales Department, or that allows users to post comments on an article.

A well-designed website should include tools that enable and invite its visitors to engage in interactive, two-way communication with the website's publisher. At a minimum, every website should include a page of contact information—phone numbers, mailing addresses, physical location addresses, and email addresses. To encourage interactivity and communication, a website should include links to its blog, Twitter feed, or Facebook page, and enable users to share website content with others. Figure 2-3

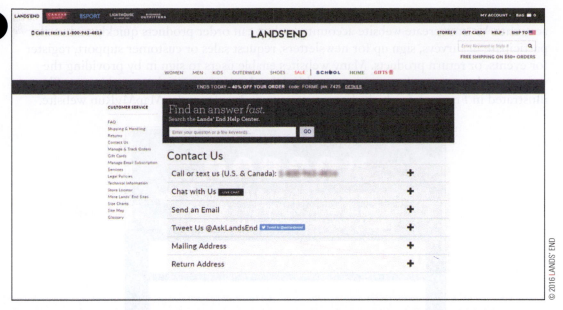

Figure 2-3 A website's contact page encourages communication between the website and its visitors.

shows the contact page for Lands' End's website, which includes several methods by which a user could contact Lands' End. In addition, some contact information typically is included in a webpage's footer or elsewhere on the webpage.

Depending on the purpose of its website, a company could use other tools to promote interactivity and communication. For example, blogs are an important internal and external tool for promoting interactivity and communication between companies and their vendors, customers, and other business partners. Companies such as Ballard Designs host blogs (Figure 2-4) that encourage interactivity and communication. Blogs help a company to provide information about their products, services, and related news topics that may be of interest to customers. By encouraging customers to reply or comment to blog posts or share with others, a company can help build a community of customers.

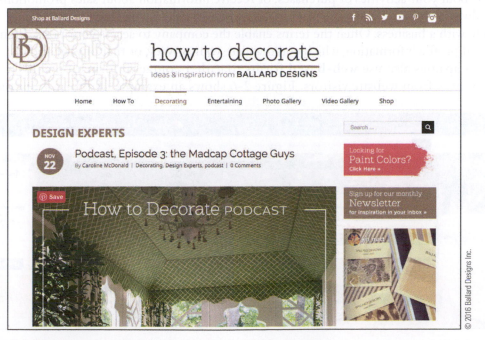

Figure 2-4 Blogs are an important communication tool for businesses.

Q&A

Do other advantages exist to using social networking and other interactivity tools?

Yes. Website administrators rely on data such as the number of users who commented on, shared, viewed, or "liked" webpage content to gauge success. This type of data is called **analytics**. To learn more, use a search engine to search for *web analytics*.

Many websites, such as e-commerce websites, encourage website visitors to create accounts. Visitors create website accounts so they can order products quickly and easily, participate in surveys, sign up for newsletters, request sales or customer support, register for events, or return products. Many websites enable users to sign in by providing the website with access to the user's personal Facebook or other social networking profile, as illustrated in Figure 2-5, which shows a sign in window from the MapMyRun website.

Figure 2-5 Setting up an account on a website can provide a custom experience and save user data.

The advantage of using your social networking profile to sign in is that you can save time by not having to retype the information. Other benefits can include the ability to share posts about your activities or purchases, or receive information about sales promotions. You always should read the fine print when agreeing to share your social networking profile with a business. Often the terms enable the company to access your posts, friends list, and profile information, which could violate your privacy, or that of your friends.

Companies also use **web-based forms** to gather contact information and preferences from website visitors. Figure 2-6 shows an example of a form from the

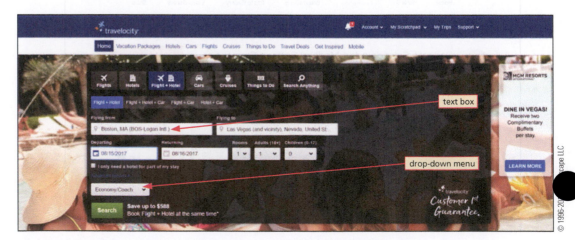

Figure 2-6 Web-based forms are used to gather information from website visitors.

Travelocity website. Common web-based form elements include text boxes, check boxes, option buttons, drop-down list boxes, and a Submit or Send button. To use a web-based form, a visitor simply types information, clicks a check box, selects an option button, or selects an item from a drop-down list and then clicks the Send or Submit button to send the information to the website. Forms can be just a few questions, or broken out into several pages to make entering and validating the data easier. Web development tools and web hosting services provide tools to create forms efficiently. Working with web-based forms is discussed in more detail in Chapter 6.

Q&A

How does a website store form data? Webpages collect form data in databases, which store data in searchable records that companies can use for mailing lists, tracking purposes, and more.

After you publish your website, plan to review the website's content for credibility, accuracy, and timeliness on a regular basis and update the content as necessary.   **DESIGN TIP**

Websites of all types promote interactivity and communication using methods beyond traditional contact pages, blogs, and web-based forms. News-oriented websites, such as FOXNews.com, often promote interactivity by allowing visitors to comment on articles or by permitting visitors to submit their own breaking news stories and images. Some businesses and organizations promote interactivity by offering chat rooms on their websites, such as Zooniverse, where visitors can comment on and discuss science projects in real time.

Build into your website appropriate ways to promote interactivity, such as a contact page, web-based form, or blog.   **DESIGN TIP**

Exploring Connectivity

YOUR TURN

1. Use a search engine to search for examples of the following types of websites: news, e-commerce, and blog.
2. Open each website in a different tab.
3. Explore each website and answer the following questions:
   a. What social media tools are included in the website to promote connectivity? Give examples to support your answer.
   b. What contact information appears on each page of the website? Is there a separate contact page?
   c. Can you create an account on the website? What advantages might you have if you created an account on the website? What privacy settings exist?
4. Submit your results in the format requested by your instructor.

The Cost Advantage

Compared with print, updating web content is more cost effective. However, the costs associated with developing and maintaining a website can be quite expensive. A website budget may include the following costs:

- Web design
- Content writing or adaptation
- Multimedia development
- Website hosting
- Domain name registration
- Promotional services

Publishing web content has some **cost advantages** over print. Print costs include purchasing paper and ink, printing, and distribution. Unlike print, the cost of publishing web content does not vary based on its length, color composition, or design complexity. Whereas each printed piece incurs an individual cost, a website's expenses are not affected by the number of visitors. To add interest to your webpages and break up text, you should add images or other multimedia. You may be able to find free downloads for photos, animations, video, and sound clips for use at your website; however, you might incur some additional cost to prepare these types of content elements for the best display and quality. You also can purchase reasonably priced photos and multimedia elements.

As with print, the complexity of the colors and layout of your web content may increase the design costs. The technological specifications of the web mean that it does not matter whether your design is a simple one-color text piece or a sophisticated piece with hundreds of colors—the cost to publish on the web is the same. Note, however, that whenever you incorporate multimedia in your webpages, the pages generally are larger and your website might require more storage space. You also might be limited by the amount of web server space your website hosting service provides or by budget constraints if you must lease extra web server space to support your website's multimedia elements. For example, a website hosting service might limit server space for website files to 10 GB for a flat monthly fee; if you need more space, you might incur additional cost. Chapter 6 discusses adding multimedia to a website in more detail.

The Delivery Advantage

The web's **delivery advantage** enables the fast and inexpensive distribution of published information over the Internet and the web. For instance, imagine that as a volunteer for your school's health center, you need to publicize the upcoming flu shot clinic. Because you want to get the information out quickly to as many people as possible, you use your website and connectivity tools to reach current and former students, faculty and staff members, and local residents. You can use the web and the Internet to promote the webpage containing information about the clinic in many ways, including:

- Adding a link to the event to the calendar on the school's website.
- Sending email messages with a link to the event details at your website to last year's participants as well as all current students, staff, and faculty.
- Posting links to the website on your Twitter feed and Facebook page and creating ads or promotions using social media.

- Creating a landing page specifically for the clinic.
- Querying related websites, such as the elementary school, or local health and fitness clubs, to ask them to include a link to the clinic's webpage on their website, or to email their database of contacts.

These methods cost very little, and the news about the event would be available almost immediately. Distributing the same content using print takes more time because the content must go through a printing process, then be distributed using the mail or by hanging posters.

Basic Web Design Principles

Webpages should be visually attractive, convey a powerful message, and leave a distinct impression. Successful web publications that accomplish these objectives combine creativity with the basic design principles of balance and proximity, contrast and focus, and unity and visual identity. Responsive web design ensures that the content is viewable on multiple devices and screen sizes.

Balance and Proximity

In design, **balance** is the harmonious arrangement of elements. Balance, or the absence of balance, can significantly impact the effectiveness of a webpage to express its message. Web elements in a **symmetrical** arrangement appear centered or even; symmetry suggests a conservative, safe, and peaceful atmosphere. The Whole Foods Market home page (Figure 2-7) illustrates a symmetrical arrangement of web elements.

Q&A

Do web design principles change? Yes. As new web technologies, programming languages, apps, and tools develop, so do the current principles of web design. For more information about the most up-to-date web design principles, use a search engine to search for *web design principles* and filter or sort the results to show only the most recent articles.

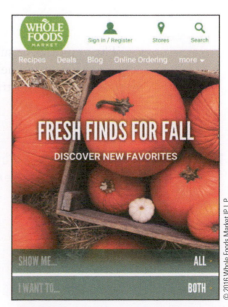

Figure 2-7 Responsive web design techniques recommend symmetrical, or balanced, layout.

TOOLKIT

Responsive Web Design
To learn more about responsive web design principles, see Appendix C.

Asymmetrical, or off balance, design creates an energetic mood. Asymmetrical designs typically do not adapt well to mobile devices. Responsive web design guidelines recommend using grids to lay out content so that you can easily move, resize, and reorder it to fit the device.

Proximity, or closeness, is associated with balance. Proximity, as applied to webpages, means that you place related elements close to each other. For example, position a caption near an image, an organization's name near its logo, and headings and subheadings near related body copy. Doing so visually connects elements that have a logical relationship, making your webpages more organized. Elements on the Martha Stewart home page (Figure 2-8) illustrate proximity: images appear above or to the left of explanatory text or captions, and headings and subheadings appear above related links.

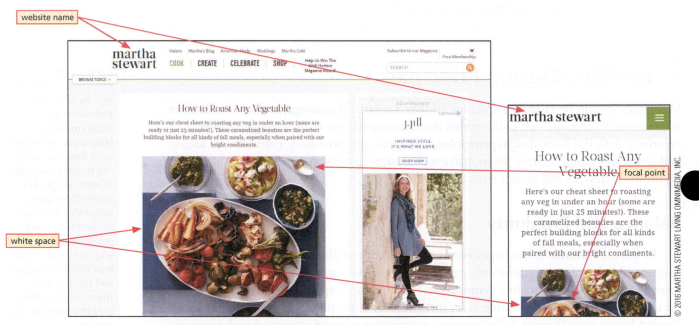

Figure 2-8 Place related webpage elements in proximity to each other and allow sufficient white space.

The empty space surrounding text and images, called **white space** in design, also can define proximity and help organize webpage elements, eliminate clutter, and make content more readable, as illustrated in the Martha Stewart home page.

DESIGN TIP You can create and adjust consistent white space by using the CSS to specify indents and line spacing for text, and space around tables and images.

Contrast and Focus

Contrast is a mix of elements to stimulate attention. Contrast also establishes a **focal point**, which is a dominating segment of the webpage that directs visitors' attention to a center of interest or activity. What do you want your website's visitors to focus on and to remember—a company name, a tag line or logo, a powerful photo, or some combination of these? Determine first what element on your webpage is the most important and then use contrast to establish that dominance visually.

> **DESIGN TIP**
>
> Using a slide show or gallery enables you to have one central focal point with content that changes automatically or as a result of user intervention. You can feature several articles at once in a small amount of space.

Pages that lack contrast, such as those with a solid block of text or a jumble of competing elements, are uninteresting or confusing. You can create contrast by using text styles, color choices, element size, and more. For example, setting a company name in a larger typeface distinguishes it from subheadings and body text, which typically are a smaller typeface. Similarly, a dark background with light, brightly colored text might draw more attention than a cream background with black text. By varying the size of webpage elements, you can establish a visual hierarchy of information that will show your visitors which elements are most important. Element size and typeface on The College of William & Mary home page (Figure 2-9) create contrast and establish a focal point for the page.

Figure 2-9 Use contrast on a webpage to stimulate attention and establish the page's focal point.

> **DESIGN TIP**
>
> Use balance, proximity, and white space to create effective, organized webpages. Use contrast to stimulate interest and establish a focal point for your webpages.

Unity and Visual Identity

All the pages at a website must have **unity**, or a sense of oneness or belonging, to create and maintain the website's **visual identity**—the combination of design elements identified with the website and its publisher. Especially important to businesses, visual identity must be consistent, not only throughout a website, but also with the business's TV or radio ads, or print publications, such as brochures, business cards, and letterheads.

Creating and maintaining a visual identity is an important aspect of branding a business or organization. A general definition of the term **brand** is the assurance or guarantee that a business or organization offers to its customers. Businesses and other large organizations take care to develop and reinforce their own brand over time, generally with the guidance of marketing professionals. Some brands, such as Ford Motor Company (assurance of quality vehicles), are decades old; others, such as Chobani (guarantee of nutritious all natural food), are relatively new.

The consistent application of **branding specifications** for color, images, and text applied to all of the entity's media strengthens and promotes the brand. Examples of design elements that promote unity, create a visual identity, and contribute to branding an entity both in print media and on webpages include logos, fonts, colors, and tag lines. A **tag line** is a concise statement that a consumer readily associates with a business, organization, or product. An example of a tag line is Verizon's "Can you hear me now?"

To help promote unity, visual identity, and branding, web designers use consistent placement and repetition of elements, such as the company name, logo, and tag line, and application of the same color scheme across all pages at a website, as shown at the Subway website (Figure 2-10). Chapter 4 discusses unity, visual identity, and branding in more detail.

Figure 2-10 Consistent placement and repetition of elements and application of a color scheme across all webpages at a website promote unity and visual identity.

Generate a sense of unity, maintain visual identity, and promote your brand at your website by using consistent alignment, branding elements, and a common color scheme across all pages at the website.

Alignment is the placement of objects in fixed or predetermined positions, rows, or columns. Applying consistent alignment will ensure that your webpages have a coherent, structured presentation. Visitors to a webpage expect page elements to line up in a consistent, meaningful way; for example, the text in a photo caption should line up with the left edge of the photo beneath which it appears. If elements on a webpage do not align, the page will look jumbled and be perceived as inconsistent and unprofessional. When the elements on a webpage align horizontally, they appear consistently to the left, right, or centered. When webpage elements align vertically, they are also top-justified, assisting in readability and ensuring an organized appearance, as shown on the GeneLab home page (Figure 2-11). As previously mentioned, the use of grids for responsive web design layout ensures pages will adapt to different screen sizes and device types.

Figure 2-11 Horizontal and vertical alignment of webpage elements ensures a consistent presentation and increases readability.

Web designers use grids and horizontal layouts, as well as simplified typography, single-page layouts, and an "app-like" interface as part of responsive web design.

Color as Web Design Tool

Color can be a powerful design tool for creating attractive, effective websites. Color reinforces a brand identity, helps bring focus to and differentiate webpage sections, increases contrast, and improves readability. The use of color helps to set a website's mood as well as provide contrast between page elements. To use color as a design tool effectively, you must understand color basics: the color wheel, how monitors display colors, and visitors' expectations for color on the web.

The Color Wheel

A basic tool for understanding color as a design tool is the **color wheel** (Figure 2-12), which is a visual representation of the relationship between colors. The color wheel can help you choose effective and appealing color combinations. The basis of the color wheel is the set of **primary colors**—red, yellow, and blue. The **secondary colors**—orange, green, and purple—result from combining two primary colors. The green, blue, and purple colors are **cool colors**, which suggest tranquility and detachment. The yellow, orange, and red colors are **warm colors**, which are associated with activity and power. **Complementary colors** are those directly opposite each other on the color wheel. A combination of complementary colors creates a significant amount of contrast. Conversely, a combination of colors adjacent to each other generates significantly less contrast.

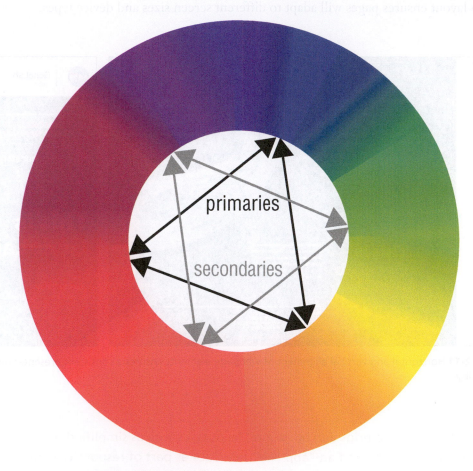

Figure 2-12 The color wheel is a representation of relationships between colors.

The RGB Color System

Computer monitors project color using the **RGB color system**, which combines channels of red, green, and blue light. The light from each channel is emitted in various levels of intensity. These levels are **values** and measure from 0 to 255. To ensure exact color specifications, use different values from the channels. For example, combining values

255 (red), 102 (green), and 153 (blue) produces a dusty rose color. Specifying color values provides an exact match that ensures consistency of colors across platforms and devices; this is especially important in branding.

Because each light channel can emit 256 levels of intensity, an RGB system can produce more than 16.7 million possible colors (256 red × 256 green × 256 blue = 16,777,216). A monitor's **color depth** is the actual number of colors that a monitor displays, stated in bits. For example, an 8-bit monitor can display 256 colors, a 16-bit monitor can display 65,536 colors, and a 24- or 32-bit monitor can display 16.7 million colors.

If you are using a text editor to create a webpage by manually entering markup tags, you specify a color for a webpage element by entering the color's hexadecimal code, which is the equivalent of the color's RGB values. The **hexadecimal system** uses 16 symbols, the letters A–F and digits 0–9, to signify values. For example, the hexadecimal code for the light green color with the RGB values of 153:255:153 is 99FF99. If you are using a web development tool, you do not need to understand the hexadecimal system in detail; simply select a color and the editor will determine and enter the appropriate hexadecimal code for you (Figure 2-13).

Q&A

What is the browser- or web-safe palette?
The web-safe palette is a set of 216 of the available 256 colors displayed by an 8-bit monitor. Fewer and fewer web visitors today have 8-bit monitors; therefore, many web designers no longer restrict their color choices to the web-safe palette.

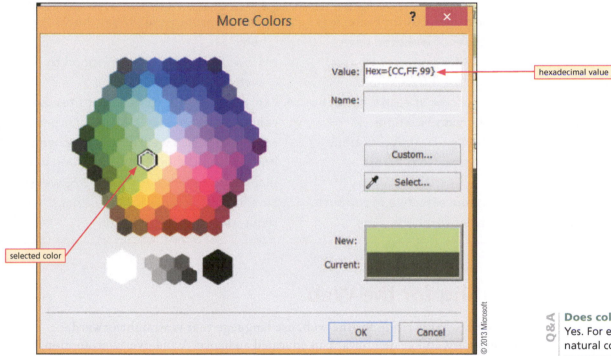

© 2013 Microsoft

Figure 2-13 Web design tools enable you to pick colors without having to know their hexadecimal value.

Target Audience Expectations

Over time, certain colors have come to symbolize particular qualities. Also, color symbolization differs across various cultures. Keep in mind the qualities generally associated with different colors when selecting colors for your website. If your website's target audience is global, research color associations in various countries to ensure that you are not creating a connotation that you do not intend.

Q&A

Does color matter?
Yes. For example, natural colors, such as greens and brown, might be a good fit for a website with an eco-friendly agenda. Some colors have cultural meanings in different countries. For more information about using color as a design tool, use a search engine to search for *website color palettes*.

DESIGN TIP Before making color choices for your website, visit several commercial and noncommercial websites to find examples of color schemes you like that fit with your website's branding. Consider using a color scheme generator to find compatible colors and color trends.

Consider the intended purpose of your website, the experience you desire for your targeted audience, and their expectations. When selecting colors for your website, allow yourself some leeway in making color decisions. Certain combinations produce different results and responses. Then choose an attractive color scheme and apply colors from this scheme to webpage elements, such as the background, text headings and subheadings, and links. When designing webpages for a commercial entity or other large organization, be sure to follow the entity's branding specifications for the use of color.

YOUR TURN

Exploring Webpage Color Schemes

1. Use a search engine to search for examples of the following types of websites: news, e-commerce, and B2B.
2. Open each website in a different tab.
3. Analyze the color scheme at each website by answering the following questions:
   a. Is the color scheme attractive, visually appealing, and consistent across pages?
   b. Is the color scheme effective in supporting the website's overall message and main purpose? If yes, how? If no, why?
   c. How do you personally respond to the website's color scheme?
4. Explain how each of these websites uses color as a design tool. Discuss your personal response to each website's color scheme and how your response might guide you when planning a color scheme for a B2C website.
5. Submit your findings in the format requested by your instructor.

Writing for the Web

In general, when writing for the web, use language that is straightforward, contemporary, and geared toward an educated audience. Avoid overly promotional language that might not appeal to visitors and avoid the use of industry jargon or slang. With responsive web design, a visitor might only see a list of headings and article titles on a webpage, which they click to expand articles they wish to read. Use wording in headings that communicates the content of a webpage or section clearly. Avoid misleading or clever headings that might confuse or annoy visitors. Be cautious regarding the use of humor. Small doses of humor correctly interpreted can enliven content and entertain. Remember, though, humor can be taken out of context and might be misunderstood or misinterpreted, especially if your audience includes visitors whose first language is not English.

DESIGN TIP To help web users more easily find your website, carefully consider the text that you place in headings to use search engine optimization techniques to their best advantage. To learn more about SEO techniques for headings, see Appendix D.

Whatever the particular circumstances of a user's web needs, an interesting webpage competes with distractions such as conversations, other electronic communications, and time constraints. Consequently, website visitors generally scan webpage text quickly to find useful information that is accurate and current, easy to read, and well organized.

> To keep webpage text succinct, place information that is not crucial, such as historical backgrounds or related topics, on subsidiary pages, either within the content as linked text, or as a separate link or list of links at the bottom or side of an article. For example, in a business news article about a company, you can include links to the company's website, the NASDAQ website to show the company's current stock price, and a related story from a previous day.
>
> **DESIGN TIP**

Accuracy and Currency

When writing or curating content for your website, confirm its accuracy using reliable sources. Refer to respected subject experts, professional organizations, trade journals, and other resources with a proven track record. Typographical and spelling errors can embarrass you and diminish your website's credibility. If you publish your webpages with such errors, your visitors might question how closely you checked your content and how committed you are to your purpose. To avoid these types of errors, perform spelling and grammar checks by writing the text content for your webpages in a word processor, content management system, or web development tool that includes proofing features. Proofread your content and then ask at least one other person to review it before you add the text to a webpage.

As noted earlier in this chapter, after you publish your website, you must keep the content on your webpages current. To demonstrate the currency and freshness of your website's content, you can add the last updated date and/or time to your webpages.

> Consider hiring a copywriter or content expert to create or adapt your web content. Content that reads well for the web and is accurate and error-free can help position your website as a valuable resource.
>
> **DESIGN TIP**

Scannability

Most website visitors, especially those using mobile devices, prefer to quickly scan webpages for useful information, and not read long passages of onscreen text. The **chunked text technique** breaks webpage text into small sections with headings, subheadings, and bulleted lists that adequately but concisely cover the topic. For example, consider the same information presented in Figure 2-14 as dense paragraph text and then as chunked text. Chunked text is much easier to scan, and will adapt better to devices with smaller screens, as the content under the headings and subheadings can be hidden until a website visitor clicks on it.

Q&A

Is chunked text appropriate for all webpage text? In some situations, a webpage might contain lengthy text articles that are intended to be printed and read offline. In these situations, you should present the text in its entirety and not chunked.

Dense Paragraph Text Example

When writing or curating content for your website, confirm its accuracy using reliable sources. Refer to respected subjec[t] professional organizations, trade journals, and other res[o] proven track record.

Typographical and spelling errors can embarrass you[r] ish your website's credibility. If you publish your webpag[e] errors, your visitors might question how closely you che[ck] content and how committed you are to your purpose.

To avoid these types of errors, perform spelling and checks by writing the text content for your webpages in processor, content management system, or WYSIWYG that includes proofing tools. Proofread your content, an[d] at least one other person to review it before you add the webpage.

Chunked Text Example

To ensure accurate and credible webpages:

- Confirm content accuracy with reliable sources.
- Refer to respected subject experts and others with a proven track record.
- Use proofing tools to check for spelling and grammatical errors.
- Ask at least one person to proofread content.

Figure 2-14 Chunked text is much easier for readers to scan online than dense paragraph text.

Q&A

How long do website visitors spend deciding whether to read content or move on? Website visitors spend an estimated 20–30 seconds on a webpage deciding whether the content meets their needs or whether they should go to another website for the desired information or products.

Remember that visitors to your website likely will scan your webpages rather than taking the time to read every word. Also, be aware that many website users assume that colored or underlined text represents a hyperlink. To ensure **scannability**, you should write your webpage content with the following guidelines in mind:

- Use chunked text, where appropriate, to create short paragraphs and bulleted lists.
- When it is necessary to write longer paragraphs, begin each paragraph with a topic sentence that summarizes the general idea of the whole paragraph. A visitor who scans only the first sentences of each paragraph will still get the overall picture of your webpage's purpose.
- Avoid using colored text or underlines for emphasis because they are associated with links. Be consistent with how you format links so that website visitors can identify links easily.
- Use of only uppercase characters can reduce scannability. Some visitors might also consider text in uppercase characters to be the equivalent of shouting.

Scannability also is affected by the choice of navigational elements, color scheme choices, and fonts. You learn more about these topics in Chapters 4 and 5.

 DESIGN TIP   Website visitors typically scan online text looking for useful information instead of reading the text word for word. Chunking text allows your website visitors to quickly scan your webpages. This makes your page content more easily readable on a mobile device.

Organization

The **inverted pyramid style** is a classic news writing style that places a summary (or conclusion) first, followed by details, and then any background information. Web content writers use the inverted pyramid style by placing summary chunked text at the top of the home page. Related details and background information appear further on the same page, or on linked subsidiary pages.

Sometimes using chunked text for scannability is inappropriate; for example, for a press release, where it is necessary to retain the press release's dense text paragraphs. Writing the press release text in the inverted pyramid style is particularly useful in helping visitors quickly understand the text's general idea. Figure 2-15 shows an example of the inverted pyramid style as shown in this article on the CNN website, viewed in a mobile browser.

Figure 2-15 The inverted pyramid style is a classic newswriting style.

© 2016 Cable News Network

Q&A

How can you ensure your web content will be well received and not offend readers?
Netiquette is a list of guidelines that help web users and developers to interact and create content. Netiquette rules govern the use of certain words, phrases, and formatting. For more information, use a search engine to search for *netiquette*.

TOOLKIT

Appendix D: SEO
Within the summary text are key terms that improve a website's SEO rankings. To learn more about SEO, see Appendix D.

Web Publishing Issues

Successful web publishing further includes recognizing certain technical, legal and privacy, accessibility, and usability issues, as well as the design techniques that can effectively manage them.

Technical Considerations

You must weigh a number of technical considerations when creating your website. Before creating your website, you should understand the balance between technical concerns and good web design. These issues include bandwidth, differences among browsers, resolution, and mobile-friendly practices.

BANDWIDTH   **Bandwidth** is the quantity of data transmitted in a specific time frame, measured in bits per second (bps). You learned about transmitting data over a network and the data's transfer rate in Chapter 1. A larger bandwidth indicates a higher data transfer rate. Visitors' Internet access methods and device types can affect transfer rates. The bandwidth or transfer rate of the Internet connection, the amount of traffic on the Internet at a specific time, and a webpage's file size all affect how quickly the webpage downloads in a visitor's browser.

As a web designer, you have no control over how your target audience members access the Internet and web or the amount of traffic across the Internet. You do have control over the file size of the webpage, which includes all its elements such as text, images, and multimedia. A visitor to your website generally will wait no longer than 5–10 seconds for a webpage to download before moving on to another website; therefore, you must take bandwidth into consideration when you choose elements to include on your webpages. Even with the increased access to high-speed Internet access methods, the file size of your pages should always be a consideration when designing effective websites.

Use images sparingly and consider using **thumbnail** images, which are miniature versions that link to larger images. In addition to careful image choices, you can take steps to optimize images for quick download time by reducing image file sizes using image-editing programs such as Corel™ PaintShop® Pro X9 or Adobe Photoshop CC. Chapter 5 discusses optimizing graphics in more detail.

BROWSER DIFFERENCES   In Chapter 1, you learned that Google Chrome, Microsoft Edge, and Mozilla Firefox are today's most widely used browsers for desktop and laptop computers. These popular browsers, along with most mobile browsers and mobile browser versions, are **graphical display browsers**. Along with text, graphical display browsers can display elements such as photographs, clip art, animations, and video. You can assume that visitors will view your website with a graphical display browser. Browsers can vary as to the support levels they offer for HTML tags, CSS, and scripting languages. Because of these varying support levels, webpages might appear differently when viewed with different browsers or with different versions of the same browser. You should test your webpages with different browsers and browser versions before publishing your website.

A visually impaired visitor using adaptive software to convert webpage text into audio might choose to turn images off in his or her graphical display browser. When adding images to a webpage, you should specify an alternative text description for each image. **Alternative text**, also called *alt text*, is language that briefly describes each image that loads in a webpage; such information appears in place of turned-off images and helps visitors better understand a page's content. If you are using a text or HTML editor, you can add the HTML *<img> </img>* tag attribute *alt=text* to add alternative text to the image. If you are using a web development tool, you can use an option provided by the editor to specify an alternative text description for each image.

> **DESIGN TIP**
>
> Webpages will appear quite differently when viewed with different devices, platforms, browsers, and browser versions. For this reason, use responsive web design techniques, and test your webpages using multiple devices and browsers before publishing your website.

SCREEN RESOLUTION   **Resolution** is the measure of a display device's sharpness and clarity, related directly to the number of pixels it can display. A **pixel**, short for *picture element*, is a single point in an electronic image. The pixels on a display device are so close together that they appear connected. To express resolution, graphic images use two numbers—the number of columns of pixels and the number of rows of pixels that a display device can display. At higher resolutions, the number of pixels increases while their size decreases. Page elements appear large at low resolutions and decrease in size as resolution settings increase.

When designing websites, you must account for a smaller screen size and the auto-rotate feature included in many smartphones and tablets. **Auto-rotate** enables the user to change the angle of a rectangular screen in order to change the screen orientation from landscape (wider) or portrait (higher). Figure 2-16 shows the Amazon webpage viewed on a smartphone in both orientations. In addition, by using finger gestures such as pinching, many mobile devices enable users to zoom in and out to better view images or text.

TOOLKIT

Appendix C: RWD
For more information about designing webpages that accommodate mobile devices' rotation and zoom features, see Appendix C.

© 1996-2016, Amazon.com, Inc. or its affiliates

Figure 2-16 Mobile devices use auto-rotate to change from portrait to landscape orientation.

When designing a webpage, use techniques that adapt to multiple resolutions. For example, design for a lower resolution and then add an attractive background that appears on either side of the page when viewed at a higher resolution.

What is the mobile-first strategy?
Mobile-first is a web design trend that encourages web designers to first design for mobile devices, rather than standard laptop or desktop monitor sizes. Mobile-first techniques include RWD principles, as well as other trends such as one-page websites, and expandable or hidden content or navigation. For more information, use a search engine to search for *mobile-first web design*.

MOBILE-FRIENDLY PRACTICES   Most mobile web browsers can identify changes you specify to the website to adapt its content, navigation, and multimedia to the smaller screen size and bandwidth. The most important consideration when creating a mobile-friendly website or applying RWD practices is to simplify the navigation and content to accommodate a smaller screen size and the use of a stylus or touch screen. You can address the bandwidth differences by reducing the number of images, replacing paragraphs with lists, and removing unnecessary or duplicate HTML code. Ensure that interactive website experiences, such as shopping or commenting, are easy to do on a mobile device.

Web design experts discourage the creation of separate mobile website versions and recommend responsive web design techniques to create device-independent websites. When working with an older website design, or one that is complex, you can create a mobile version of your website as a temporary, or easier, choice until you can complete a major redesign of the website.

YOUR TURN

Viewing Websites on Multiple Devices

1. Using devices with differing screen sizes and bandwidths (such as a desktop or laptop computer and a tablet or smartphone), display the same webpage on both devices.
2. Document the differences in how the webpage appears when viewed on different devices.
3. Does the website have difficulty loading images, multimedia, or animations when viewed on a smaller device or one with lower bandwidth?
4. Discuss differences in navigation, content, and number of images and animations.
5. Submit your findings in the format requested by your instructor.

What is Creative Commons?
Creative Commons is a nonprofit organization that provides guidelines for artists and others to protect and license creative content, including images, music, and more. Creative Commons allows content and media creators to establish permissions for use of their works, such as enabling use for entertainment or recreation purposes, but not for any commercial use.

Legal and Privacy Issues

You should take the time to familiarize yourself with legal and privacy issues related to publishing a website. Legal issues include copyright infringement and content liability. Criminal activity based on identity theft is a major problem for both businesses and consumers. If you gather visitor information—names, addresses, credit card numbers—at your website, you must take steps to protect the privacy of that information and secure it from unauthorized access or theft.

LEGAL ISSUES   At some time, you might see an image on a webpage that would be perfect for your website. To use it, all you need to do is download a copy of the image to a storage device on your computer, right? Although it is relatively easy to copy an image, doing so potentially is illegal, and definitely is unethical. By downloading and using the image without permission, you could violate the creator's **copyright**, or ownership right to the image. You are responsible for obtaining all permissions for content on your website, and can be subject to fines or prosecution for any violations.

U.S. laws protect published and unpublished intellectual property, such as webpage text or images, by copyright, regardless of whether the content owner registers the property with the U.S. Copyright Office. In general, the law states that only the owner may print, distribute, or copy the property. To reuse the property, the user must obtain permission from the owner. The owner may also request compensation for the usage or acknowledgment of the source.

A **copyright notice** is text that includes the word *copyright* or the © symbol, the publication year, and the copyright owner's name. Many websites today, especially commercial websites, add a copyright notice at or near the bottom of the home and subsidiary pages. Figure 2-17 illustrates a copyright notice at the bottom of the Chase home page.

Figure 2-17 Webpages at commercial websites generally include a copyright notice.

Publishing a website might expose you to potential liabilities, such as copyright infringement, defamation, or libel, especially when you use website content from different sources or include links to webpages at other websites. For protection against these potential liabilities, you can post on your website a disclaimer of liability notice prepared by an attorney. Figure 2-18 illustrates the disclaimer of liability notice at the U.S. Department of the Interior website.

Q&A

What are phishing and spoofing?
Phishing and spoofing are methods of misleading people into revealing personal or financial information. In a **phishing** scheme, a perpetrator imitates a legitimate company, such as an ISP or online bank, and sends an email message requesting that the user verify account information. The message directs users to a fraudulent website, which may look authentic but is actually a fake. The fraudulent website then collects the user's information using forms and other collection methods that appear to be legitimate. **Spoofing** is the creation of a fraudulent version of a website that appears to use the original website's URL by **masking**, or hiding the actual URL while displaying the URL the visitor intended to reach. Visitors to a spoofed website may be fooled into entering account information, or downloading content that contains a virus.

Using connectivity tools to allow website visitors to share your content helps to protect you from copyright concerns. These tools direct the visitor back to your website, which allows you to share your content or connect to other websites' content while crediting the source clearly.

DESIGN TIP

How can I protect my webpage content?
Include the following on your website: a copyright notice, a policy for using images or content from your website, and contact information for those who want to use your work. For more information about protecting your webpage content from copyright violations, use a search engine to search for *protecting webpage copyrights*.

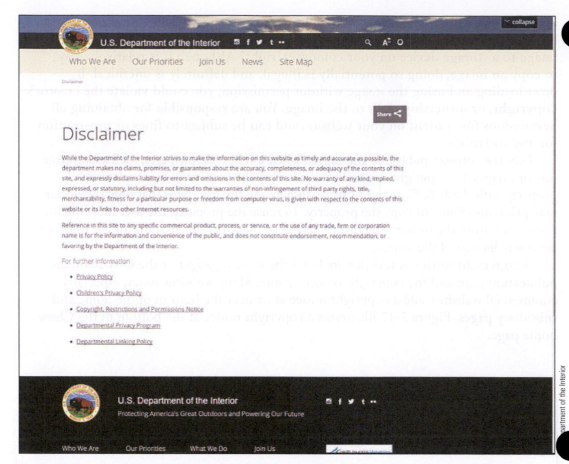

Figure 2-18 A disclaimer of liability notice can protect website owners against potential liabilities.

What are digital certificates and signatures?
Digital certificates and signatures are methods for verifying a content's source. For more information about these tools, use a search engine to search for *digital certificates and signatures*.

PRIVACY ISSUES AND DATA SECURITY Many websites, especially e-commerce websites, collect sensitive **personally identifiable information (PII)**, such as Social Security numbers, credit card numbers, names, addresses, and telephone numbers. To provide security for transmission of personal or confidential information, such as credit card transactions, e-commerce websites use encryption, which prevents unauthorized recipients from reading data. **Encryption** is a process that encodes data into illegible content. To restore the usability of encrypted data, users apply **decryption** techniques, which remove the encryption and return data to its original format. The **Secure Sockets Layer (SSL)** protocol safeguards and encrypts confidential information as it travels over the Internet. Webpages with the *https://* protocol designation instead of *http://* in their URL use SSL to transmit customers' data.

Websites often use tracking tools to customize a website visitor's session, or to collect a user's personal information. Most often, the tracking occurs without the user's permission or knowledge. When used positively, web tracking tools can make it more convenient for visitors to return to their favorite websites by storing their login data or webpage customization preferences. Web tracking tools also can collect information about a user, such as personal information or website visits, and report that information back to the website owner or to a third party. A common web tracking method is the use of **cookies**, which are small text files stored on a visitor's hard drive. Chapter 7 discusses in more detail various methods of tracking visitor statistics, including Google Analytics and the use of server logs and cookies.

Protecting sensitive information that a user provides voluntarily is only part of the privacy issue. The server's transaction log records every request for a page from a web browser to a web server. Many websites automatically collect certain information from visitors, such as domain names, browser types, and operating systems from these server transaction logs. Although the content of this information is not sensitive, websites collect it without a visitor's approval or control, violating the privacy of users without their knowledge.

Website visitors have legitimate concerns about how all their information, whether willfully submitted or automatically gathered, is being used. Additionally, visitors are concerned about the steps being taken by website publishers to ensure that their information remains secure and out of the hands of unauthorized parties. Privacy advocates have been working to come up with guidelines and practices for website owners and visitors to protect personal data from being misused. The term **big data** refers to large and complex collections of information from a variety of sources, including website statistics, e-commerce transactions, social media profiles, databases, and other personally identifiable information about a person available through public records and other sources.

To ease visitors' concerns, many websites, especially e-commerce websites, include a **privacy policy statement** that explains the use of information submitted by a visitor or gathered automatically through server logs and cookies. For example, such a statement might explain that the website owners use the information only to gather demographic data about website visitors and will not release data to any third party. Figure 2-19 illustrates a portion of the privacy policy statement on the Privacy webpage at the American Student Assistance website.

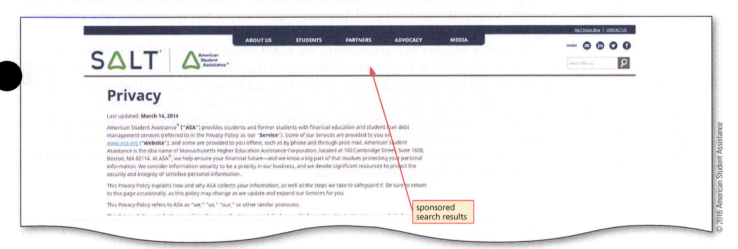

Figure 2-19 A privacy policy statement explains how the organization uses visitor information.

Establish privacy and data security policies for your website operations. Make sure that everyone associated with designing, maintaining, and operating the website is aware of the policies. Explain your policies to website visitors by publishing a privacy policy statement.

DESIGN TIP

In addition to posted privacy and security statements, many commercial and organizational websites also participate in the privacy and security standards certification programs offered by entities such as TRUSTe and BBBOnline. Members in good standing of these certification programs may indicate compliance with the program's privacy and security standards by displaying program seals, or graphic symbols, on their webpages.

Exploring Website Privacy and Data Security Issues

1. Use a search engine to search for websites for the following organizations: TRUSTe, Verisign, and National Consumers League.

2. Open each website in a different tab.

3. Review the privacy and data security issues and tools discussed at each website.

4. Explain how you would use this information to ensure the privacy of visitors' information and the security of visitors' data at your website.

5. Submit your findings in the format requested by your instructor.

Accessibility and Usability Issues

Web designers incorporate features called web **accessibility** to ensure that their websites are usable by people with various types of special needs, such as lost or impaired vision or color blindness. Web accessibility is an important issue for the World Wide Web Consortium (W3C), which sets web standards. To advance web accessibility, the W3C sponsors the Web Accessibility Initiative (WAI), a consortium of government agencies, IT industry representatives, and nonprofit organizations representing people with special needs. The WAI encourages accessibility through technology, guidelines, and research. Currently, the WAI guidelines are specifications, not regulations, which many organizations choose to adopt for their websites.

To further support web accessibility, the U.S. Congress instituted Section 508 of the U.S. Rehabilitation Act. Section 508 requires that all U.S. government agencies use accessibility technologies and follow accessibility guidelines to ensure that people with special needs can acquire the public information posted to the agencies' websites. Many e-commerce and educational websites and most U.S. government websites now provide a statement of commitment to web accessibility, including information describing how accessibility issues are handled at the website. Figure 2-20 illustrates the web accessibility statement at the City of Houston website.

Q&A

What are some accessibility guideline examples? For more information about web accessibility guidelines, use a search engine to search for *WAI* and *Section 508*.

Figure 2-20 Many commercial and educational websites and most government websites affirm their web accessibility compliance.

Design your website to be accessible by people with various types of special needs, such as lost or impaired vision or color blindness, by following the WAI and Section 508 guidelines for web accessibility. If using a web development tool, use the tools provided by the program to check for potential accessibility issues.

DESIGN TIP

Although some people use the terms web *accessibility* and web *usability* interchangeably, they are related, but different, concepts. Whereas web accessibility deals with ensuring access to web-based information, web **usability** involves designing a website and its pages so that all visitors to the website can easily and quickly satisfy their goals. Web designers incorporate **user experience (UX)** practices into webpage design. The goal of UX is to enhance the user's website experience in order to meet the user's needs and make the user feel their visit was worthwhile.

Q&A

What are UX principles?
UX incorporates all elements of good web design, including website structure, the use of text, color, and images, navigational elements, and other design guidelines discussed throughout this text.

Chapter Review

Print publishing cannot match the benefits of the web for delivering current, interactive content and for efficient, cost-effective distribution of information. The objective of web publications is to deliver a specific message and leave a distinct impression. Achieving these objectives requires combining creativity with the fundamental design principles of balance and proximity, contrast and focus, and visual identity and unity. Website visitors quickly want to find accurate, easy-to-read, well-organized, and concise information that they can use. Writing content with these attributes requires applying specific techniques including chunked text and inverted pyramid-style content. Color can powerfully enhance a website's message and personality. Persuasive, effective color use involves being aware of established color principles and conventions. Using the principles of responsive web design ensures your webpages can be viewed on multiple devices. Successful web publishing further includes recognizing certain technical, legal, privacy, accessibility, and usability issues, and applying the design techniques that can manage them effectively and responsibly.

TERMS TO KNOW

After reading the chapter, you should know each of these Key Terms.

accessibility (64)
aggregator (41)
alignment (51)
alternative text (59)
analytics (44)
asymmetrical (48)
auto-rotate (59)
balance (47)
bandwidth (58)
big data (63)
brand (50)
branding specifications (50)
chunked text technique (55)
color depth (53)
color wheel (52)
complementary colors (52)
connectivity advantage (41)
connectivity tools (40)
contrast (49)
convergence (42)
cookies (62)
cool colors (52)
copyright (61)
copyright notice (61)
cost advantage (46)
currency advantage (40)
decryption (62)
delivery advantage (46)
encryption (62)
focal point (49)

graphical display browser (58)
hexadecimal system (53)
interactivity advantage (42)
inverted pyramid style (57)
masking (61)
netiquette (57)
personally identifiable information
　(PII) (62)
phishing (61)
pixel (59)
primary colors (52)
privacy policy statement (63)
proximity (48)
resolution (59)
RGB color system (52)
scannability (56)
secondary colors (52)
Secure Sockets Layer (SSL) (62)
spoofing (61)
symmetrical (47)
tag line (50)
thumbnail (58)
unity (50)
usability (65)
user experience (UX) (65)
values (52)
visual identity (50)
warm colors (52)
web-based form (44)
white space (48)

TEST YOUR KNOWLEDGE

Complete the Test Your Knowledge exercises to solidify what you have learned in the chapter.

Matching Terms

Match each term with the best description.

_____ 1. accessibility

_____ 2. alignment

_____ 3. auto-rotate

_____ 4. big data

_____ 5. color depth

_____ 6. contrast

_____ 7. convergence

_____ 8. cookies

_____ 9. focal point

a. The creation of a fraudulent version of a website and masking its URL.

b. Small text files stored on a website visitor's hard drive.

c. A dominating segment of a webpage that directs visitors' attention to a center of interest or activity.

d. A feature that changes the screen orientation from landscape to portrait.

e. Large and complex collections of information from a variety of sources, including website statistics, e-commerce transactions, social media profiles, and databases.

_____ 10. RGB color system

_____ 11. spoofing

_____ 12. symmetrical

f. The trend of connecting information and accounting between devices.

g. The actual number of colors that a monitor displays, stated in bits.

h. A mix of elements to stimulate attention.

i. Web layout where elements appear centered or even.

j. Combination of channels of red, green, and blue light, which computer monitors use to project color.

k. Web design guidelines applied to websites and pages to ensure ease of use by people with special needs.

l. Arrangement of objects in fixed or predetermined positions.

Short Answer Questions

Write a brief answer to each question.

1. List and explain the advantages of web publishing over print.

2. Identify the basic design principles that help webpages deliver a powerful message and leave a distinct impression.

3. Discuss how responsive web design principles influence web design.

4. Discuss the role of branding in promoting unity and maintaining visual identity.

5. Define chunked text and discuss reasons for using chunked text to create scannable web content.

6. Explain the role of color as a web design tool.

7. Describe the color wheel and identify primary colors and secondary colors.

8. Explain how to incorporate UX into the web design.

9. Briefly discuss each of the following web publishing issues:

   a. Bandwidth

   b. Resolution

   c. Legal and privacy concerns

   d. Usability and accessibility

TRENDS

Investigate current web design developments with the Trends exercises.

Write a brief essay about each of the following trends, using the web as your research tool. For each trend, identify at least one webpage URL used as a research source. Be prepared to discuss your findings in class.

1 | Section 508

Research the latest developments in accessibility standards. Make a list of three important accessibility considerations, and note whether they are new or existing issues. Visit two websites to see whether these websites meet the considerations.

2 | Big Data

Research types of information collected as part of big data. Find articles stating pros and cons of big data practices by companies and other institutions. What concerns do you have about big data? How could big data practices benefit you? Will you take measures to protect yourself from big data? If so, how and why?

@ISSUE

Challenge your perspective of the web and web design technology with the @Issue exercises.

Write a brief essay in response to the following issues, using the web as your research tool. For each issue, identify at least one webpage URL used as a research source. Be prepared to discuss your findings in class.

1 | Personally Identifiable Information

Make a list of at least three websites into which you have entered personally identifiable information. Think about the information you have entered into each source and whether you feel comfortable knowing that others could access this information. Find privacy statements on each website. Does the statement provide assurance to your concerns?

2 | Accuracy

Explain how accuracy affects the overall user impression and contributes to the success or failure of a website. How can you ensure accuracy with your content? What measures can you take to reassure your audience that your content is accurate?

Use the World Wide Web to obtain more information about the concepts in the chapter with the Hands On exercises.

1 | Explore and Evaluate: Branding

Browse the web to find an example of a webpage whose branding, in your opinion, is inconsistent or ineffective. How does the website successfully incorporate its branding? Suggest changes to logos, layout, fonts, colors, and other design principles to improve the website's branding.

2 | Search and Discover: Writing for the Web

Find news articles on two different websites on the same topic or current event.

1. Explain how each article incorporates techniques discussed in this chapter, including the inverted pyramid and chunked text.

2. Does one article have better web writing in your opinion? Why?

3. How might you suggest changing the writing style to make the article more web-friendly?

Work collaboratively to reinforce the concepts in the chapter with the Team Approach exercises.

1 | Rate History Museum Websites

Form a team with three of your classmates. Have each team member visit the home page plus three subsidiary pages of a different history museum website, including one for a large museum such as the Museum of Natural History in New York, one of the history museums associated with the Smithsonian museums in Washington, D.C., and a local historical museum, such as the Salem Witch Museum. Rate each website on how well the website incorporates the basic design principles presented in this chapter:

- Balance and proximity
- Contrast and focus
- Unity and visual identity

a. Use a rating scale of 1 through 5, where 5 is the highest rating. Meet as a team and summarize your ratings; using your summary, rank the three websites from highest to lowest.

b. Explain how you would use the design principles embodied at the highest-ranking website to plan the design for your website. Be prepared to discuss your findings with the class.

2 | Compare Interactivity at E-Commerce Websites

Form a team of three or four classmates to evaluate how the following e-commerce websites use web design to promote interactivity with their customers, potential customers, partners, and other interested parties. Which of the e-commerce websites is the most successful at promoting interactivity? Which is the least successful? Why? Suggest ways that the least successful website might better promote interactivity.

   a. Amazon

   b. Dell

   c. IKEA

   d. etsy

Write a report of your team's findings and be prepared to discuss your report in class.

CASE STUDY

Apply the chapter concepts to the ongoing development process in web design with the Case Study.

The Case Study is an ongoing development process using the concepts, techniques, and Design Tips presented in each chapter.

Background Information

As you progress through the chapters, you will learn how to use design as a tool to create effective webpages and websites. At each chapter's conclusion, you will receive instructions for completing each segment of the ongoing design process.

In this chapter's assignment, you are to identify methods and tools to manage currency, encourage connectivity, and promote interactivity and communication at your website. Discuss costs associated with the development of your website. Create a tag line, describe how you plan to use color at your website, find resources for your website's topic, practice writing and editing scannable text, apply responsive web design techniques, and create a plan for handling accessibility and usability issues.

Chapter 2 Assignment

1. In the format requested by your instructor, do all of the following:

   a. Identify the element(s) that you could include on your website that would convey to its audience that the website's content is current.

   b. Identify the connectivity tools you will use to encourage users to share or promote your content, and explain how you will use them.

   c. Identify ways you can promote interactivity at your website.

   d. Create an appropriate tag line for your website and describe how you will use it in the website's design.

   e. Describe how you plan to use color at your website.

   f. Write three paragraphs about your website's topic in inverted pyramid style. Then rewrite the paragraphs as chunked text.

   g. Describe how you plan to use RWD principles to enhance your website's usability.

   h. List ways you plan to make your website accessible.

2. Submit your findings in the format requested by your instructor and be prepared to share your plan with the class.

3 Planning a Successful Website: Part 1

© 2016 FCA USA LLC

© 2016 Trader Joe's

Introduction

Chapters 1 and 2 introduced you to the Internet and the World Wide Web, different types of websites, and basic web design tools and roles. You also learned about important techniques for writing text for webpages, using color as a design tool, and addressing privacy and security considerations.

Chapters 3 and 4 explain important steps in website planning. In this chapter, you explore some of the first steps in the website development process: defining the website's purpose and target audience; determining the website's general content; and specifying the website's structure. Then, using what you have learned about the website planning process, you begin to develop a plan for your own website. You complete your website's plan in Chapter 4. Completing the steps in Chapters 3 and 4 helps you to create a comprehensive website. The order of the steps may overlap or switch depending on the complexity of your website and the number of people involved in its planning. It is important to think of the website as a complete project, where each step and component must complement and align with the plans for other steps. Before finalizing your website plan, you should review all steps to ensure that there is no conflict between later steps and decisions made earlier in the project.

Objectives

After completing this chapter, you will be able to:

1. Describe the website development planning process

2. Complete Step 1: Identify the website's purpose and target audience

3. Complete Step 2: Determine the website's general content

4. Complete Step 3: Select the website's structure

The Website Development Planning Process

The best way to ensure the success of any project is to plan it carefully. It takes thorough preparation to develop a website that will achieve its goals and attract and influence its audience. Creating a website requires you to invest significant time and other resources; planning helps ensure that the website development process is efficient, cost-effective, and successful. Before you begin to create your first webpage, you must develop a solid, detailed plan for the website, called a **website plan** or **design plan**. This plan determines the purpose, audience, content, structure, navigation system, visual design, and publishing and maintenance strategy. Following the six major steps illustrated in Figure 3-1 is a good way to approach the development of a detailed website plan.

STEP 1: Define the website's purpose and target audience

STEP 2: Determine the website's general content

STEP 3: Select the website's structure

STEP 4: Specify the website's navigation system

STEP 5: Design the look of the website

STEP 6: Develop a plan to test, publish, and maintain the website

Figure 3-1 Creating a successful website begins with developing a detailed website plan.

DESIGN TIP When creating a design plan, be sure to have colleagues, managers, or other stakeholders review the plan. Although you might think that visual design would be the most important aspect of a website, you first need to determine the purpose, audience, content, and structure. These conclusions influence the decisions regarding creating a visual design that meets the needs of your website.

Because planning is critical to the development of a successful website, this book devotes two chapters to a thorough discussion of the six steps illustrated in Figure 3-1. This chapter discusses Steps 1 through 3. Chapter 4 discusses Steps 4 through 6. In this and subsequent chapters, a specific web design example is used to explain the concepts related to developing a detailed design plan. In this scenario, you are the head of the web design department at Fit4U, a new B2C e-commerce company that focuses on selling fitness-related products and services. You need to work with your team of web designers to develop a website plan for the new company.

Step 1: Define the Website's Purpose and Audience

Your first step in developing a solid website design plan is to define the website's goals, objectives, and audience, and then formulate a written purpose statement for the website. **Goals** are the results you want your website to accomplish within a specific time frame; you might set separate goals for the first weeks, months, or years of business. Goals might include sales, number of visitors, or social media interactions. **Objectives** are those methods you will use to accomplish the website's goals. Although anyone has the potential to visit your website, you must identify the specific group of visitors you want to reach. Recognizing the website's **target audience**, and knowing their wants, needs, and expectations, enables you to create a website that provides the most value for that audience. A formal, written **purpose statement** summarizes your website's goals and objectives to ensure that they meet the audience's expectations and needs.

Website Goals

Although a website has a primary goal, it likely will have additional secondary goals. For example, in this chapter's example, your website's primary goal is to sell products or services. You can set secondary goals that support your website's primary goal, such as providing customer service, educating customers about new products or services, promoting communication between employees and customers, informing shareholders of business developments, or keeping customers informed about business changes in your industry.

In the example, your team has identified a primary goal and multiple secondary goals for the new website:

- Primary goal:
  - Increase sales of fitness-related products, clothing, and services.
- Secondary goals:
  - Promote awareness of the company and its products and mission, and build a community of engaged customers and potential customers.
  - Establish the company's credibility in the field of fitness-focused businesses.
  - Educate website visitors about incorporating fitness into daily life.
  - Inform shareholders and potential investors of business developments and plans.
  - Encourage visitors to return to the website by providing updated information in the form of a blog with articles by fitness experts.

Website Objectives

After identifying the website's goals, your next step is to determine the website's objectives—the methods your development team will use to accomplish the goals. For example, if the primary goal is to sell a product or service, the objectives to accomplish that goal might include posting testimonials from customers who have purchased a product or service or offering a 20 percent price discount for customers who purchase the product or service in the next 30 days.

You and your team have defined the following objectives for the Fit4U website to accomplish the new website's primary and secondary goals:

- Develop an attractive, informative, and easy-to-use website that follows RWD principles to promote an online awareness of the company.
- Provide authoritative information and advice at the website to establish credibility.
- Include links to articles and quick tips to educate website visitors about the importance of being fit and healthy.
- Employ social media tools to inform and engage current and potential customers and investors.
- Offer online tools to encourage website visitors to make changes to increase their fitness levels.

Every website should include a call-to-action in its objectives list. A **call-to-action (CTA)** is a suggestion or offer that requires the website visitor to interact with the website by purchasing a product, following the company's social media account(s), making a donation, sharing or commenting on an article, requesting an appointment, signing up for an account, or registering for an event or program.

You and your team identify the following calls-to-action that you will incorporate into the Fit4U website in order to help reach its objectives:

- Purchase products
- Sign up for an account profile
- Follow the website's social media profiles

Q&A

Why is a CTA important?
A CTA helps you to measure your website's success by providing methods for visitors to interact with the website. CTAs are a measure of **return-on-investment (ROI)**, which is a comparison of costs spent and income generated. For more information, use a search engine to search for *website call-to-action*.

YOUR TURN

Exploring Calls-to-Action

1. Search for three of your frequently visited websites and open each website in a new browser tab.
2. Make a note of any calls-to-action you find. Make a note of whether the call-to-action is on the home page or a subsequent page. What is the purpose of the call-to-action?
3. Make a note of additional calls-to-action you might add to the home page or subsequent webpages on the website. How might these suggestions further the website's goals?
4. Submit your findings in the form requested by your instructor.

DESIGN TIP

You will refer back to your goals and objectives constantly as you complete the website plan. Before publishing the website, you should evaluate how well the website's content, structure, and design help to meet the website's goals and objectives.

Target Audience Profile

To begin the process of creating a profile of your website's target audience, imagine the ideal visitor for your website: *who* they are, and *why* they visit your website. Think of what visitors' website experience will provide them and how their actions may help you reach your website goals. A **target audience profile** is a research-based overview that includes information about potential website visitors' demographic and psychographic characteristics. **Demographic characteristics** include gender, age group, educational level, income, location, and other characteristics that define who your website visitors are. **Psychographic characteristics** include social group affiliations, lifestyle choices, purchasing preferences, and political affiliations. These and other characteristics explain why visitors might want to access your website, and how they might interact with your website. A target audience profile is crucial when making decisions regarding user interface (UI) and user experience (UX).

> **DESIGN TIP**
>
> Make sure that your target audience profile aligns with your goals and objectives. You might need to revise your website plan to ensure that the target audience will interact with your website in a way that helps your website meet its goals.

Using research and reports prepared and sold by companies who specialize in demographic and psychographic research, you can ask and answer questions similar to the following to develop a formal target audience profile for your website:

- What is the age range for your likely audience members?
- What are audience members' gender, educational background, and marital status?
- What are the typical careers and income levels of audience members?
- What types of devices do your audience members typically use to access the website?
- What social media profiles do your audience members typically use?
- Where do audience members live?
- What are audience members' social group affiliations, lifestyle choices, interests, and purchasing preferences?
- What would be the audience members' primary and secondary reasons for accessing and interacting with the website?

Based on this information, your team has developed the target audience profile for the new website for the Fit4U example, as shown in Figure 3-2.

Fit4U Website
Target Audience Profile

The typical website visitor

- Is between 20 and 45 years old
- Is 60% likely to be female and 40% likely to be male
- Has a minimum of two years of college
- Has an annual income of at least $40,000
- Lives primarily in suburban areas
- Uses social media frequently, primarily through a smartphone
- Is single or newly married, without kids
- Is aware of current fitness trends and is committed to a healthy lifestyle

Figure 3-2 A target audience profile identifies potential website visitors by defining *who* they are and *why* they might visit your website.

After you identify the members of your target audience, your next step is to determine the audience members' wants, needs, and expectations.

Q&A

Can a website have more than one target audience?
Yes, many websites have multiple target audiences. For example, the Office Depot e-commerce website promotes its brick-and-mortar stores for walk-in customers, sells office equipment and supplies online to individual consumers, and offers specialized services directed to business customers.

Q&A

How do I create a target audience profile?
Sources such as the U.S. Bureau of Labor Statistics, the U.S. Census Bureau, and the Small Business Administration provide resources for identifying general audience demographics. Industry-specific resources exist, such as the Sports & Fitness Industry Association for fitness websites such as Fit4U. For more information about developing a target audience profile, use a search engine to search for *creating a website target audience profile*.

Q&A

How does a target audience profile affect UX?
User experience (UX) decisions based on an audience profile include font, color, and other mood-setting design-related choices, as well as the use and delivery of multimedia, and structural and navigational decisions. For more information, use a search engine to search for *UX considerations web design*.

Target Audience Wants, Needs, and Expectations

A successful website fulfills its audience's wants, needs, and expectations in both general and specific ways. In general, all audiences expect an attractive, interesting, and well-organized website that conveys useful information and is easy to use. An audience's specific expectations for a website will vary based on the website's purpose. For example, a B2C website must offer the products or services that visitors want to purchase in order to meet its audience's specific expectations. If a website does not meet its target audience's various expectations, visitors will take their business elsewhere.

After you identify your website's target audience, conduct a **needs assessment** by answering questions such as the following to determine your target audience's wants, needs, and expectations:

- What do audience members expect to gain from a visit to your website?
- Do audience members frequently use social media tools to share and comment on website content?
- What usability or accessibility issues are important to audience members?
- Are audience members generally experienced or inexperienced web users?
- Will audience members have any cultural biases, norms, or customs that you must accommodate in the website's design and organization?

Your team has performed a needs assessment and identified the target audience's major wants or behaviors, needs or requirements, and expectations for the new website example, as shown in Figure 3-3.

Fit4U Website
Target Audience Wants, Needs, and Expectations

The typical website visitor:

Behaviors
- Frequents websites that include current content, articles, and product tips
- Seeks advice on how to make fitness-conscious choices
- Shares articles and products with others using social media

Requirements
- Accesses the web using multiple device types
- Favors websites that meet web accessibility standards
- Chooses websites that have easy-to-use site navigation

Expectations
- Attractive, professional-looking websites containing credible content
- Websites that emphasize UI/UX, and meet standards for RWD and accessibility
- Social media integration to build community and enable content sharing

---

Figure 3-3 A successful website meets its target audience's expectations by creating a content-rich, attractive, and usable website.

DESIGN TIP
To create a successful website, you should assess your target audience's wants, needs, and expectations. These factors determine how your audience will interact with your website, enabling you to design your website to satisfy them.

If you have limited resources and a tight time frame for your initial website development, begin by identifying your target audience's top two or three needs and plan your website to satisfy those needs. Then after you publish the website, continue to solicit feedback from your target audience to establish additional wants, needs, and expectations and update your website to satisfy them as necessary.

Website Purpose Statement

After determining your website's goals, objectives, and audience, you should create a purpose statement, which is a formal written summary of reasons for publishing the website. A well-written purpose statement synthesizes into a few words the reason or reasons you are publishing your website and explains a website's overall goals and the specific objectives designed to achieve those goals. It also includes a brief summary of the target audience's demographics and expectations. Figure 3-4 illustrates the approved purpose statement for the new Fit4U website.

Q&A

Is determining target audience wants, needs, and expectations a one-time process?
No. After creating your website, you should continually gather feedback from your target audience to update your target audience profile and fine-tune the website's content.

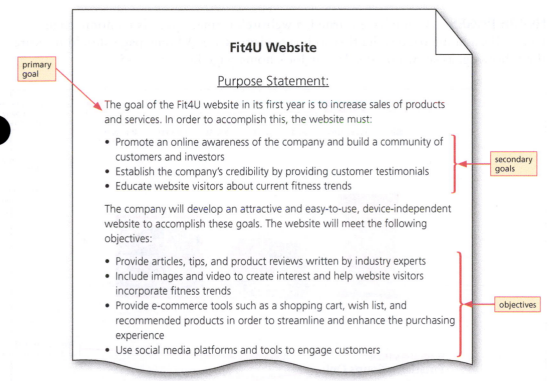

Fit4U Website

primary goal

Purpose Statement:

The goal of the Fit4U website in its first year is to increase sales of products and services. In order to accomplish this, the website must:

- Promote an online awareness of the company and build a community of customers and investors
- Establish the company's credibility by providing customer testimonials
- Educate website visitors about current fitness trends

secondary goals

The company will develop an attractive and easy-to-use, device-independent website to accomplish these goals. The website will meet the following objectives:

- Provide articles, tips, and product reviews written by industry experts
- Include images and video to create interest and help website visitors incorporate fitness trends
- Provide e-commerce tools such as a shopping cart, wish list, and recommended products in order to streamline and enhance the purchasing experience
- Use social media platforms and tools to engage customers

objectives

Figure 3-4 A purpose statement explains a website's overall goals and the specific objectives that will be used to achieve those goals.

A purpose statement can function as an agreement between the web designer and the client, to ensure that the website meets not only the audience needs, but also the goals of the website owner.

DESIGN TIP

Step 2: Determine the Website's General Content

A website likely will consist of multiple webpages including a combination of text, images, audio, video, animations, and multimedia. This section provides an overview of three types of webpages: the home page, subsidiary pages, and a landing or entry page. Additionally, this section introduces the content that might appear on these pages.

Home, Subsidiary, and Landing Pages

Most websites consist of a home page and subsidiary pages. The home page is the anchor for the entire website, and the **subsidiary pages** provide detailed content and interest. Website visitors will access subsidiary pages using the navigation tools your website provides, a search box, or links from the home or landing page. You will learn more about how to structure subsidiary pages later in this chapter. Some websites also have a landing page, which is the page that your browser navigates to when you click a link in an ad, email, or other online promotion from a different website.

HOME PAGES   As you have learned, a website's primary page is its home page. Generally, a home page is the first webpage visitors see. A home page should indicate the following, as shown on the Trader Joe's home page in Figure 3-5.

Figure 3-5 A website's home page should answer visitors' Who?, What?, Why?, and Where? questions.

- Who: Company name in text format, graphic logo, tag line, copyright notation, and similar elements that clearly identify *who* owns and publishes the website.
- What: Summary text and images that show visitors *what* content is available at the website, and what call-to-action is requested or required.

- Why: Text, images, or links that establish the website's value, and provide a reason *why* one should visit and interact with the website.
- Where: Easily identifiable navigational links to indicate *where* specific information or features are found, and/or a method to search website content.

The answer to the *Who?* question should be evident throughout the website by use of corporate logos, a contact link, and copyright notices. An e-commerce website's home page could answer the *What?* question using a slide show or tabbed window to show a variety of the types of products or services sold at the website, or explain how a user can create an account and follow the website's social media profiles. Providing website visitors with information about accreditations or awards for an informational or organizational website or sharing customer quotes for an e-commerce website encourages visitors to choose your website over others, and answers the *Why?* question. The home page of a B2B website that sells web hosting services could have links to pages that detail the types of hosting services provided, fees, customer support information, privacy and security policy information, and so forth to answer the *Where?* question. A home page for a large website should include a **search feature**, which is a text box into which users enter a search term; the search tool then searches the website for that term. Search features function as search engines, but only search within the website for matching results.

DESIGN TIP

A website's home page should contain elements that draw in the visitor and encourage further exploration or interactivity. The home page also should be different enough to stand out as the primary page, but still visually connect with other pages at the website.

Additionally, a website's home page should contain elements that establish the website's visual identity. Chapter 2 introduced the concepts of branding and using design elements to create and maintain visual identity. Organizations and companies spend a large amount of time and money defining, creating, and maintaining a positive, recognizable brand. As you learned in Chapter 2, you can exploit the power of branding on a home page using design elements—images, logo, font, and color scheme—alone or in combination to establish and maintain visual identity.

One way to add content to a home page without creating clutter is to use a tabbed window, slide show, or carousel to provide access to several articles, videos, or other content at once. On most pages, these elements display a rotation of articles or images and automatically advance to the next tab or screen, as well as provide user controls to navigate to or pause at a certain screen (Figure 3-5). Clicking a screen in the tabbed window, slide show, or carousel opens the complete content page in the browser. A **card layout** such as the one on the Hallmark homepage (Figure 3-6) also provides a method to showcase multiple topics or articles by presenting each topic in a square or rectangular area. Card layout content can be influenced by a website visitor's past searches or website visits and providing custom content views.

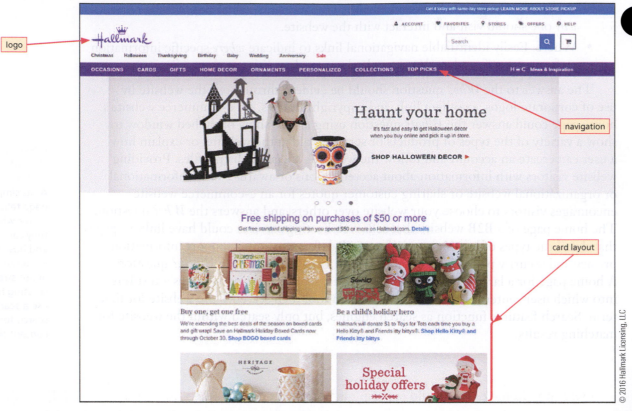

Figure 3-6 A card layout provides clickable areas to showcase multiple topics or articles.

© 2016 Hallmark Licensing, LLC

YOUR TURN

Exploring Home Page Content

1. Use a search engine to locate the home pages for the following: Guggenheim Museum, AutoZone, and Uvault. Open each home page in a separate browser tab. Make a note of who the target audience might be for each website.

2. Review each home page and determine how well each page's content answers the Who?, What?, Why?, and Where? questions.

3. Summarize your home page review. Discuss the content employed at each website to address these four questions.

4. Note the website that, in your opinion, does the best job of answering these four questions and the one that does the poorest job. What design recommendations would you make to improve each home page in terms of answering these questions?

5. Submit your findings in the format requested by your instructor.

SUBSIDIARY PAGES In Chapter 2, you also learned that a website generally includes multiple subsidiary or underlying pages that provide details to the summary information shown on the website's home page. Links connect the home page with a subsidiary page and, where necessary, connect one subsidiary page to another subsidiary page. For example, typical subsidiary pages found at an e-commerce website include pages that provide the following:

- Product catalogs
- Shopping cart and checkout information
- Customer account information
- Customer service information
- Contact information
- Privacy policy and security information
- A blog

Each subsidiary page at a website should include the same elements—name, logo, font, color scheme—as its home page to provide unity and promote visual identity. Figure 3-7 depicts two subsidiary pages at the Hallmark website; comparing these pages with the home page shown in Figure 3-6 illustrates how Hallmark has implemented visual unity throughout its website. Additionally, like the two Hallmark subsidiary pages, each subsidiary page at a website should provide a link back to the website's home page.

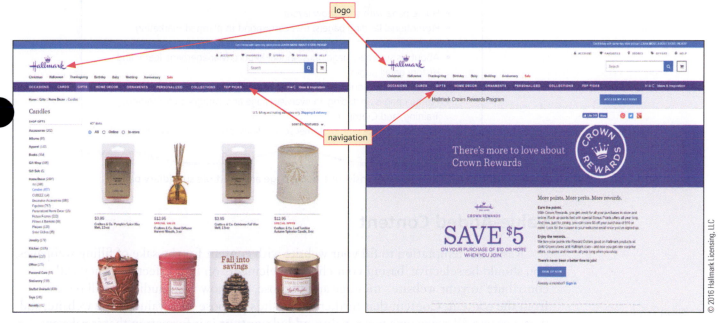

Figure 3-7 Subsidiary pages should include most of the same visual identity elements as the home page.

Exploring Types of Subsidiary Pages

YOUR TURN

1. Use a search engine to locate at least five commercial websites. Include two B2C and two B2B websites, and one C2C website. Open each website in its own tab.
2. Review the types of subsidiary pages offered at each website. Evaluate the webpages for branding and consistency. How do the webpages differ from and relate to the home page?
3. List the typical categories of subsidiary pages found at each type of commercial website. Be prepared to discuss your findings in class.

Q&A

What should I put on my landing page?
A landing page should include text that directly relates to the search query or ad that the website visitor uses to get to the landing page. For more information about creating effective landing pages, use a search engine to search for *landing page content*.

LANDING PAGES As you learned in Chapter 1, a *landing page* is a page that appears when a visitor reaches a website by clicking a link, advertisement, or search result. Web marketers use social media, email campaigns, and search engine optimization (SEO) techniques to generate leads to the landing page. Websites use landing pages as marketing tools to measure the effectiveness of the advertisement by evaluating the number of times the page is visited and whether the visitor goes on to complete a transaction on the website. Landing pages generally have one of two purposes: to provide reference and specific information to customers about a product or event, or to encourage website visitors to complete a sales transaction or other specific interaction.

In the Fit4U website example, you and the team agree on a structure for the new website, which will consist of a home page and multiple subsidiary pages, as shown in Figure 3-8.

Fit4U Website
Website Pages

The website will contain the following page types:

- Home page with slide show layout
- Promotional landing page(s) that correspond to planned marketing campaigns
- About Us summary page, plus Annual Report, Management Team, and History detail pages
- Customer Testimonials page
- Product pages, including an overview page and categories for Videos, Training, and Clothing
- Contact Us page with customer service links, phone numbers, and social media links

Figure 3-8 The Fit4U website will consist of a home page and multiple subsidiary pages.

Value-Added Content

Resist the temptation to fill your website with content for the sake of filling webpages. You should be selective, basing your choice of elements on how effectively they will contribute to your website's message and purpose, and how your audience will benefit from the content. Content that furthers a website's purpose adds value to the website, and does not just fill space on a page. **Value-added content** is information that is relevant, informative, and timely; accurate and of high quality; and usable.

Q&A

What is an infographic?
An **infographic** is data or information presented visually, such as in a chart or pyramid, or to show a sequence of events.

In general, you should create original content elements prepared specifically for the web instead of choosing existing content elements designed for print. For example, on the website's About Us page, incorporate a short video clip of the CEO explaining the company's history and mission, rather than a timeline or other text.

If you must use an existing content element from another medium, you should **repurpose**, or modify, the element for the web. Repurposing content frequently involves shortening or rewriting text, adding hyperlinks to background or additional information, rescanning or altering photos, creating an infographic, and editing or segmenting audio and video. Most importantly, it requires creative thinking and keeping in mind the web environment and audience needs and expectations.

DESIGN TIP

Create new content or repurpose print content so that it will add value. Add visual branding to your text content to fit with the rest of your website.

The following criteria help you determine if the content you plan to add is worthwhile, regardless of whether you are considering images, animation, interactivity, or dynamically generated content at your website. Respect copyrights and give credit to content you repurpose from another source, where appropriate.

The availability of cutting-edge technology alone is never a valid reason to use it. The content element should meet all of these criteria:

- It adds value to the website.
- It furthers the website's purpose.
- It enhances visitors' experiences at the website.
- It encourages interactions.

TEXT   Remember, visitors typically scan webpage text for information rather than read the text word for word. Avoid long paragraphs, and break up text with images, links, and multimedia. When writing original text, follow the guidelines for writing for the web introduced in Chapter 2. You can also follow similar guidelines to repurpose print publication text for the web:

- Chunk text for scannability.
- Place explanatory or detailed information on linked, subsidiary pages.
- Keep content to one page where possible to avoid scrolling.
- Use active voice, action verbs, and a friendly tone.
- Remove transitional words and phrases such as *as stated previously*, *similarly*, and *as a result*, which might not be relevant for the chunked text.

Q&A

What are public domain materials?
The rights to public domain materials belong to the public at large. Examples include older material on which the copyright has expired, newer material explicitly placed into the public domain by its creator, and U.S. government work, such as publications or photographs not covered by copyright protection. Copyrights or patents do not protect public domain materials. For more information, search for *public domain materials*.

Exploring How to Repurpose Text for the Web

YOUR TURN

1. Use a search engine to search for tips and advice about repurposing text for the web.
2. Open a report or document you created for this or another class that includes several pages of text. How should you change the text to repurpose it for the web?
3. Using the guidelines for repurposing print text for the web, repurpose at least four paragraphs from the report or document. As an acknowledgment, cite the source of the repurposed text in a line below the text.
4. Submit the original report or document, along with the repurposed text, to your instructor. Be prepared to compare your repurposed text with the original text in class.

IMAGES   Images are files including graphic elements such as clip art, illustrations, infographics, diagrams, and photographs. After text, images are the most commonly used content element on webpages. Photographs on a webpage can familiarize the unknown and aid in decision making.

You can deliver a message and/or prompt an action beyond the capabilities of text alone using images, such as clip art or photographs. Suppose you are an avid rock climber and need to lease a four-wheel-drive vehicle that can handle difficult terrain.

Before you visit a dealership, you decide to shop online and visit the Jeep website. As you click through to view the photos of different Jeep models, the photo of the sleek Jeep® Wrangler poised in the forest (Figure 3-9) captures your interest. The compelling images

Figure 3-9 Powerful imagery can contribute to a website visitor purchasing or inquiring about your products.

encourage you to search the website to find information on available Jeep options (Figure 3-10). The images prompt you to read the vehicle specifications on the website, and contact your local dealership to set up a test drive.

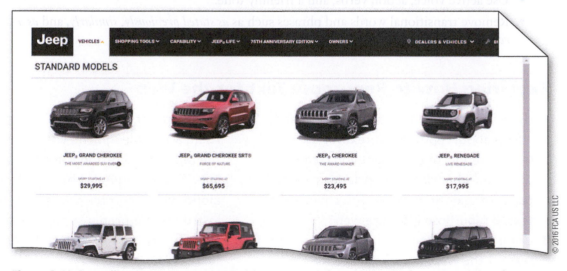

Figure 3-10 Compelling imagery encourages visitors to search for additional information and perform actions.

DESIGN TIP Webpage images can communicate and motivate powerfully. Select relevant, high-quality images that support the website's purpose. Make edits, such as cropping, to relevant images, and view the images' appearances on multiple devices and screen sizes.

You can draw your own illustrations and diagrams using illustration software or take your own photographs using a digital camera. Large corporations will pay for professional photography of their products to showcase them in the best light. You can find free or low-cost **stock images**—clip art and photographs—from a variety of online sources. In Chapter 5, you learn more about webpage images and the tools you can use to create and/or edit them.

Whether you create your own images or acquire them from another source, preselecting high-quality, relevant images that add value to your website, is part of the website planning process. In the ongoing example for Fit4U, the team asks you to research appropriate photographs to accompany articles on the website.

Remember to ensure that content elements you use at your website are free of copyright restrictions.	**DESIGN TIP**

Exploring Stock Photographs

YOUR TURN

1. Search the web using keywords such as *stock photos* or *stock images* to locate at least six sources of stock photographs. Include sources of royalty-free and low-royalty photographs as well as those for which you must pay a standard licensing or royalty fee.

2. Research the selected sources' offerings for fitness-related images and identify four photographs in total from the six sources suitable for the Fit4U website. Why did you choose these images? For what purpose might you use these images?

3. Compare all stock photograph sources. Create a comparison table, including the following columns of information: source name, type of photographs offered, and typical cost. Add a second table that lists the four photographs selected for the Fit4U website. Include the photograph name or other identifying reference, description, source name, and cost.

4. Submit your findings in the format requested by your instructor. Be prepared to discuss the results of your research in class.

AUDIO AND VIDEO   **Audio**, or sound, can vary in both form and intensity—from a child's whisper to the president's State of the Union address, or from a heavy metal band to the U.S. Navy Choir. Audio can persuade, inspire, personalize, motivate, or soothe.

Audio also enhances memory recall or invokes a reaction. Does a lyric that keeps playing in your head remind you of a significant life event? Does a stirring speech make you feel as if you are listening to the speaker's words live? Think of the ways that audio—with its capability of evoking emotion, prompting action, and triggering memory—can benefit your website. Imagine, for example, the persuasive effect of a glowing testimonial about your product from a satisfied customer, or recall the possibilities of a catchy jingle.

Inform visitors when a website link launches an audio file, or a video that includes sound, so that they can use a headset or turn off their speakers so as not to disturb those around them. Repetitive sounds can be irritating to frequent website visitors, so use sound sparingly.	**DESIGN TIP**

Q&A

Should I use streaming or downloadable media on my webpage? Downloadable media that you do not own can come with copyright restrictions. For more information, use a search engine to search for media copyright restrictions.

Typically, **video**, or moving imagery, incorporates the powerful components of movement and sound to express and communicate ideas. Delivering quality video over the web efficiently can present challenges. The primary problem is the extremely large size of video files, resulting from the enormous amounts of data required to depict the audio and video. One solution is to embed streaming video, or links to streaming video. As you learned in Chapter 1, streaming media, such as audio or video, begins to play as soon as the data begins to stream, or transfer, to the browser. By contrast, a user must transfer **downloadable media** in its entirety to the user's computer or device before viewing or listening to it. Linking or embedding a video from an outside source, such as YouTube, keeps the webpage size down and provides a platform to play the video. Requiring the website visitor to click Play to start the video helps keep the webpage download time down and ensures that the video does not start playing without the visitor's interaction.

DESIGN TIP Embed streaming video or links to streaming video, and require user interaction to start a video playing in order to avoid bandwidth issues that might discourage website visitors.

What is a plug-in? Animated and interactive elements might require that your visitors install web browser plug-ins, software that allows these elements to play in the visitors' web browsers. Many, if not most, of your website visitors will have already downloaded and installed browser media players. Most plug-ins needed to run media are free. Some users are wary about installing plug-ins because of security concerns. For more information about plug-ins work, use a search engine to search for *website plug-ins*.

INTERACTIVITY AND ANIMATED ELEMENTS Although definitions vary, **multimedia** can combine text, images, movement, audio, or video, and also frequently can involve interactivity. **Interactivity** refers to elements that encourage website visitors to click, answer questions, make comments, search, or perform other actions.

Animated elements are popular because they can add action, excitement, and interactivity to webpages. Examples of **animated elements** include images that rotate, appear in 3D, or that pop up as you scroll in a webpage. Figure 3-11 shows the website for the documentary *Eat: The Story of Food*, which includes enticing animated graphics. Web tools such as JavaScript, the *<canvas>* element in HTML5, and more make the addition of animation to static images easy to incorporate.

How do multimedia and animation affect web accessibility? Some users have visual, learning, or other differences that influence their website experience. For information about how multimedia and animation can impact web accessibility, use a search engine to search for *web accessibility multimedia and animation*.

Figure 3-11 Animated elements can add action, excitement, and interactivity to a website.

Animated elements can add interest and appeal to your webpages. Use them sparingly and only in support of your website's purpose—and only when doing so meets your target audience's expectations for content at your website. For example, a topical website promoting sports activities to a young target audience might benefit from the use of animations that encourage them to participate. However, the target audience for a B2B e-commerce website offering consulting services might find repeated or multiple animations distracting and annoying.

Simple animations and movies are not difficult to create, as you will learn in Chapter 6. Additionally, many online vendors offer free or low-cost animations.

DESIGN TIP

As with any element, excessive use of animation at your website can shift your audience's focus away from the other content and mask your website's purpose. Overuse of rotating objects, scrolling text, animated advertising banners, or videos that play automatically could annoy website visitors to the extent that they might exit your website and not return.

Although viewers might find your website's animated elements intriguing and entertaining, developing animated elements for your website internally can require considerable expertise, time, and money. Therefore, it might be more cost-effective to purchase appropriate multimedia elements from a professional multimedia developer.

DESIGN TIP

Web designers without the necessary programming resources and expertise can purchase ready-made multimedia elements from professional multimedia developers.

You can add interactive elements to your website such as polls, quizzes, comments features, and more. Survey or polling websites such as Survey Monkey or Doodle (Figure 3-12) can provide a quiz structure that you can link or embed into your website, and even track and project the results back to the website. Comment features are popular additions to blog posts and articles. Someone at the website should monitor comments and other interactive features to ensure comments and posts are relevant and not inflammatory. You will learn more about comments and other interactive website elements in Chapter 6.

TOOLKIT

Appendix C: RWD
For information about how the use of images, animation, and other forms of multimedia can impact responsive web design, see Appendix C.

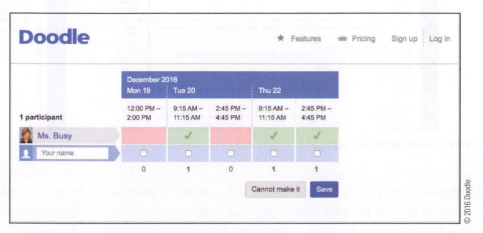

Figure 3-12 Surveys and polls add interactivity to your website.

Exploring Animated Features

1. Use a search engine to locate the home pages for NBC Universal, Golf Channel, Zappos, and VisitCalifornia.

2. Open each website in a new tab. Review the home page and three of the subsidiary pages at each website. Make note of the type and target audience of each website.

3. Evaluate how well, in your opinion, each website uses animated elements on the home and subsidiary pages that support the website's purpose and meet target audience needs and expectations.

4. Summarize your findings by identifying each website and its purpose, and select one animated element for each website that best fits the purpose of the website. Be prepared to discuss your findings in class.

5. Search for websites from which you can purchase animations and multimedia for a fee. Visit one of the websites, and locate at least one element you feel would be appropriate for the Fit4U website. Make a note of the cost, technical requirements, and quality of the element. Determine whether the element meets the criteria for inclusion.

DYNAMICALLY GENERATED CONTENT   **Dynamically generated content**, unlike static information, updates periodically and can appear on a website's pages when triggered by a specific event, such as the time of day or by visitor request. Webpages that display dynamically generated content typically acquire the information from a database. A **database** is a file that stores data, such as a store's inventory or a library's card catalog, so that the contents are searchable and easily updated. Websites that use databases to generate dynamic content are **database-driven websites**. Figure 3-13 illustrates the result of a request for dynamically generated content—course and schedule information—from a Portland Community College database.

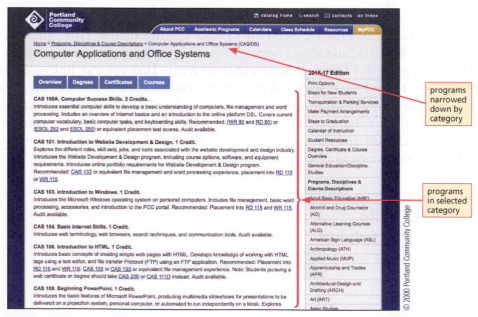

Figure 3-13 Dynamic content is updated to reflect changing conditions.

DESIGN TIP   Use databases to provide dynamic content to e-commerce websites to keep track of items sold and update product availability and inventory, or for an academic website to make sure that online enrollment of classes falls within class-size guidelines.

Continuing with the Fit4U example, you and the team agree that the value-added content for your website will include text articles and tips, appropriate photos and a logo image, product information, and video clips of client testimonials. Dynamically generated content is necessary to populate the product catalog. Figure 3-14 illustrates further development of the planning document for the Fit4U website.

Fit4U Website
Value-Added Content

The website's value-added content will include the following:

- Company logo
- Photos of products
- Video clips of customer testimonials and employee comments
- Current news pages with articles, press releases, and columns
- Fitness tips and tricks on most pages

Figure 3-14 Value-added content for the Fit4U website includes text, images, video clips, and dynamically generated content.

Organizing Website Files

As you develop your website, you should organize the resulting files, including HTML, image, animation, and multimedia files, to make it easier to maintain them and to publish your website. If your website is small—fewer than 5–10 total files—consider creating a single folder for all the files. If your website will exceed 10 files, consider creating separate, logical subfolders; for example, include subfolders for HTML code, photographs, audio, video, animation, and multimedia files. Remember that a single webpage can comprise many files because each graphical element and article or document is its own file.

You can store the files on your computer's hard drive, or, if using a content management system (CMS), the files will be stored on the CMS platform's server. When creating a website on your own computer, back up your files regularly, and store the backups at a location separate from your local hard drive. A CMS typically stores your image files in a gallery, which is a folder or series of folders, specifically for the website's media.

> Plan an organized file system for your website files. You will work more effectively, minimize the risk of losing or misplacing content elements, and facilitate the publishing of your website if you are organized.

DESIGN TIP

Step 3: Select the Website's Structure

After you define a website's purpose and identify its target audience, you are ready to plan the structure of the website—the linked arrangement of the website's pages from the home page. The website's structure should support the website's purpose and make it easy for visitors to find what they want at the website in as few clicks as possible. The website should use navigation, links, breadcrumb trails (discussed in Chapter 4), and other methods to show website visitors their location within the website, and also should show how to return to the home page or previously visited webpages.

Planning the website's structure before you begin creating its pages has several benefits, such as the ability to do the following:

- Visualize the organization of the website's pages and linking relationships.
- Organize the pages by level of detail.
- Follow the links between pages to make certain visitors can click through the website quickly to find useful information—fewer clicks mean more satisfied website visitors.
- Detect **dead-end pages**, which are pages that currently do not fit into the linking arrangement.
- Rearrange pages and revise linking relationships, identify missing elements or webpages, and then visualize the changes before you create the website.

An outline of a website's structure can serve as a blueprint and illustrate how visitors can follow links from page to page. Some designers use a text outline to plan a website's structure, whereas others use a **site map**, a visual representation of the website's structure. Figure 3-15 is an example of a site map used to plan a website's structure.

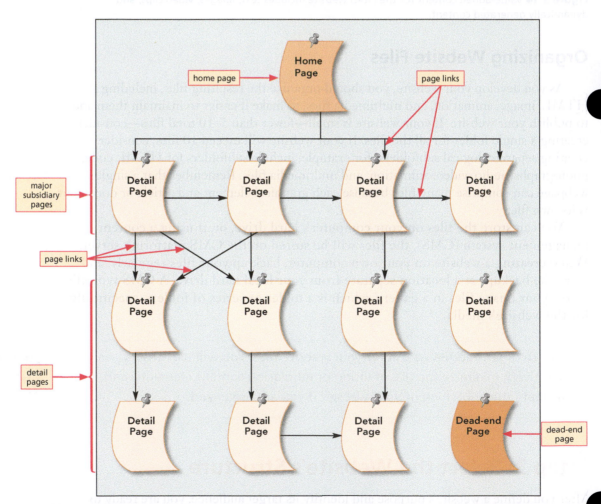

Figure 3-15 A site map is a useful tool for planning a website's structure and defining the links between pages.

To create a site map, draw an arrangement of shapes and lines where each shape indicates a page and each line indicates a link from page to page. You can manually draw the site map, use application tools such as Microsoft® Office® SmartArt graphics, or use drawing software such as Microsoft® Visio Pro for Office 365.

As a web designer, you should choose the method that you find most flexible to outline your website's structure. Regardless of the tool you use, your website's structure will likely follow one of three structural themes: linear/tutorial, webbed, or hierarchical.

Exploring Tools for Planning Website Structure

YOUR TURN

1. Search the web to identify at least three apps you can use to create a formal outline or plan for a website's structure. Locate a content management system that also offers outlining and planning tools.

2. Use a table to summarize your research. Include the following columns in your table:

vendor name, app name, brief description of features, and cost.

3. Include a discussion of which tool you would prefer to use to create the formal plan for your website's structure and why. Be prepared to discuss your research in class.

Linear/Tutorial Structure

A **linear/tutorial website structure** organizes and presents webpages in a specific order, as shown in Figure 3-16. A training website could use this structure to ensure that users do not miss steps or perform steps out of sequence. For example, a website that illustrates how to serve a tennis ball properly would use this structure to demonstrate the necessary range of motions in the correct order. The linear/tutorial structure controls the navigation of users by progressing them from one webpage to the next. This structure is also appropriate for information presented in a historical or chronological order; for example, a website that details the explosive growth of e-commerce might benefit from this structure.

Figure 3-16 A linear/tutorial website structure organizes webpages in a specific order.

Webbed Structure

A **webbed website structure**, also called a **random website structure**, does not arrange its pages in a specific order. From the home page of a website organized around a webbed structure, visitors can choose any other webpage according to their interests or inclinations. Figure 3-17 illustrates a webbed website structure and shows how a visitor to this type of website could navigate to different webpages as he or she sees fit. Websites that use a webbed structure need to provide a search feature so that website visitors easily can find the information they need. Webbed structures work well for some informational websites, catalogs, and other websites that use search features or dynamic content.

Q&A

Do all websites have multiple pages?
No. Some web designers create one-page websites, where information is all on one scrollable page, or all of the information is viewable within a standard screen view. This is not appropriate for any content-heavy websites, and can make it difficult to apply search engine optimization (SEO) and responsive web design practices. For more information, use a search engine to search for *one-page website SEO* and *one-page website responsive web design*.

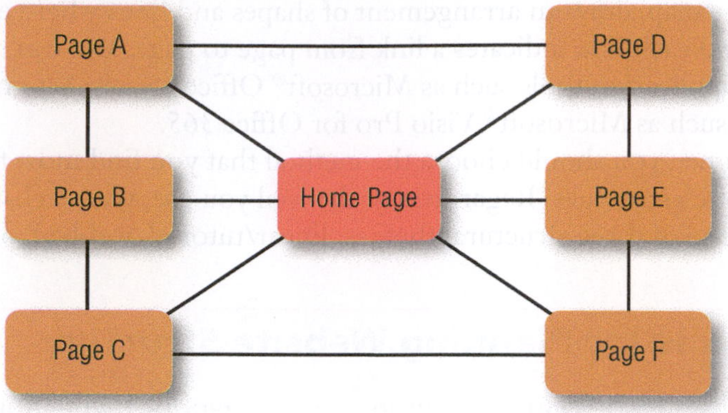

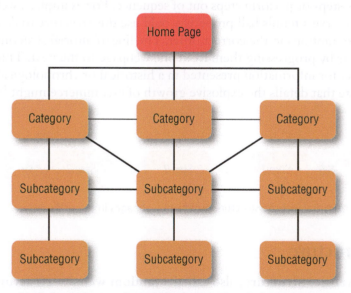

Figure 3-17 A webbed website structure does not arrange its pages in a specific order.

Q&A

Which website structure should I choose?
The type of structure you use is an important choice. Base your decision on the website content and how website visitors will look for information on your website. For more information about planning website structure, use a search engine to search for *website structure*.

Hierarchical Structure

A **hierarchical website structure** organizes webpages into categories and subcategories by an increasing level of detail, as shown in Figure 3-18. Organizational and topical websites usually are well suited to a hierarchical structure. A university website, for example, might structure its webpages in three categories with multiple subcategories:

- Academics category with departments and majors subcategories
- Athletics category with teams and schedules subcategories
- Students category with current and prospective students and alumni subcategories

Figure 3-18 A hierarchical structure organizes webpages into categories and subcategories by increasing level of detail.

Websites with many pages and multiple objectives, such as an e-commerce website, might use a combination of the three primary website structures rather than adhering to a single website structure to organize its pages. Returning to the Fit4U website example, you and your team agree on a website structure that combines the hierarchical and linear structures. Figure 3-19 illustrates the update to the design plan to include the structure site map.

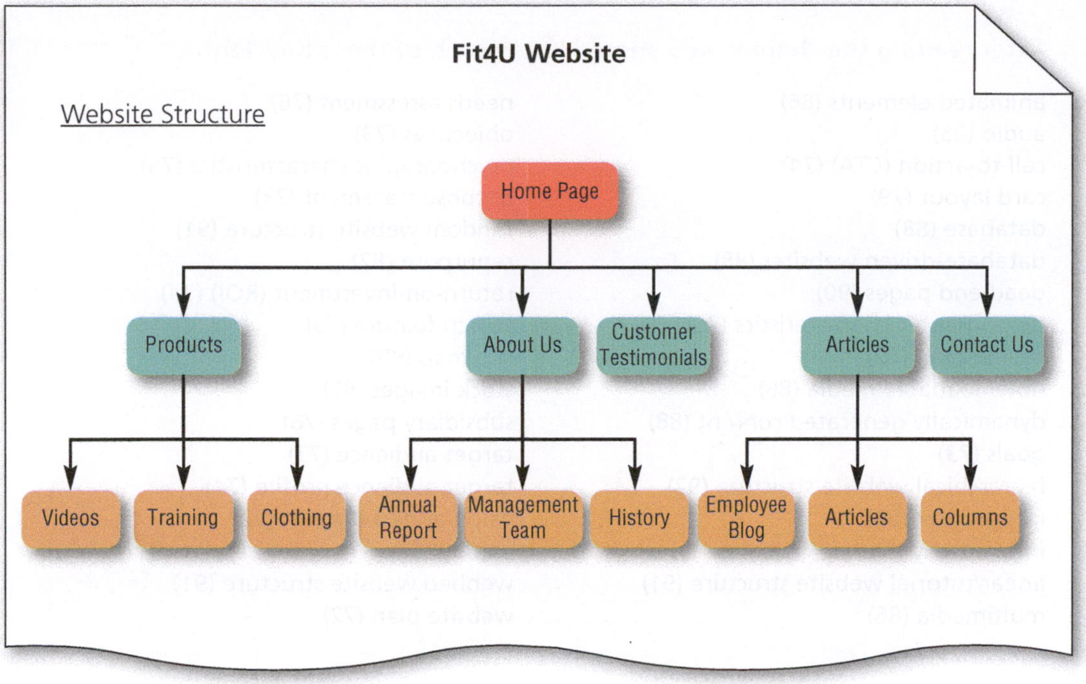

Fit4U Website

Website Structure

Figure 3-19 The Fit4U website's structure combines the hierarchical and linear structures.

Chapter Review

Creating a website demands a considerable investment of time and other important resources. To ensure a website's success, a detailed website plan is essential. Website planning incorporates six general steps, the first three of which you learned about in this chapter. Step 1 defines the purpose of the website, which entails determining goals and objectives. Step 1 also identifies the website's target audience, including developing a target audience profile and needs assessment. Step 2 identifies the general content of the website, including webpage selection and types of value-added content to be used. Content types include text, images, audio, video, animation, multimedia, and dynamically generated content. As you develop a website, having an organized electronic filing system for files and folders will help you work more effectively, minimize the risk of losing or misplacing elements, and smooth the process of publishing your website. Finally, Step 3 involves planning the website's structure: linear/tutorial, webbed, or hierarchical.

TERMS TO KNOW

After reading the chapter, you should know each of these Key Terms.

animated elements (86)
audio (85)
call-to-action (CTA) (74)
card layout (79)
database (88)
database-driven websites (88)
dead-end pages (90)
demographic characteristics (75)
design plan (72)
downloadable media (86)
dynamically generated content (88)
goals (73)
hierarchical website structure (92)
infographic (82)
interactivity (86)
linear/tutorial website structure (91)
multimedia (86)

needs assessment (76)
objectives (73)
psychographic characteristics (75)
purpose statement (73)
random website structure (91)
repurpose (82)
return-on-investment (ROI) (74)
search feature (79)
site map (90)
stock images (85)
subsidiary pages (78)
target audience (73)
target audience profile (74)
value-added content (82)
video (86)
webbed website structure (91)
website plan (72)

TEST YOUR KNOWLEDGE

Complete the Test Your Knowledge exercises to solidify what you have learned in the chapter.

Matching Terms

Match each term with the best description.

_____ 1. call-to-action

_____ 2. card layout

_____ 3. database

_____ 4. dead-end pages

_____ 5. dynamically generated content

_____ 6. hierarchical website structure

_____ 7. linear/tutorial website structure

_____ 8. psychographic characteristics

_____ 9. purpose statement

a. Content updated periodically that can appear on a website's pages when triggered by a specific event, such as the time of day or by visitor request.

b. Webpages arranged in no specific order.

c. Webpages organized by categories and subcategories.

d. Social group affiliations, lifestyle choices, purchasing preferences, political affiliations, and other characteristics that explain why visitors might want to access your website.

e. A webpage that currently does not fit into the linking arrangement.

f. Information that is relevant, informative, and timely; accurate and of high quality; and usable.

g. A file that stores data, such as a store's inventory or a library's card catalog, so that the contents are searchable and easily updated.

h. Clip art and photographs available for free or to purchase.

_____ 10. stock image

_____ 11. value-added content

_____ 12. webbed website structure

i. Something that requires the website visitor to interact with the website.

j. Showcases multiple topics or articles by presenting each topic in a square or rectangular area.

k. A formal written summary of your website's goals and objectives to ensure that they meet the audience's expectations and needs.

l. Webpages that must be viewed in a specific order.

Short Answer Questions

Write a brief answer to each question.

1. Differentiate between goals and objectives when planning a website. What is the goal of a purpose statement?

2. Identify the first three steps in developing the website plan for a website.

3. Discuss how to develop a target audience profile and target audience needs assessment. How does the audience profile influence UX?

4. Define the four primary questions visitors want answered by home page content and identify the types of content on a commercial website's home page that can answer visitors' questions.

5. Define psychographic characteristics. What is their role in creating a target audience profile?

6. Discuss the functions of a home page, landing page, and subsidiary pages.

7. Discuss how the following content types can add value to a website: text, images, audio and video, animated and interactive elements, and dynamically generated content.

8. Explain what a database-driven website is, and give two examples of such websites.

9. Define the term *site map* and explain its role in the website development process.

10. Describe three basic website structures. When is each appropriate?

TRENDS

TRENDS

Investigate current web design developments with the Trends exercises.

Write a brief essay about each of the following trends, using the web as your research tool. For each trend, identify at least one webpage URL used as a research source. Be prepared to discuss your findings in class.

1 | Card Layouts

Use a search engine to find examples of websites that use card layouts. Search for articles that recommend or argue against the use of card layouts. What other website trends do the articles recommend that might fit the same purpose? What are the goals and purposes of a card layout? Do you find them to be effective? Why or why not? As a web designer, when would you use a card layout?

2 | One-Page Websites

The websites with which you are familiar typically consist of several linked pages with a clear organization and an easy-to-use navigation system. However, some websites consist of only one page. Research the trend of creating one-page websites. Find an article that reviews or advises how to use one-page websites. View a few one-page websites. Are they effective or too long? How much scrolling do you have to do to view the entire page? As a web designer, what type of client would you advise to have a one-page website? How does responsive web design affect the decision to create a one-page website?

@ISSUE

Challenge your perspective of the web and web design technology with the @Issue exercises.

Write a brief essay in response to the following issues, using the web as your research tool. For each issue, identify at least one webpage URL used as a research source. Be prepared to discuss your findings in class.

1 | Website Purpose Statements versus Website Mission Statements

A commercial or noncommercial organization often develops an organizational mission statement to succinctly explain to its constituencies (members, customers, employees, shareholders, business partners, government agencies, and so forth) why the organization exists. The use of succinctly worded website mission statements is an outgrowth of the use of these organizational mission statements. However, some business and web critics consider formal organizational or website mission statements to be useless. After researching the arguments for and against website mission statements, create a report that accomplishes the following:

a. Compares website *purpose* statements as described in this chapter with examples of website *mission* statements. How are they alike? How are they different?

b. Describes how, as a web designer, you would advise a client on the inclusion of a website purpose and/or website mission statement at a B2B website.

2 | Web Accessibility

Research web accessibility issues with using multimedia in websites. What kinds of multimedia may cause website visitors to have difficulty viewing or interacting with your website? What types of adaptive devices and software are available for users with accessibility issues to use with mobile devices, or desktop and laptop computers? What can you do, as a web designer, to create a website that is accessible to all or most users?

Use the World Wide Web to obtain more information about the concepts in the chapter with the Hands On exercises.

1 | Explore and Evaluate: Database-Driven Websites

Browse the web to locate three examples of either e-commerce or academic websites that use databases to provide dynamic content. How does the website enable users to interact with the database? What user interactions may cause information in the database to update or change? Using what type of format(s) does the user interact with the database both to retrieve and input data?

2 | Search and Discover: Embedding Videos

Use a search engine to identify at least three sources for videos that can be embedded for use on webpages. Write a brief description identifying each source, the types of videos offered, and, if not free, the typical cost. List any restrictions imposed on the use of videos. Select one video from each website and describe a situation in which you, as a web designer, might include it on a webpage.

Work collaboratively to reinforce the concepts in the chapter with the Team Approach exercises.

1 | Value-Added Content

Good web design involves using value-added content that attracts, informs, and entices website visitors. Team up with two other students to examine the content on the following websites. List the different types of content that appear on the home page and two subsidiary pages for each website. Think about what might be the target audience for each website, and the design and content choices that the website owners made to meet the audience's expectations.

a. JuicePlus

b. DogVacay

c. houzz

Explain how each website uses value-added content. Cite examples that support the teams' decision on how well each website uses value-added content.

2 | Website Goals, Objectives, and Purpose Statement

Join with two other classmates to create a team for this activity. Select two of the team members to form a web design team. The third team member will assume the role of the client who hires the web design team to develop his or her website.

a. The client develops an idea for a B2C website of his or her choice, for example, a bike shop or a pet grooming business.

b. The design team works with the client to develop a list of website goals and objectives, write a formal purpose statement, and develop the target audience profile and needs assessment for the website.

c. As a team, search for two websites that are similar to the one you have planned. Create a presentation for the instructor and other classmates that compares the team's website plan with the sample websites. Include in the presentation an evaluation of how the sample websites met their objectives and what changes you would make to their websites or your website plan after doing the comparison.

CASE STUDY

Apply the chapter concepts to the ongoing development process in web design with the Case Study.

The Case Study is an ongoing development process using the concepts, techniques, and Design Tips presented in each chapter.

Background Information

The three steps described in this chapter covered a lot of material—from defining the website's goals, objectives, and audience, to planning a website's content and structure. If you have carefully explored the information in each step and have worked your way through the end-of-chapter materials for this chapter, you are ready to tackle this chapter's assignment.

Chapter 3 Assignment

In this assignment, you will begin to create your own formal website plan by defining the website's goals and objectives, writing a formal purpose statement, and creating a target audience profile and needs assessment. You will also plan its general content and structure.

1. Using the report you created in the Chapter 2 Case Study as your starting point, create a formal website plan.

    a. Determine your website's goals and objectives and draft the website's purpose statement.

    b. Identify your website's target audience(s) and determine the wants, needs, and likely expectations that your website's design and content should satisfy for that audience.

    c. Identify the pages you initially plan to include at your website.

    d. Add to your website plan a list of value-added content that will help achieve your website's purpose and satisfy target audience needs. Identify possible sources for the content, keeping in mind the copyright issues discussed in Chapter 2.

    e. Determine which of the three website structures—linear/tutorial, webbed, or hierarchical (or a combination of structures)—will best meet your website's purpose. Use a text outline, manually draw the structure, or use software to illustrate your website's structure as part of your design plan.

2. Submit your partial design plan to your instructor. Be prepared to discuss the elements of your partial design plan in class.

4 | Planning a Successful Website: Part 2

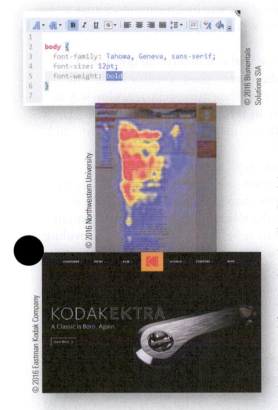

© 2016 Blumentals Solutions SIA

© 2016 Northwestern University

© 2016 Eastman Kodak Company

Introduction

In Chapter 3, you completed the first three of the six steps required to develop a solid website design plan: you defined the website's goals, purpose, and target audience; planned the website's general content; and specified the website's structure. In this chapter, you continue the development of your website plan by discovering how appropriately using two variables—page length and content placement—can enhance webpage usability. Then you complete Steps 4 through 6, in which you plan the navigation, select design options for your website, and plan for how you will test, publish, and maintain the website. Finally, you use a checklist to review your completed website plan.

Objectives

After completing this chapter, you will be able to:

1. Discuss the relationship between page length, content placement, and usability

2. Complete Step 4: Specify the website's navigation system

3. Complete Step 5: Design the look of the website

4. Complete Step 6: Develop a plan to test, publish, and maintain the website

5. Use a checklist to review your web design plan

Page Length, Content Placement, and Usability

When a website visitor views your website for the first time, what he or she sees at a glance provides a sense of the website's contents and its ability to meet visitor needs and expectations. Because you cannot control visitors' screen resolution and size, you should take care to position visual identity content, such as logos and names, calls-to-action, and important links, above and to the left of the potential scroll lines or the **scroll zone**, which is the area beyond the initial visible screen. Placing identifying page content and navigational tools above and to the left of the scroll zone not only is important for your website's home page but also for all subsidiary pages to ensure consistency. As you learned in Chapter 3, your home page introduces your website by informing visitors *who* you are, *what* you offer at the website, and *where* they can find specific information or website features.

As you learned in Chapter 2, the screen resolution and size determine how much of a page is visible. At lower resolutions, and with smaller screen sizes, a visitor likely will need to scroll vertically and perhaps horizontally to view the entire webpage. One way to maximize the initial visual content is to employ content layouts such as cards, carousels, or slide shows. In this chapter, you also will learn about collapsible and hidden menus and navigation tools that maximize visual space.

You also learned in Chapter 2 that desktop visitors typically dislike unnecessary scrolling and often avoid doing so. Mobile users are more used to having to scroll due to small screen sizes. Page length is less of a concern now than in the past, due to mobile influences. You still should consider page length for the following reason: shorter content tends to be better focused. By answering key questions (*why*, *where*, *who*, etc.) and providing links to subsidiary or background information, you will maximize your content's impact while minimizing its space.

The web designers of the Dell home page (Figure 4-1) positioned content important for visual identity and links to major areas of the website above and to the left of the potential scroll lines, and used a carousel to display content.

TOOLKIT

Appendix C: RWD
Carousels, card layouts, and slide shows help prevent webpage scrolling, but may affect your webpage's SEO results and accessibility. See Appendix C for more information about using responsive web design techniques to create these space-saving elements.

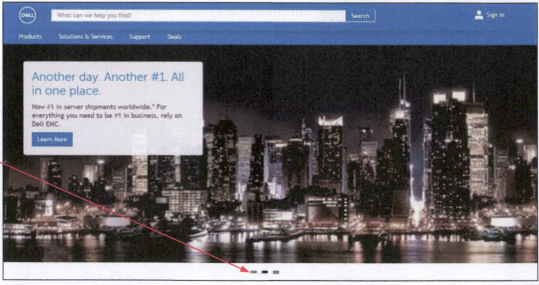

carousel navigation

Figure 4-1 Place content important for visual identity and navigation at the top left.

You have no control over visitors' monitor resolution, screen size, or scrolling habits. To increase usability, take care to place important content, such as logos, names, calls-to-action, and major links, above and to the left of potential scroll lines, and use mobile-first, RWD techniques. Using these methods maximizes the content visitors see, potentially enticing them to read more or visit other webpages on your website.

To increase usability and promote unity, you follow the same guidelines on subsidiary pages by placing identifying and navigational elements above and to the left of potential scroll lines. Subsidiary pages provide greater detail in support of a specific topic or website feature and might not lend themselves to a single page of text, graphics, and other content. When it is necessary to extend webpage content beyond a single visible screen, consider limiting the page length to two screens of content for a typical desktop view, as mobile users are more likely to scroll to view content.

Ensure that your visitors will not need to scroll excessively to view the page's entirety, and easily can return to the top of the page and the navigation area.

Another important UX issue to consider in content positioning is *where* visitors typically first look when viewing a webpage. **Eye-tracking studies** use various technologies to analyze the movement of a visitor's eyes as he or she views a webpage and produce **heat maps**, an analytical tool that uses color to represent data. The resulting heat maps, as shown in Figure 4-2, suggest that a website's visitors typically follow an **F-pattern**: they first look at the top and left areas of a page, and then look down and to the right. Eye-tracking is one more example of the importance of understanding your audience's behavior when making design choices. Eye-tracking studies add support to the concept of placing calls-to-action, visual identity content, and major links at or near the top and

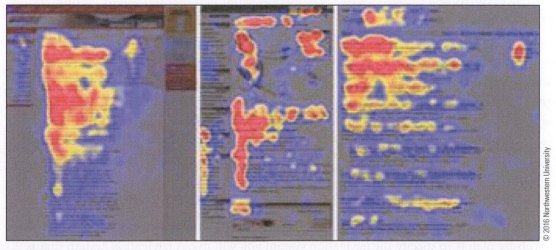

© 2016 Northwestern University

Figure 4-2 An F-pattern heat map shows that visitors look at the top and left areas of a page, then down and to the right.

left side of a page to improve usability. Calls-to-action should be placed prominently to ensure visitors focus on them. Consider providing visual clues, such as arrows, shading, or a person pointing or viewing the content to draw visitors' eyes. Web marketing relies on data from eye-tracking studies. You learn more about website marketing in Chapter 7.

When designing a webpage, you need to decide how to manage page width. A **liquid** or **flexible page layout** sets the width of the page as a percentage of the browser window. The benefit of a liquid layout is that the page expands to fill the entire window, maximizing the viewable content. However, liquid layouts allow for less control over size or placement of images and text, which can result in awkward or unreadable placement or content. A **fixed-width page layout** sets a specific pixel width for the page. The benefit of fixed-width pages is that the layout is consistent no matter the resolution. Fixed-width page layouts can create problems, however. On screens with lower resolution or smaller sizes, visitors may need to scroll a fixed-width page horizontally. A **hybrid page layout** uses a combination of fixed-width and liquid page layouts and takes into consideration responsive web design (RWD) techniques. One aspect of a hybrid page layout may be to set a maximum screen width at which the webpage displays.

DESIGN TIP Consider the needs of your likely website visitors and current RWD practices when deciding on a page layout format. Make sure to test your pages at different resolutions and screen sizes. Consider using a hybrid page layout to ensure flexibility in page width.

YOUR TURN

Exploring Webpage Width Options

1. Use the search tool of your choice to research width options using keywords such as *liquid layout, fixed-width layout,* or *responsive web design*. Locate three articles that discuss the benefits and downsides of different techniques.

2. View webpages of different types (for example, government, business, and entertainment) using multiple devices or screen sizes. For each website, does the page width adapt as the screen size changes?

What techniques might the web designers have used to make the page readable across differing page widths?

3. Summarize your research. How might you apply what you learned about webpage width to the design of a website? Take into consideration audience needs and how the page will look at different resolutions.

4. Submit your findings in the format requested by your instructor.

Step 4: Specify the Website's Navigation System

Once you have determined the structure of your website, the next step in developing your website plan is to specify the navigation system you will use. A navigation system that is easy for visitors to understand and follow will draw them deeper into your website to view detail pages with content that can satisfy their needs and expectations. A website navigation system consists of different types of links: text links; hidden links; image links; related link groups presented as menus, bars, or tabs; and breadcrumb trails. Websites often use a combination of these link types. A large website with many pages also should include a search capability, which allows visitors to search for content within the webpage. You also should keep in mind the needs of touch screen users when deciding on navigation options. In addition, make sure that your use of links meets current WAI guidelines for accessibility.

User-Based and User-Controlled Navigation

In Chapter 3, you learned about the three common structures used to organize the pages at a website: linear/tutorial, webbed, and hierarchical. In our ongoing example, the Fit4U website team has selected a combination of hierarchical and linear website structure. In Chapter 3, you also created a site map (see Figure 3-19) that illustrated the organization of website pages and the major links between pages. With this structure in mind, you are ready to select the link types for your pages. No matter what combination of link types you use for your website's navigation system, the links should be both user-based and user-controlled.

A **user-based navigation system** provides a linking relationship between pages based on the website *visitors'* needs rather than the website *publisher's* needs. To develop a user-based navigation system, you consider the target audience profile information you developed in your website plan's Step 1, and the basic website structure developed in Step 3, with an understanding of UX practices. One way to get a better understanding of how visitors will use your website—and to ensure that your navigation system is user-based—is to perform usability tests as you develop the system. You will learn more about usability testing later in the chapter.

A **user-controlled navigation system** provides a variety of ways visitors can move around a website beyond the major links from the home page. User-controlled navigation allows visitors to move around a website in a manner *they* choose—and not be restricted to the website publisher's opinion of how visitors should move from page to page. For example, some visitors to a B2C website might go straight to the product catalog. Some visitors might prefer to search for a specific product. Others might prefer to learn more about the company first.

> **DESIGN TIP**
> Include navigation back to the home page on all subsidiary pages. Include page-to-page navigation as well as a search feature within a product catalog. Offering various types of links in your navigation system allows website visitors the freedom to choose how they want to move from page to page at your website.

> **DESIGN TIP**
> Create a user-based navigation system to match the way visitors move from page to page at your website. Consider all types of users and their different needs, including how they search for content and what type of devices they use.

Link Types

To create a well-designed, user-controlled navigation system for your website, consider combining different types of links: text links; hidden links; image links; groups of related links presented as menus, bars, or tabs; and a breadcrumb trail. You also should consider adding a search capability to your website.

Q&A **What are the WAI guidelines?** WAI is the Web Accessibility Initiative, an open standard developed by the World Wide Web Consortium (W3C). The WAI develops guidelines to ensure all website visitors can access content on webpages. For more information about WAI guidelines for links and other webpage elements, use a search engine to search for *WAI web guidelines*.

Q&A **What are the WAI guidelines for links and navigation?** WAI guidelines for links specify to identify the target for a link clearly, and not to use color alone to identify links. Group related links together in navigation bars consistently across all pages at a website.

Q&A

What is a tooltip?
A **tooltip** is a small textbox that may appear when you point to a link. Web designers use tooltips to provide a description of the link target to avoid confusion.

TEXT LINKS **Text links** are hyperlinks based on a word or words. Text links are a common way to navigate between sections on the same page, between webpages at the same website, or from a webpage at one website to a webpage at another website. A text link should clearly identify its **target**, which is the webpage or content to which the link points. When including text links to related content, such as an article that provides background information, create the text link using existing text that flows within the page content. This technique frequently is used in news articles, such as the one in the CNet article shown in Figure 4-3.

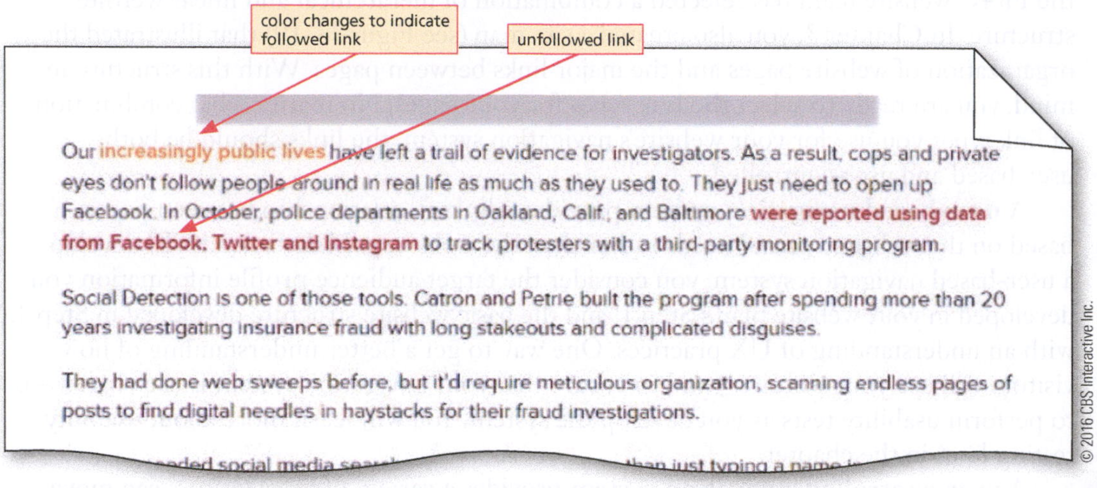

Our increasingly public lives have left a trail of evidence for investigators. As a result, cops and private eyes don't follow people around in real life as much as they used to. They just need to open up Facebook. In October, police departments in Oakland, Calif., and Baltimore were reported using data from Facebook, Twitter and Instagram to track protesters with a third-party monitoring program.

Social Detection is one of those tools. Catron and Petrie built the program after spending more than 20 years investigating insurance fraud with long stakeouts and complicated disguises.

They had done web sweeps before, but it'd require meticulous organization, scanning endless pages of posts to find digital needles in haystacks for their fraud investigations.

Figure 4-3 Within an article, use existing text to create links.

Q&A

How can I make my website touch screen-friendly?
Some menus can be difficult for touch screen users to navigate. Touch screens do not have a pointing device that changes to a hand pointer when positioned over a link, so links and navigation must be obvious to all visitors. For more information about making your website accessible for touch screen users, use a search engine to search for *touch screen-friendly website navigation*.

Use formatting to indicate a text link, rather than adding instructional text, such as *click here*. For example, formatting for a text link might be colored and bold, as seen in Figure 4-3. Including both formatting and color to indicate a text link helps to meet website accessibility standards. After a visitor clicks a text link, the text remains formatted, but the color traditionally changes (such as from blue to purple) to indicate a followed link. Consider using colors for your links that match your webpage design. Be consistent with how text links are treated throughout your website. Avoid using the same formatting you use for links to emphasize text.

DESIGN TIP

Use descriptive language in a text link to indicate the target page content. Use consistent formatting for text links throughout your website. Add formatting in addition to color to meet accessibility standards for text links.

HIDDEN LINKS Some navigational options are collapsed or hidden by default. Called **off-canvas** or **hamburger menus**, when a website visitor points to or clicks the menu, it expands, showing a menu of links. Figure 4-4 shows an off-canvas menu at the Slate

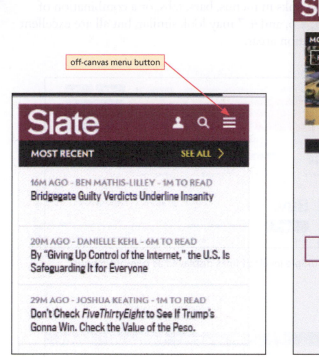

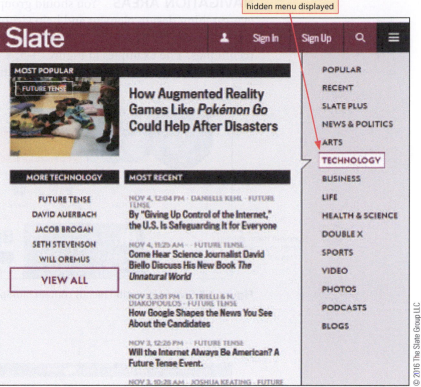

Figure 4-4 Hidden menus save screen space by expanding only when pointed to or clicked.

website. Proponents of off-canvas menus argue that they save screen space. Other web designers avoid them because a website visitor might not notice or click on them, potentially missing out on accessing the content available from the menu. You also might find text links that look like body text until you point to it, at which time it changes color and/or is underlined indicating a link. This type of hidden link is a **rollover link**. Use caution when creating rollover links or using different color scheme colors for your text links. User-based navigation requires that you first consider the effect of hidden or differently formatted fresh and followed text links on the usability and accessibility of your website's pages.

TOOLKIT

Appendix B: CSS
If you decide that hidden navigation serves a purpose to your website while still accommodating visitors' navigation needs, you can create the effects with scripts or CSS. See Appendix B for more information.

> During the testing phase, ensure that any hidden navigation links satisfy your target audiences' expectations and there is no adverse effect on the usability and accessibility of your website's pages.

DESIGN TIP

IMAGE LINKS   An **image link** assigns a link to a visual element, such as an illustration or a photograph. A common use of an image link is an image map. An **image map**, sometimes referred to as a *clickable map*, is an image that contains **hot spots**, which are areas on the image to which a link is assigned.

Q&A

When might I use an image map?
A common use of an image map is a clickable geographic map. For more information about image maps, use a search engine to search for *when to use image maps*.

NAVIGATION AREAS   You should group related links into a navigation area to create an eye-catching design element and help visitors identify links to a website's major subsidiary pages quickly. Navigation areas can group links in menus, bars, tabs, or a combination of techniques. The examples in Figures 4-5, 4-6, and 4-7 may look similar, but all are excellent examples of different approaches to navigation areas.

pop-out menu appears when you point to "Plan a trip" tab

© 2016 JetBlue Airways

Figure 4-5 Some navigation menus contain multiple levels of links displayed as pop-out menus.

navigation button with hover color applied

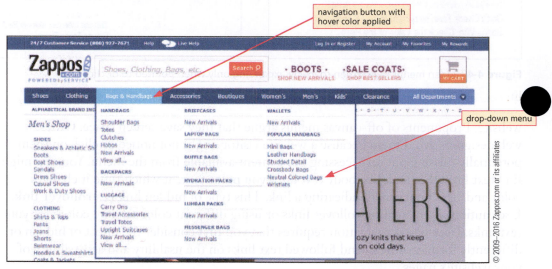

drop-down menu

© 2009–2016 Zappos.com or its affiliates

Figure 4-6 A navigation bar uses graphic buttons to present links; some navigation bar buttons display drop-down menus of additional links.

drop-down menu appears when you point to "Academics"

© 2016 Clemson University

Figure 4-7 Tab with drop-down menu that appears when hovering.

- A **navigation menu** is a list of related links. A navigation menu might contain multiple levels of links displayed as **pop-out menus**. Figure 4-5 shows a pop-out menu from the JetBlue website.

- A **navigation bar** generally uses graphic buttons to present links. Pointing to some navigation bar buttons displays **drop-down menus**. Some websites add navigation bars with text links instead of button links at the bottom of each page. Figure 4-6 shows a navigation bar with a drop-down menu from the Zappos website.

- **Navigation tabs** present links as small tabs. Navigation tabs work best when linking to alternative views of the content. Figure 4-7 shows the Clemson University website, which uses navigation tabs.

No matter which navigation elements you include at your website, basic design rules still apply. Use navigation elements consistently across all pages at your website. Navigation element colors should follow the website's overall color scheme to maintain visual identity. Make certain to indicate the target page clearly.

DESIGN TIP

BREADCRUMB TRAIL   A **breadcrumb trail** is a hierarchical outline or horizontal list that shows a visitor the path from the home page to the currently viewed page. A breadcrumb trail (as shown in the Centers for Disease Control and Prevention webpage in Figure 4-8) provides a visitor with a visual understanding of the linking relationship between pages. A visitor can click any link in the breadcrumb trail to move back to that link's target page.

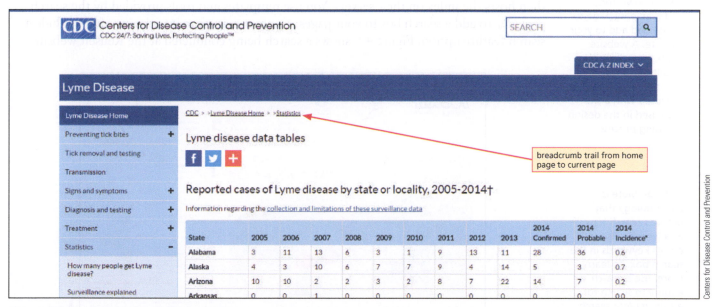

Figure 4-8 A breadcrumb trail shows the path between the home page and the current page.

Centers for Disease Control and Prevention

Breadcrumb trails are best suited to large websites with a hierarchical structure. Use a breadcrumb trail in combination with other navigation elements, such as navigation menus or bars.

DESIGN TIP

YOUR TURN

Exploring Navigation

1. Locate six websites: two e-commerce websites, two blogs about web design, and two organizational websites. Familiarize yourself with the navigation on each website.
2. Examine how each website presents text links.
   a. Does the link text clearly identify the link's target webpage or content? Do tooltips appear when you point to a text link?
   b. Does the website use both color and formatting to define text links? How are fresh and followed links differentiated? Are hidden or rollover text links used?
3. Examine how each website presents menus.
   a. What type(s) of menus does the website use?
   b. Do any examples of hidden menus exist? Were they easy to find and use?
4. Will the results of your research determine what type(s) of navigation you would use as a web designer? If yes, how? If no, why not?
5. Summarize your findings and submit in the format requested by your instructor.

Q&A

What is a website index?

A **website index** is a summary page of links to major pages at the website. With the use of search features, a website index might seem like an unnecessary feature. However, it can be helpful to visitors, and is an easy page to create and add to your website. A website index sometimes also is called a *site map*, but it should not be confused with a site map used in the design planning process.

Q&A

What is autocomplete?

Autocomplete is a technology that predicts search terms as a website visitor enters keywords in the search box. To learn more, use a search engine to search for *autocomplete search feature*.

SEARCH CAPABILITY   Adding a keyword search capability and a search box to all of your website's major pages allows visitors to locate pages at your website that contain specific keywords without browsing your website page by page and maintains visual consistency across pages. A **website search feature** is another popular navigation tool for websites with many pages. A large business or organization that manages its own web servers can use scripts to create and maintain a searchable website index on its servers. If you do not manage your own web servers, you can contract with a hosted website search provider to provide search services. A **hosted website search provider** is a third-party company that uses spiders or other tools to build a searchable index of your website's pages and then hosts the index on their servers. You use templates and tools provided by the search provider to add a search box to your pages. Content management systems often include a search feature option. Figure 4-9 shows a search being conducted at the Reuseit website.

Figure 4-9 Adding search capability to your website allows visitors to locate specific information quickly.

DESIGN TIP   Provide a text link-based website index for large websites with many pages. Organize a website index's text links in a logical way, such as alphabetically or by topic.

Exploring Custom Website Search Providers

1. Use the search tool of your choice to search for the keywords *adding custom search to a website* or similar keywords. Identify five B2B companies that offer hosted website search services.

2. Compare the services offered by each company. Summarize the special features and cost for each company's service.

3. Choose a hosted website search service you could recommend to a client for whom you are developing a B2C e-commerce website. Give the reasons for your recommendation.

4. Submit your findings in the format requested by your instructor.

Create a user-controlled navigation system by combining in your navigation system text links; hidden links; image links; navigation menus, bars, and tabs; a breadcrumb trail; and search capability as appropriate for your target audiences.

DESIGN TIP

Levels of Website Navigation

There are several categories of website and webpage navigation, all with different purposes and functions. **Primary navigation** provides an overview of the website, and generally remains consistent from page to page, such as a menu bar. **Local** or **subsidiary navigation** provides navigation within an area of the website, such as a pop-out menu, or a breadcrumb trail. **Contextual navigation** is specific to the content webpage being viewed. Examples of contextual navigation include text links within an article, or a list of related links. **Adaptive navigation** refers to links that use a website visitor's browsing or search history to provide content suggestions that might be of interest.

Your Fit4U website design team agrees that to meet your visitors' needs, the website's navigation system must be both user-based and user-controlled and should follow WAI guidelines. The navigation system will consist of a navigation bar at the top of each page, a navigation menu on the left side of each page, formatted text links, links that identify their target pages, and links to the home page on subsidiary pages. You also will contract with a hosted website search provider to add a search feature to the website's pages. Figure 4-10 illustrates the update to the website plan.

Fit4U Website

Step 4: Specify the Website's Navigation System

Navigation System

- Top navigation bar
- Left side navigation menu
- Formatted text links
- Search capability supported by a hosted website search provider

Figure 4-10 A user-based and user-controlled navigation system enhances your website's usability.

Q&A

What is the *look* and *feel* of a website? As described in this chapter, the *look* of a website is the combination of design aspects. The *feel* of a website is the behavior of its elements, such as the navigation or animation. The **look and feel** combine to display the emotion or reaction the website invokes in its visitors.

Step 5: Design the Look of the Website

At this point, you have determined the website's purpose and audience, developed a plan for the website's general content, structure, and navigation, and gained an understanding of the roles of page length and content placement in usability. Now you are ready to tackle the next step, which is planning your website design. Chapter 2 introduced you to the concepts of unity and visual identity and the importance of following an entity's branding specifications when planning the design of a website. To promote unity and maintain brand identity across pages at your website, use visual consistency when choosing color and typeface and when positioning content across all pages at your website.

Visual Consistency

Website visitors might feel confused if a website's subsidiary pages fail to include common content and design features found on the home page. They might even conclude that a subsidiary page belongs to an entirely different website. To avoid confusing visitors, all pages at a website must share a visual consistency that reinforces the company's brand identity as visitors move from page to page.

You can create **visual consistency** by repeating design features across all pages at a website, including:

- Font and typeface
- Content position
- Color scheme
- Placement of company or website name, logo, and navigational elements

Repeating design features and content, as shown at the Orange Leaf website in Figure 4-11, unifies a website's pages, strengthens a website's visual identity and brand, and maintains visual consistency.

Figure 4-11 Repetition of design and content elements promotes unity, maintains visual identity, and creates visual consistency.

DESIGN TIP Repeating design features across all pages at a website is one technique you can use to create visual consistency. Use repeated elements such as color, logo, and major links.

Color and Visual Contrast

In Chapter 2, you learned about the principles of color as a design tool and that a well-chosen color scheme creates unity among pages at a website. As you consider color options for a website's pages, remember the power of color to influence moods, the cultural implications of color, and your target audience's expectations for the use of color at your website.

Apply the same color scheme to the background, navigation and other visual elements, and text for all webpages to build visual consistency throughout your website. Page length, content positioning, and use of color come together to create attractive and usable pages.

Choose background and text colors that provide sufficient contrast to enhance readability and that permit print legibility. Studies have shown that, in general, greater contrast leads to better readability. Web designers commonly use light colors (white, gray, or cream) as background colors, contrasted with black- or dark-colored text colors. Alternatively, some websites use darker background colors, such as black or dark blue or dark red, and create contrast with light-colored text, as in the Kodak website (Figure 4-12).

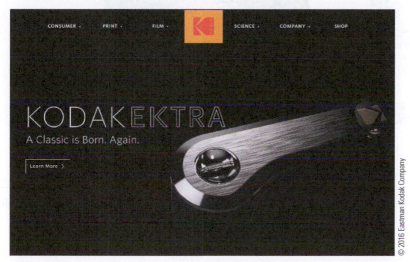

© 2016 Eastman Kodak Company

Figure 4-12 Contrast between background and text ensures readability.

Exploring the Use of Color: Visual Consistency and Visual Contrast

1. Use a search engine to search for the following websites. Open each home page in a new browser tab.
   a. Napster
   b. Adobe
   c. Anthropologie
   d. Huffington Post
2. Review the home page and at least three subsidiary pages at each website to determine how each website uses color.
3. Describe how each website uses color—including overall color scheme and individual background, graphic element, text, and image colors. Does the color scheme offer sufficient contrast between the background, foreground, and text? Does the website use its color scheme to create visual consistency across pages? Discuss how you would modify the color, if necessary, to improve readability and visual consistency.
4. Identify any messages or reasons why the website designer may have chosen the color palette. For example, if the colors reinforce a company's brand or identity, or if the colors provoke an emotional response such as feeling calm.
5. Submit your findings in the format requested by your instructor.

What are the WAI guidelines for color usage?
The WAI specifies that the contrast between background and foreground colors should be sufficient for visitors with vision problems or those using a monochrome monitor. Color alone should not be used to indicate information such as the presence of a text link. A common practice is to combine color and formatting for a link.

As you learned in Chapter 2, webpages can use color to evoke mood, stimulate interest, support a website's purpose, and meet audience expectations for the type of content found at a website. One way to select an appropriate color scheme and apply it across all webpages is to use a template. In Chapter 1, you learned that some web design tools, such as Adobe Dreamweaver CC, content management systems, such as WordPress, and websites such as SquareSpace, shown in Figure 4-13, offer web templates with predetermined color schemes. Color-matching and analysis tools also are available. Using templates or color-matching tools can help ensure visual consistency among all pages at your website.

Figure 4-13 Web templates can help ensure consistency of layout and color schemes across all pages at a website.

 DESIGN TIP   Limit your website color scheme to three contrasting, yet compatible colors. Choose a text color for titles, headlines, and so forth to attract the appropriate amount of attention. Test the background and text colors in your color scheme to ensure both on-screen readability and print legibility.

Another way to choose an effective color scheme with appropriate contrast between background and text colors is to use inexpensive or free color-matching software, such as Adobe Color CC, or Color Hunter (Figure 4-14). **Color-matching software** and color-matching websites contain tools you can use to create sample website color schemes based on color theory, preview the color schemes in a browser, and then apply the colors in the selected scheme to your webpages.

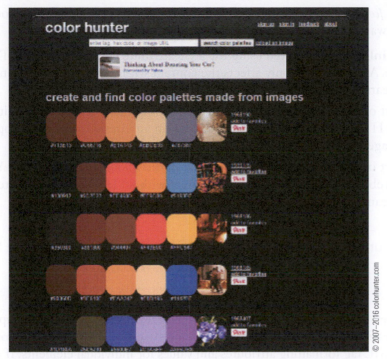

Figure 4-14 Color-matching apps and websites use color theory to select complimentary and contrasting colors.

> Images that you include on webpages, such as illustrations and photos, will add more color to your pages. Choose images with colors that match or complement your website's color scheme, as well as provide contrast.

DESIGN TIP

Continuing with the Fit4U example, your team meets to discuss potential color schemes that promote professionalism and the educational tone of the website's content. To assist in the discussion, your team reviews the company's print media—for example, letterhead, business cards, and brochures—that illustrate the company's branding specifications for the use of color. Based on this material and your discussions with your team, you use color-matching software to experiment with website color schemes.

CSS and Formatting

As you learned in Chapter 1, web designers use CSS specifications to create text documents, called style sheets, to control the appearance of one or more pages at a website.

A **style** is a group of formatting properties, such as bold, italic, font type, font size, or font color, applied as a group to selected text. When you use CSS, you create a style sheet containing style rules. **Style rules** are specifications that define one or more formatting properties and their values (declarations) for specific HTML tags (selectors). For example, suppose you want all the top-level heading text surrounded by the *<h1>…</h1>* HTML heading style tag pair to be a blue color. You could create a style rule for the *<h1>* heading tag consisting of the heading tag itself, called the *selector*, and the CSS property: value

TOOLKIT

Appendix B: CSS
For more information about the W3C standards for CSS, see Appendix B.

What is the current W3C standard for CSS?
The current W3C style sheet standards include modules for both CSS Levels 3 and 4. To learn more, use a search engine to search for *W3C style sheet standards.*

combination *{color: blue}*, called the *declaration*. You can add this style rule to your pages in one of three ways:

- As an **inline style** inserted using the style attribute within the *<h1>* HTML tag on a page. An inline style only affects the content within the *<h1>···</h1>* tags in which it appears.
- As part of an **internal style sheet** inserted using the *<style>* element within a page's HTML heading tags. CSS rules within an internal style sheet apply only to that page.
- As part of an **external style sheet** saved in the folder with the website's pages. The webpages are linked to the style sheet with an HTML tag. An external style sheet can be applied to multiple HTML documents across a website.

DESIGN TIP Because no current browser supports all CSS specifications, be sure to test how the webpages you format using CSS appear in different browsers.

What does *cascading* mean for style sheets?
CSS prioritizes style rules to determine priority in case of conflicting rules. The first priority is for specifications the author sets in the form of inline styles. The second priority includes internal and external style sheets. The lowest priority is default styles specified by the browser. Style rules are applied in cascading order based on priority.

Appendix B: CSS
To learn more about how CSS prioritizes conflicting style rules, see Appendix B.

Style sheets standardize formatting of a webpage, which saves time and simplifies the process of creating and modifying webpages. Using style sheets prevents you from having to insert HTML tag formatting attributes and values for individual elements. If you make a style change to the style sheet, such as changing the font color for all headings, the associated webpages update automatically. Using style sheets also helps you maintain visual consistency across all pages at your website. Web design programs provide CSS tools you can use to create and edit style sheets and link style sheets to your pages. Web templates have style sheets already linked. You also can create style sheets using **CSS editor software**, such as Stylizer or Rapid CSS Editor (Figure 4-15).

```
1
2  body {
3      font-family: Tahoma, Geneva, sans-serif;
4      font-size: 12pt;
5      font-weight: bold
6  }
7
```

© 2016 Blumentals Solutions SIA

Figure 4-15 Web designers use CSS editors to create style sheets they can apply to websites.

Page Layout

Earlier in this chapter, you learned how page length and content placement, as well as UX, affect usability. With page length, content placement, and usability in mind, you should create a logical, standardized **page layout**, or arrangement of content elements, that ensures visual consistency across your website's pages. A standardized page layout fosters a sense of balance and order that website visitors find appealing and reassuring. Figure 4-16 shows the layout of the Target website. Observe that in both the desktop and

Figure 4-16 A logical, standard page layout provides visual consistency across all pages at a website.

mobile versions, the branding appears in the upper left and major navigation links are at the top of the page. Layout grids and Cascading Style Sheets are used to create attractive, visually consistent, and responsive page layouts.

Once you determine the navigation options and repeated page elements, you can start planning how webpages will function. **Wireframing** is a method of creating documentation that plans the arrangement of page elements. Several wireframing tools exist, including Adobe InDesign® CC, and UXPin. Wireframing separates page layout and functionality from design. UX principles recommend the wireframing process to ensure that the placement of navigation and other page elements benefit the user. Figure 4-17 shows an example of a wireframe that shows the placement of the logo, search feature, navigation, and content. The logo placement is important for branding, as well as ensuring to the visitor that he or she has not left the website. Navigation and search affect the usability of each page in the website. Consistent content placement helps the readability of your website. Think of wireframing as a sketch or blueprint of a layout. After the blueprint is complete, you can begin the layout process, and choose colors, fonts, and other design elements to add to the layout.

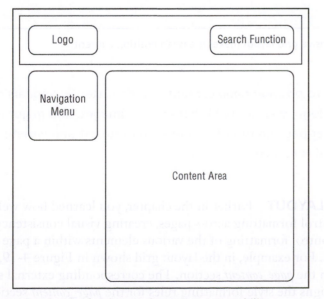

Figure 4-17 A wireframe is a sketch of webpage elements to test usability.

LAYOUT GRIDS Many designers use a fluid or responsive grid layout to position content on a page using an underlying structure of rows and columns. **Fluid grid layouts** determine the size of page elements based on a percentage of the screen. The page elements resize proportionally to fit whatever size screen on which the page displays. **Responsive grid layouts** use a combination of percentages and fixed limits to adapt page elements by size and position. Unlike fluid grid layouts, a responsive grid layout may remove or replace certain screen elements once the page reaches a certain size. You can position and align content precisely, set margin width, and make more adjustments using a layout grid. A layout grid is not visible when a webpage appears in a browser, but it determines both how the webpage will appear in a browser and how it will respond to a variety of screen sizes.

With a web design tool, such as Adobe Dreamweaver CC (Figure 4-18), you can use a responsive grid layout to add and reposition content. You can change grid line color, spacing (pixels, inches, or centimeters), and style (dotted, solid, dashed). Additionally, you can set a command to have content automatically "snap to," or align precisely with, the closest grid line.

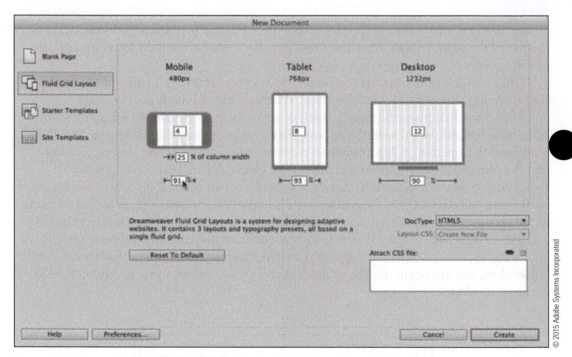

Figure 4-18 A responsive grid layout makes it easy to position content.

DESIGN TIP Use a layout grid to position page content that consistently appears on all pages, for example, the logo, website publisher's name, images, and major links. Then carefully add other page content that generates interest and variety while maintaining visual consistency.

CSS AND PAGE LAYOUT Earlier in the chapter, you learned how web designers use style sheets to control formatting across pages, creating visual consistency. Style sheets are also used to control formatting of the various elements within a page layout, such as a navigation section. For example, in the layout grid shown in Figure 4-19, the article content is displayed in the *page_content* section. The corresponding external style sheet shown in Figure 4-20 assigns the style formatting rules for the *page_content* section.

Figure 4-19 Webpage sections are specified in a layout grid.

Figure 4-20 Style sheets set rules for webpage sections.

Exploring CSS Editor Software

1. Using the search tool of your choice and the keywords *CSS editor software* or similar keywords, research different options for CSS editor programs used to create CSS style sheets.

2. Compare the features and costs of three different programs. Find and read reviews on each program if possible. Describe which you, as a web designer, might use to create style sheets for your webpages, and why.

3. Discuss whether you might prefer to use this type of software program as opposed to other methods of creating style sheets, such as text editors and web design programs.

4. How does each program conform to responsive web design standards?

5. Submit your findings in the format requested by your instructor.

Continuing with the Fit4U example, your team agrees on a page layout for the visual identity content and major links on each page. You also agree on pursuing a responsive grid layout for the pages and to CSS for both formatting and layout. Figures 4-21 and 4-22 illustrate the update to your formal website plan for Step 5.

Fit4U Website

Step 5: Design the Look of the Website

Color Scheme

- Will follow company's branding specifications for color
- Will be consistent across all pages at the website

Page Layout

- Pages will use a liquid layout controlled by CSS
- Header at the top of each page containing logo, tag line, company name, search tool, and Contact Us link
- Major navigational links down left side of page
- Content area in the center of the page
- Contact Us page link, social media icons, privacy and security policy statement page link, and copyright notation at the bottom of each page

Figure 4-21 Apply a color scheme and layout to establish the look of the website.

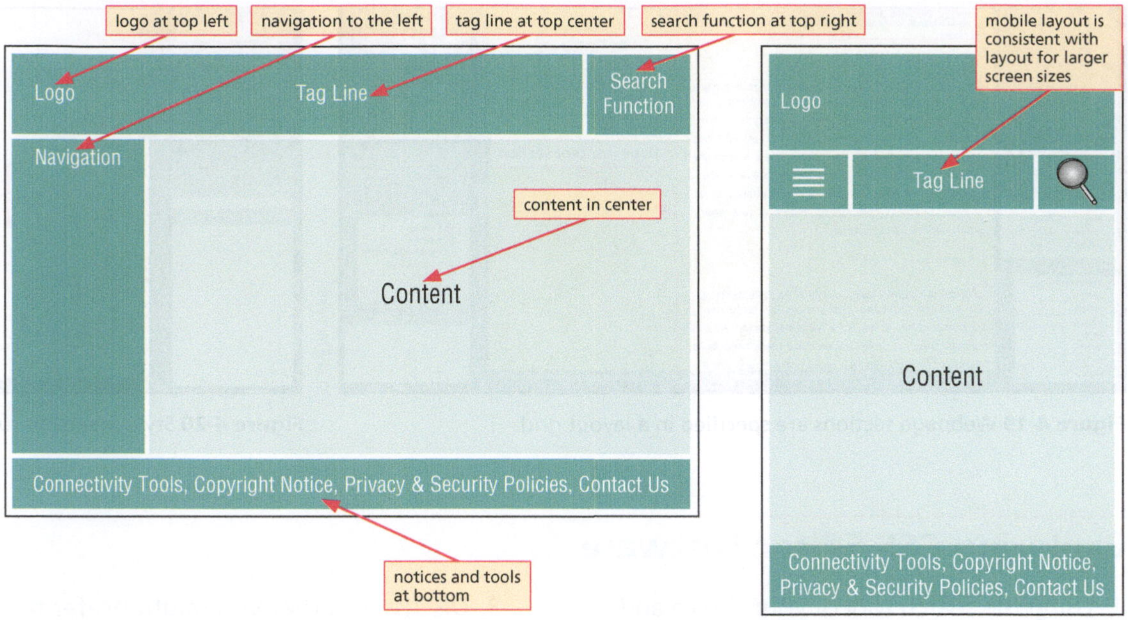

Figure 4-22 Use a consistent and logical page layout across all pages at a website.

Step 6: Develop a Plan to Test, Publish, and Maintain the Website

A complete web design plan includes details outlining how and when you will test the website, how you will publish the website, where you will host it, and the necessary measures to maintain and update the website. These factors affect the budget and timing of your website, as well as its ultimate success. Without testing, you cannot determine if your website will work properly, or if it contains errors or broken links. If you design a website that exceeds the limit of your host web server's allotted size, you cannot publish the website. Without a plan for updating content, your website is static, and visitors have no reason to return.

Testing

A formal website **usability test** is an evaluation that generally takes place in a structured environment, such as a testing laboratory. During the test, usability and design professionals observe exactly how visitors use a website, then use the research to create a report containing design recommendations. Formal website usability tests can be very expensive, costing perhaps several thousand dollars, and might be well beyond your budget. An informal usability test, however, involves using a team of friends, family members, coworkers, or other interested parties to test a website's navigation system or other website features and then report on their experiences. Testers should use a variety of devices, screen sizes, resolutions, and browsers to make the results more complete. Informal usability testing generally is very inexpensive, perhaps even free, but the feedback you gain can be invaluable.

You begin by having a testing team evaluate the navigation system using a website prototype as part of the planning process to ensure that it meets your needs before publishing. In Chapter 7, you learn more about testing your website before and after publishing it.

Q&A

Does testing end when the website is published?
No. It is important to ensure that the links on your website's pages continue to work as intended. You should plan to conduct periodic testing of the website's navigation system, making sure your website works with new devices, platforms, and browser versions.

Publishing and Maintaining

You will learn more about the steps involved in publishing and maintaining your website in Chapter 7. It is crucial to include these steps in your web design plan to create a website that meets the needs of your hosting service, and ensure that you can update and monitor the content to keep your website relevant and entice visitors to return frequently. Some questions you should answer include:

- Will you host the website on an internal web server or will you contract with an external vendor?
- What size limits exist for the website?
- How often will you update the content?
- Who updates the content?
- What budget restrictions exist for publishing and maintaining the website?
- How will you monitor your website to determine what changes, if any, need to be made?

Continuing with the Fit4U example, your team plans strategies and budgets for testing, publishing, and maintaining the website. To ensure a focus on user-based and user-controlled navigation, your team conducts usability testing with a group of participants consisting of two employees, two Fit4U trainers, and two longtime customers. They will test the navigation system's usability on a regular basis during both website development and prepublishing testing. You will contract with an outside web server hosting company. The content will be updated by adding blog posts, weekly sales and coupons, and maintaining the product catalog by using a database. The updates to the website plan are shown in Figure 4-23.

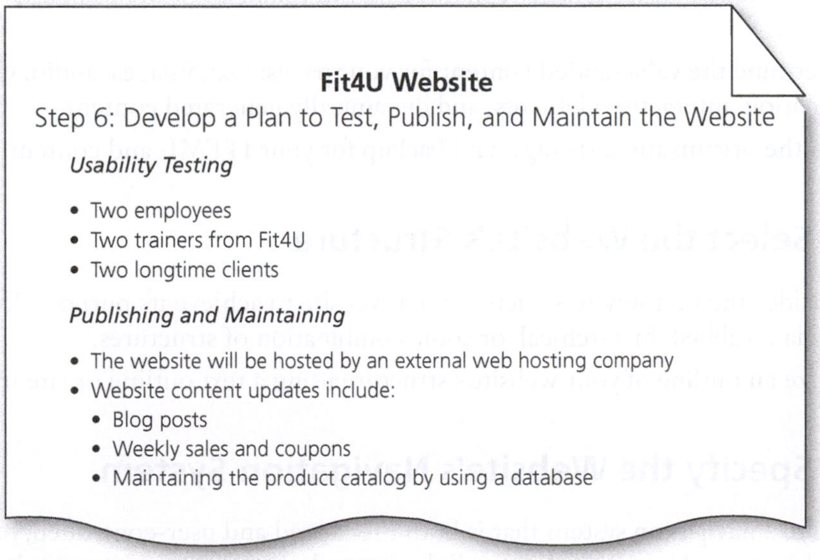

Fit4U Website

Step 6: Develop a Plan to Test, Publish, and Maintain the Website

Usability Testing

- Two employees
- Two trainers from Fit4U
- Two longtime clients

Publishing and Maintaining

- The website will be hosted by an external web hosting company
- Website content updates include:
  - Blog posts
  - Weekly sales and coupons
  - Maintaining the product catalog by using a database

Figure 4-23 Plan website testing, publishing, and maintenance to ensure your website meets user needs and falls within your resources.

Site Plan Checklist

Detailed planning is a vital step in website development and should occur before you invest time and money. Planning helps to ensure that the website will meet your goals as well as the expectations of website visitors. To ensure a successful website, use the following checklist when completing your web design plan.

Step 1: Identify the Website's Purpose and Target Audience

- Identify the primary and secondary goals for your website.
- Determine the objectives necessary to meet the website's goals, including its call-to-action.
- Develop a target audience profile that identifies the demographic and psychographic characteristics of audience members.
- Perform a needs assessment to determine the target audience's wants, needs, and expectations that can be satisfied by your website to ensure your website employs UX.
- Write a formal purpose statement for the website.

Step 2: Determine the Website's General Content

- Determine your website's home and subsidiary pages, and any necessary landing pages.
- Ensure that the content on your website's home page answers visitors' *who*, *what*, *why*, and *where* questions.
- Determine the visual identity content that will brand all of the webpages in your website.
- Determine the value-added content for your pages: text, images, audio, video, animation, interactive elements, and dynamically generated content.
- Plan the organization, storage, and backup for your HTML and content files.

Step 3: Select the Website's Structure

- Consider the best way to structure your website to achieve its purpose: linear/tutorial, webbed, hierarchical, or some combination of structures.
- Create an outline of your website's structure using a text outline or site map.

Step 4: Specify the Website's Navigation System

- Create a navigation system that is both user-based and user-controlled, offering a combination of text links; hidden links; image links; navigation menus, bars, and tabs; a breadcrumb trail; and a search feature.
- Follow WAI guidelines for links and navigation elements.

Step 5: Design the Look of the Website

- Position visual identity and vital page content above and to the left of potential scroll lines.
- Maintain visual consistency across pages with a color scheme, page layout, and placement of navigation elements.
- Follow WAI guidelines for the use of color.
- Consider RWD when designing page layout.

Step 6: Develop a Plan to Test, Publish, and Maintain the Website

- Perform usability testing on the navigation system during the planning and development phases.
- Determine how and where you will publish the website, and identify any technical or budget limitations.
- Develop a content maintenance plan that includes a schedule and budget.

Chapter Review

Place critical visual identity and navigation elements above and to the left of the scroll zone to reduce visitors' need to scroll. The typical website visitor looks first at the top of a webpage, then to the left, and then down and to the right. Place the content you want your visitors to see first at or near the top and on the left side of a webpage. Consider the visible screen area, and how that changes depending on the visitor's computer or device, when designing subsidiary webpages. Ensure that visitors never have to scroll horizontally to view webpages and that the information on underlying webpages flows smoothly and logically.

A user-based navigation system creates links between pages based on how visitors move from page to page at a website. A user-controlled navigation system allows visitors to move between pages in the manner of their choosing and offers both major navigation links as well as other options, such as a breadcrumb trail, website index, and search capability. Common types of navigation links include text links; image links; groups of related links presented as menus, bars, or tabs.

Using color and page layout to maintain visual consistency across all pages at a website promotes unity, strengthens visual identity, and reassures visitors. Apply a uniform color scheme and a consistent page layout created with tools such as responsive grids and CSS to create visual consistency.

After completing planning Steps 1 through 6, use the checklist to review your web design plan.

TERMS TO KNOW

After reading the chapter, you should know each of these Key Terms.

adaptive navigation (109)
autocomplete (108)
breadcrumb trail (107)
color-matching software (112)
contextual navigation (109)
CSS editor software (114)
drop-down menu (107)
external style sheet (114)
eye-tracking study (101)
fixed-width page layout (102)
flexible page layout (102)
F-pattern (101)
fluid grid layout (116)
hamburger menu (104)
heat map (101)
hosted website search provider (108)
hot spot (105)
hybrid page layout (102)
image link (105)
image map (105)
inline style (114)
internal style sheet (114)
liquid page layout (102)
local navigation (109)

look and feel (110)
navigation bar (107)
navigation menu (107)
navigation tab (107)
off-canvas menu (104)
page layout (114)
pop-out menu (107)
primary navigation (109)
responsive grid layout (116)
rollover link (105)
scroll zone (100)
style (113)
style rule (113)
subsidiary navigation (109)
target (104)
text link (104)
tooltip (104)
usability test (118)
user-based navigation system (103)
user-controlled navigation system (103)
visual consistency (110)
website index (108)
website search feature (108)
wireframing (115)

TEST YOUR KNOWLEDGE

Complete the Test Your Knowledge exercises to solidify what you have learned in the chapter.

Matching Terms

Match each term with the best description.

_____ 1. adaptive navigation

_____ 2. breadcrumb trail

_____ 3. contextual navigation

_____ 4. fixed-width layout

_____ 5. F-pattern

_____ 6. inline style

_____ 7. internal style sheet

_____ 8. fluid layout grid

_____ 9. liquid layout

_____ 10. navigation tabs

_____ 11. tooltip

a. A navigation system that bases linking relationships on the website visitors' needs rather than the website publisher's needs.

b. A way to evaluate exactly how website visitors will access website information and move from page to page at a website.

c. A text file containing formatting instructions saved within a webpage's HTML heading tags.

d. An underlying structure of rows and columns used to determine the size of webpage elements based on a percentage of the screen.

e. The webpage to which a link points.

f. A small textbox that may appear when you point to a link.

_____ 12. off-canvas menu

_____ 13. target

_____ 14. usability test

_____ 15. user-based navigation

g. Specifies a webpage's width specified as a percentage of the browser window.

h. A group of related links used to display alternative views of the content.

i. How eye-tracking studies suggest that a website's visitors typically view a webpage.

j. A hierarchical outline that shows the visitor the path between the home page and current page.

k. Specifies a webpage's width in pixels.

l. Hidden navigation element that expands when pointed to or clicked.

m. Links specific to a webpage being viewed, such as text links within an article, or a list of related links.

n. Links that use a website visitor's browsing or search history to provide content suggestions that might be of interest.

o. Rule inserted within the <h1> HTML tag on a page.

Short Answer Questions

Write a brief answer to each question.

1. Describe the importance of consistency of visual elements to reinforce branding.

2. Describe eye-tracking studies and heat maps, and how web designers use them to plan webpage design. What is an F-pattern?

3. Discuss WAI guidelines for the use of color and links.

4. Differentiate between inline styles, internal style sheets, and external style sheets. What tools can you use to apply CSS?

5. Describe user-based and user-controlled navigation.

6. Define several common types of links used in a navigation system.

7. Differentiate between primary, subsidiary, contextual, and adaptive navigation.

8. Explain why you would include a search feature, and how you might add one to your website.

9. List considerations when planning the testing, publishing, and maintenance of your website, and why you should include these steps in the planning process.

TRENDS

Investigate current web design developments with the Trends exercises.

Write a brief essay about each of the following trends, using the web as your research tool. For each trend, identify at least one webpage URL used as a research source. Be prepared to discuss your findings in class.

1 | Touch Screen Navigation

Use a search engine to search for *touch screen website navigation* or similar keywords to find articles or blog posts that offer recommendations for making website navigation easy to use with touch screens. List two things that you should consider that will make your website more accessible to touch screen users. If you have access to a device with a touch screen, experiment with using website navigation tools at several websites and make notes about any difficulties you encounter.

2 | Hidden Navigation

Using a search engine and the keywords *hidden website navigation* or similar keywords, locate one article or blog post that expresses a positive opinion and another that is negative about the use of hidden navigation. Summarize your findings, and discuss whether you agree with the opinions stated in the articles. Include any personal response you have based on your own experiences. Would you use hidden navigation as a web designer? Why or why not?

@ISSUE

Challenge your perspective of the web and web design technology with the @Issue exercises.

Write a brief essay in response to the following issues, using the web as your research tool. For each issue, identify at least one webpage URL used as a research source. Be prepared to discuss your findings in class.

1 | Cascading Style Sheets (CSS)

Cascading Style Sheets (CSS), a multifeatured specification for HTML, offers designers an expedient, powerful method to control the formatting and layout of webpages. Research the current level of support for style sheets by leading browsers and the current W3C recommendations for style sheet usage. Find an article that supports the use of CSS for creating websites that use responsive web design. Create a report summarizing your research. Explain the benefits of using CSS to design your website.

2 | Color-Matching Tools

Using a search engine and the keywords *best color-matching tools*, or something similar, find two current articles listing and rating color-matching tools. Create a report summarizing the articles, including any differences or similarities between the authors' lists. Conclude by stating what you might choose to use as a web designer and why.

Use the World Wide Web to obtain more information about the concepts in the chapter with the Hands On exercises.

1 | Explore and Evaluate: Levels of Navigation

Using a search engine and the keywords *levels of website navigation* or similar keywords, find at least two articles that give overviews of the levels discussed in this chapter. Note that the levels may be named slightly differently, depending on the author or source. Find examples on a large website of your choice of each level. Evaluate the use of varying levels of navigation on the website based on your own experiences.

2 | Search and Discover: Websites and Visual Identity

Using a search engine and the keywords *website visual identity* or similar keywords, locate three different visual identity topic pages or blog posts. Write an outline for a presentation to your class on the results of your research. Include in your outline a discussion of how you would use visual identity elements at your website and whether you think it is necessary to address visual identity on a page at your website.

Work collaboratively to reinforce the concepts in the chapter with the Team Approach exercises.

1 | Website Search Features

Join with two other students to research how to add a website search feature to a website. Find examples of free and hosted solutions and reviews of each. Make notes of whether any of the websites offer autocomplete as a part of the search feature, and any additional requirements or costs associated with using autocomplete. Do any of the websites address UX? If so, how? Compile the team's findings and submit in the format requested by your instructor. Be prepared to present your results to the class.

2 | Usability Tests

Join with another student to create a two-person research team. One team member should research firms that offer usability tests for a fee. The other team member should research tips for conducting usability tests on your own or with a limited budget. Create a presentation for the class in which you describe the costs, benefits, and weaknesses of each. Make recommendations as to which method might work best for small websites and large, corporate websites.

CASE STUDY

Apply the chapter concepts to the ongoing development process in web design with the Case Study.

The Case Study is an ongoing development process using the concepts, techniques, and Design Tips presented in each chapter.

Background Information

Continuing with the development of your website plan that you began in Chapter 3, complete Step 4: specify the website's navigation system; Step 5: design the look of the website; and Step 6: develop a plan to test, publish, and maintain the website. Then use your design plan checklist to evaluate your complete plan.

Chapter 4 Assignment

In this assignment, you will finalize your website's plan by completing the remaining three steps discussed in this chapter: planning the navigation of your website, planning the look of your website, and planning how you will test, publish, and maintain the website.

1. Review the related chapter material on page length, content placement, and usability.

2. Review the guidelines for user-based and user-controlled navigation systems, and then specify the individual elements of a user-based and user-controlled navigation system for your website.

3. Using what you have learned about wireframing, create a sketch or blueprint of the layout of page elements. If possible, use wireframing software.

4. Define your website's color scheme by using a web design template or color-matching software.

5. Plan the page layout for your home page and subsidiary pages. Explain how you will control page layout with CSS.

6. Create a plan for testing, publishing, and maintaining your website. Include costs and schedules in the plan.

7. After completing the final three steps of your design plan, review your design plan using the design plan checklist. After your review, make any necessary additions or edits to your design plan.

8. If time permits, meet with three classmates to compare and evaluate each other's design plans and offer constructive suggestions as applicable.

5 | Typography and Images

Introduction

Once you have developed a thorough website plan that takes into consideration your audience expectations, website goals, and design plans, you are prepared to create your website. As you learned in previous chapters, web designers use text and images to communicate messages and to set a mood. In this chapter, you learn more about typography standards and practices to ensure readability. You also learn how to select appropriate images, such as photographs, diagrams, illustrations, and more, which add value to your website and support your website's message. Then, you learn how to prepare images for the web.

Objectives

After completing this chapter, you will be able to:

1. Explain webpage typography issues

2. Discuss effective use of webpage images

3. Describe image file formats

4. Discuss how to prepare web-ready images

Q&A

What are current typography trends?
Like most web design principles, typography trends evolve constantly. One current trend is to use larger, magazine-style fonts for headers. Other trends include contrasting font sizes, and text imposed onto images. To find out more, use a search engine to search for *web typography trends* and sort or filter the results to display the most recent.

Q&A

What are leading, tracking, and kerning?
Leading refers to line spacing, or the amount of vertical space between lines of text; more line spacing generally means greater readability. **Tracking** is a spacing technique that allows designers to squeeze or stretch text, as necessary, to fit in a specific amount of space. **Kerning** adds or removes space between two individual characters.

Webpage Typography Issues

In Chapter 2, you learned the importance of composing text that is accurate, easy to read, understandable, and comprehensive. You also learned that text must be concise and written or adapted for the web. Selecting the appropriate type for your webpages' text is part of the design process. To format your text to be more readable, you follow the rules of typography. **Typography** is the study of the appearance and arrangement of characters, commonly referred to as **type**. The characteristics that define type are typeface, color, style, and size.

In this chapter, we differentiate between the typography needs of **headings** and other text meant to define, set apart, or set a mood, and webpage **content text**, such as paragraphs, image captions, and more. When selecting font and typography for headings, consider branding, color, and design, as well as size. For content text, the most important consideration is readability. For most of the typography discussion in this chapter, the considerations focus on content text.

Font Sizes and Styles

A **typeface** is a group of alphabetic characters, numbers, and symbols with the same design, such as the slant and thickness. Figure 5-1 illustrates some typefaces commonly used on the web. Five generic font types exist: serif, sans serif, cursive, fantasy, and monospace fonts.

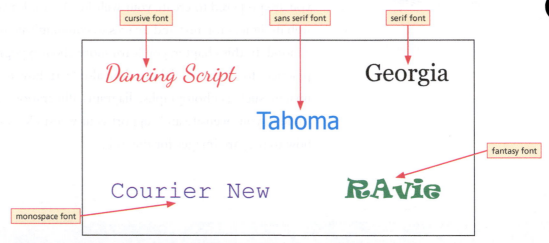

Figure 5-1 A typeface is a group of characters with a common design.

Type style refers to the variations in form such as roman (regular), italic, or bold. Desktop publishing professionals and other creators of printed materials use points to measure **type size**, where 72 points = 1 inch. Web designers sometimes measure type size in pixels, where 16 pixels equal a 12-point font, approximately. Figure 5-2 illustrates different type styles, sizes, and colors.

Segoe Print 16-point (regular)

Georgia 20-point bold

Arial 12-point italic

Century Schoolbook 18-point small caps

Figure 5-2 Style, color, and size define typeface.

Font Selection and Web Design

While web designers frequently use the terms *font* and *typeface* interchangeably, a **font** is the digital file that specifies the combination of character data used to display the typeface. Heading font selection can help establish the mood of your website—from whimsical to professional. To select the best font for your webpage content, you must consider how your font selection will affect visitors' reading comprehension.

When a webpage loads in a browser, the browser refers to the CSS specifications to determine the font the web designer specified for the text. Specialized fonts might not be available on a user's device. Using CSS to specify backup fonts or embed fonts (described later) ensures that your website text will be readable for all users. As a web designer, you should evaluate potential fonts based on readability, availability, and the mood you want your website visitors to experience.

READABILITY   The most commonly used fonts in web design are serif and sans serif. Some fonts, such as Times New Roman, have a short line extending from the top or bottom of a character called a serif; web designers refer to these as **serif** fonts. Fonts that do not have serifs, such as Arial, are **sans serif** fonts. Web designers often vary serif and sans serif fonts for heading and body text fonts to create visual contrast. Figure 5-3 illustrates characters in the Times New Roman serif font and the Arial sans serif font.

Q&A

What are the Web Accessibility Initiative (WAI) guidelines for font selection?
The WAI guidelines state that you should use CSS and the font-family, font-style, font-weight, and font-size properties to specify fonts, rather than including font choices in the HTML document.

Q&A

How do serifs affect readability?
Many web designers use serif fonts for webpage body text, although they are equally likely to apply serif and sans serif fonts to headlines. For more information about research on the sans serif and serif readability debate, use a search engine to search for *sans serif and serif UX and readability*.

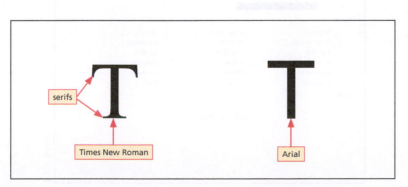

Figure 5-3 A serif is a short line extending from the top or bottom of a character.

How many different fonts should I use in my website?

Web designers have varied opinions on this topic. Many recommend limiting font choices to two or three, and having one be serif and the other sans serif. Others suggest choosing one font, and using styles, colors, or size to differentiate heading and body text. For more information about choosing fonts, use a search engine to search for *mixing fonts on webpages*.

Cursive, or script, fonts replicate handwriting. Web designers use fantasy fonts for decoration. Monospace fonts have equal spacing between characters, simulating characters created on a manual typewriter. Cursive, fantasy, and monospace fonts might not be appropriate for most webpage content text because it can be difficult to read them online. Another reason to avoid cursive or fantasy fonts is that specific examples of these fonts are less likely to be available across different computers and devices. However, these choices may be appropriate for headings. Varying fonts adds visual interest to your website, as in the For the Love of Your Biz website (Figure 5-4).

Figure 5-4 Contrasting fonts add visual interest to a webpage.

What is a web-safe font?

A **web-safe font** is a commonly available font that most website visitors' browsers will be able to display. Most web designers rely on CSS to specify web-safe backup fonts if the designer's original font choice is not available in the visitor's browser. For more information, use a search engine to search for *web-safe fonts*.

Many web designers ensure the readability of website content by using commonly available fonts, such as Georgia or Arial. Web design tools and content management systems (CMS), such as WordPress or Microsoft Expression Web (Figure 5-5), allow you

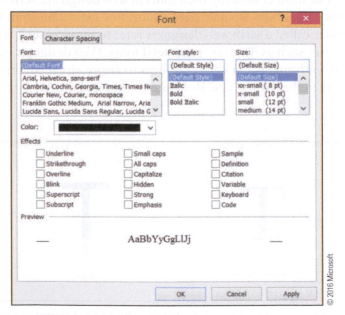

Figure 5-5 Web design tools allow you to specify a font stack.

to use CSS to specify a **font family** or a **font stack**, which identifies the preferred font as well as backup fonts. If a browser cannot locate the specified font used on a webpage, it will replace it with the next available **backup font** in the stack. Including a generic serif or sans serif font, which all browsers and devices can interpret, as the last backup font in the stack ensures that all browsers can display your webpage content.

Another method web designers use is to include **embedded fonts** in the website. Embedded fonts are identified in the CSS for the webpage and must be downloaded to the user's device before the webpage text can appear. Embedded fonts often increase the time it takes for a page to load. When using embedded fonts, web designers often will use a tool such as Google Web Font Loader (Figure 5-6) to specify backup fonts that display while the embedded fonts download. Use embedded fonts sparingly, such as for headings or other font choices where branding and design matter more than readability or speed of downloading.

Q&A

What are TrueType, PostScript, OpenType, and WOFF fonts?
TrueType is a font standard used by Windows and Macintosh operating systems. **PostScript** is a font standard developed by Adobe Systems for PostScript printers. **OpenType** is a font standard that incorporates TrueType and PostScript fonts for Windows and Macintosh operating systems. **Web Open Font Format (WOFF)** is similar to OpenType or TrueType but includes compression. The W3C recommends using the WOFF font packaging format.

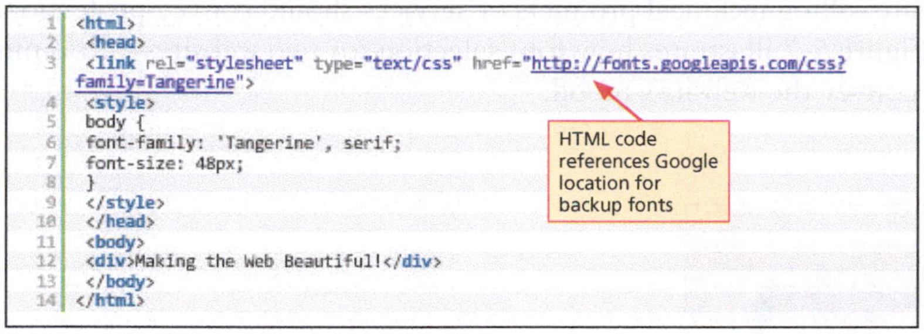

```
1  <html>
2  <head>
3  <link rel="stylesheet" type="text/css" href="http://fonts.googleapis.com/css?
   family=Tangerine">
4  <style>
5  body {
6  font-family: 'Tangerine', serif;
7  font-size: 48px;
8  }
9  </style>
10 </head>
11 <body>
12 <div>Making the Web Beautiful!</div>
13 </body>
14 </html>
```

HTML code references Google location for backup fonts

© 2016 Google Inc.

Figure 5-6 When using embedded fonts, specify backup fonts to display during download.

Despite many research studies, no clear direction exists regarding serifs and online readability. Although some early studies point to sans serif fonts as more readable for online text, more recent studies suggest that style, size, spacing between characters, contrast, white space, line length, readers' familiarity with the font, and other characteristics might play a larger role in readability than the presence or absence of serifs.

DESIGN TIP

A webpage's font size is either relative or absolute. **Relative font sizes** adjust to the user's screen and resolution. **Absolute font sizes** do not change when viewed on different screen sizes or resolutions. While absolute font sizes allow designers to maintain control over the size of page text, they do not comply with responsive web design techniques. Web designers can measure relative font sizes in two ways. First, as relative to the viewing screen, where font sizes are related to the number of pixels. Second, as a percentage of an em unit, where one **em unit** equals the font point size.

Q&A

What is a rem?
CSS3 specifications introduced the **rem** (root em). Like an em unit, a rem allows for flexible font sizing. With rems, the font size specified in the HTML document's root, or top-level heading, becomes the standard that determines relative font size.

TOOLKIT

Appendix B: CSS
See Appendix B to learn more about using CSS3 to specify relative font size.

MOOD Just as with a web color scheme, font selection can help establish an emotional connection with your visitors by suggesting a specific mood or state of mind. A website's mood can promote the website's message. For example, a topical website on snowboarding or a website that offers online games for preteens requires a heading font that contributes to a mood of fun, excitement, and challenge. However, the heading and content font used at a B2B website selling technical products or services should convey professionalism, not whimsy. Figure 5-7 illustrates how font selection for two websites—Roominate and Uber—helps convey the website's mood.

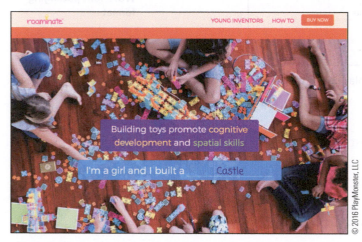

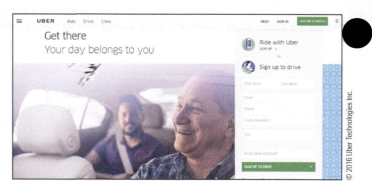

Figure 5-7 Fonts can help set a website's mood.

Exploring Fonts

1. Use a browser to open three websites in separate tabs. Choose any website in the following categories: a gaming website, a news website, and an investment website.

2. Review the home page and two subsidiary pages at each website. How do fonts and font sizes set the mood for website visitors? How do the fonts for headings and content differ? Does the design use serif or sans serif fonts, or a combination?

3. If possible, view the websites using a different device or at different resolutions. How does changing the screen size or resolution affect the readability of the fonts?

4. Explain how the website's choice of fonts, font styles, and font sizes does or does not set a mood that matches the website's content and message. Submit your findings in the format requested by your instructor.

Image Text

Image-editing software contains features that allow you to create images from text or add text to an image. For example, you can use headlines or larger text paragraphs to add to an image or create a new image, and then use editing tools to give the text shape, color, fade effects, or opacity to make the image more interesting. Web designers often save text as an image to create logos for brands, rather than embedding the fonts.

Adding text to an image, or creating an image from text, is much like working with webpage body text or text in a word-processing document. First, you select an editing tool that allows you to type the text. Then, you select the font, font size, font style, and font color options for your text. Next, click an area of the image where you want the text to appear, and type your text. The text appears in a box, called a **bounding box**. You can alter the shape of the bounding box to add interest. The JanSport webpage shown in Figure 5-8 shows an example of an image created from text. When using text images, make certain to include the image text as body text elsewhere on the webpage to ensure that it is picked up by SEO tools, and as alternative text that screen readers and other assistive technologies can read and interpret.

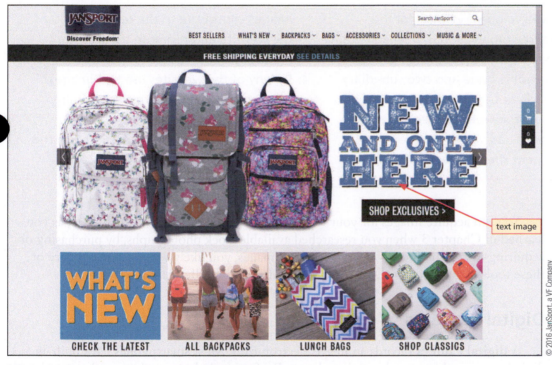

Figure 5-8 A text image can convey a supporting message.

Webpage Images

Chapter 3 introduced you to webpage images, and how they can personalize and familiarize the unknown, deliver a message, and prompt visitors' actions. Webpage images include illustrations, diagrams, and photographs. Be sure you select images that achieve the following:

- Are relevant to your content and add value to your website.
- Conform with or complement your website's color scheme.
- Support your website's message.
- Contribute to the overall mood you want to set.

Q&A Do font choices affect web accessibility? To make your website accessible, use readable fonts, relative font sizing, and sufficient contrast between background and text color, and avoid using the appearance of text to convey its meaning. For more information, use a search engine to search for *fonts and web accessibility*.

Q&A What are proprietary fonts? A **proprietary font** is a font designed especially for a brand, such as Coca-Cola or Disney. A proprietary font can distinguish a brand. The font itself is protected by copyright laws and can be used only with approval from the owner. For more information, use a search engine to search for *using proprietary fonts*.

TOOLKIT Appendix D: SEO See Appendix D for more information about ensuring image text is picked up by SEO tools.

© 2016 JanSport, a VF Company

DESIGN TIP Be creative in the use of images on your webpages. For example, tilt a photograph slightly, apply a colored filter, or add a border.

Q&A

What is a hero image? A **hero image**, also called a **background image**, is a large, banner-type image used primarily as the center image on a website's home page. To learn more, use a search engine to search for *hero image*.

Remember to follow best practices for web usability and accessibility, such as adding alternative text to your images and ensuring contrast between background images and text. Only use images to which you own the copyrights, or secure the copyrights and give proper credit to the image owner or creator if using an image from another source.

Another important consideration when selecting webpage images is file size. A higher file size means a better-quality image, but also one that may take longer to download and display in the visitor's browser. Experiment with image file sizes as a part of your website testing process to achieve a balance between image quality and download time. You will learn more about file size later in this chapter.

YOUR TURN

Exploring the Effective Use of Webpage Images

1. Use a browser to open websites for the following three organizations in separate tabs: Dana Farber, Ocean Alliance, and PBS Kids.
2. Review the home page and two subsidiary pages at each website.
3. Examine how the website uses images. Do the images add value? Do they match or complement the color scheme? Do the images contribute to the overall mood of the website and promote the website's message?
4. Do any of the websites use text images? If so, how did they address accessibility concerns?
5. Summarize your review and submit in the format requested by your instructor.

You can acquire images for your website by creating your own image files or, as you learned in Chapter 3 when you researched available stock photographs, by purchasing or acquiring images online. To create your own images, you likely will use one or more of these tools: a digital camera, screen capture software, and illustration software.

Digital Cameras

A **digital camera** records an image electronically. Most smartphones have built-in digital cameras that can take quality photos. Professional photographers or those without a camera on their smartphone can purchase a standalone digital camera. Professional photographers typically purchase digital cameras that include the ability to switch lenses, adjust settings, and produce high-resolution images. The quality and price of standalone digital cameras vary. When selecting a smartphone, camera quality often is a top consideration.

Digital cameras allow you to view the images, thereby allowing you to take as many shots as necessary to get the perfect one. Smartphone cameras are convenient and can be used to take photos that are ideal for sharing digitally. Some smartphones also have external lenses, flashes, and other photographic equipment that can be attached to the device when taking photos. You can use photo-editing apps to adjust the quality of smartphone photos (Figure 5-9).

Figure 5-9 Smartphone digital cameras can take high-quality images that you can edit using apps.

If you are purchasing a new standalone digital camera or a smartphone with a camera, you should learn about the camera's capabilities and features and how to use them to take quality photos. Most digital cameras offer default options that are adequate for general use. Use the auto options until you have mastered the potential capabilities and greater control of the customized settings. Transfer your digital images from your camera to your computer or the Internet to back them up. You can manipulate and fine-tune photos using image-editing software on your computer or using photo-editing apps directly on your smartphone.

Digital cameras store images internally or on memory cards or other storage devices. You can transfer the photos to a computer, or upload directly to social media sites. You also can upload photos directly to a **photo sharing website**, which stores the images to your account and enables you to share, print, and edit image files. Photo sharing websites are an example of a cloud resource. As you learned in Chapter 1, cloud computing stores information and software online. The transfer process from camera to computer (or other device) varies depending on the camera and the storage method. You can download internally stored images using a connecting cable from the camera to the computer. You also can transfer images stored on memory cards using a wireless or connected reading device. Many standalone digital cameras, and virtually all smartphones, include Bluetooth or wireless transfer capabilities that enable you to transfer images to a computer or a social media app such as Instagram.

Screen Capture and Illustration Software

Web designers use screen captures, also called **screen shots**, to show the contents of a computer or digital device screen at a point in time. Technical blogs, software support webpages, and instructional texts often use screen shots (like the screen illustrations in this text). You can use **screen capture software**, such as SnagIt® and FullShot®, to create an image of screen contents. Most smartphones include screen capture capabilities (Figure 5-10), or enable you to download or purchase a screen capture app. Screen

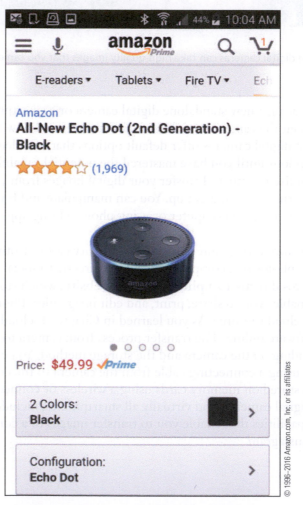

© 1996–2016 Amazon.com, Inc. or its affiliates

Figure 5-10 Screen capture software creates an image that shows the contents of a screen.

capture software also contains features for editing the images, such as cropping or adding callouts.

Web designers and graphic artists use **illustration software**, such as Adobe Illustrator CC and the Sketch mobile app (Figure 5-11), to create images, such as diagrams and drawings, by drawing shapes, lines, and curves. You learn more about images created using illustration software in the next section.

© 2011–2016 Sony Mobile Communications, Inc.

Figure 5-11 Designers use illustration software to draw and format an image.

Q&A

What are megapixels and how do they affect digital image quality?
One **megapixel** is equal to a million pixels. Professional photographers use digital cameras with higher megapixel capabilities to produce larger quality images, such as poster-sized. If you have a digital camera or smartphone with a camera, check the camera settings to see the megapixels per image.

Q&A

How can I transfer a printed photo to digital?
A **scanner** is a computer input device that reads printed text, images, or objects and then translates the results into a digital file. Three common scanner types are flatbed, sheet-fed, and drum. Many printers include scanning capabilities.

If you are unable to create your images because of restrictions on time, available resources, or expertise, you can use various sources for graphics files created and/or provided by individuals or companies that specialize in graphic design. Web design tools, image-editing software, or illustration software often provide sample images or drawing templates. You can search online by category, such as sports or medicine, and by photo type (illustration or photography, for example) to purchase individual digitized images or a library of images. You can download images offered for a fee at some websites or download free public domain images, such as those found at many U.S. government websites. Websites such as Morguefile.com (Figure 5-12) include archives of artist-provided images available for free and with limited copyright restrictions.

Figure 5-12 Searchable archives of images from multiple artists exist on the web.

> **DESIGN TIP** Before you download images or include an image on your website, locate any terms or conditions for using the image. Pay any royalty or licensing fees for the image's use. The copyright owner might require you to provide a link to the webpage that offers the image. You should add a credit line for images from other sources, even those in the public domain.

Image File Formats

TOOLKIT

Appendix C: RWD
For more information about responsive image file formats, see Appendix C.

The variety of devices used by website visitors and the range of sizes of these devices create challenges for web designers. Although most image file formats are readable on mobile devices, the size and download time can cause issues with page loading. Including an image file that has specific dimensions and file resolution means that some visitors to the webpage will see a full image, while other visitors will see a partial image or no image at all. Web designers have developed methods to address the issue. One approach includes specifying options within the HTML5 *<picture>…</picture>* tags that instruct the website to display different image sizes or formats (or no image) based on the size of the screen. Sometimes omitting the image, or providing a link to the image rather than displaying it, is the best option for small screen sizes. Considering when or if to include the option of not displaying an image is part of RWD. Per WAI guidelines, remember that you always should include text that describes the image. The alternative text displays while the image loads or if the image cannot be displayed by the visitor's browser, and can be read by screen reading devices for the visually impaired.

Image files are either raster or vector. **Raster images**, or **bitmaps**, consist of a series of individual pixels. At the optimal resolution (based on image quality and size), the pixels are not visible. A bitmap contains a specific number of pixels measured as pixels per inch (ppi) and is **resolution dependent**, meaning that resizing the image affects the image quality. Figure 5-13 illustrates a bitmap image zoomed to show the individual pixels in the image.

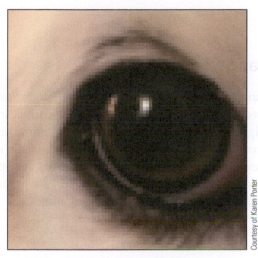

Courtesy of Karen Porter

Figure 5-13 Individual pixels are visible in a zoomed bitmap image.

A file name includes a **file extension**—a period (.) and a file format identifier. Web designers commonly refer to bitmap files by their file extensions, such as GIF or JPEG. Figure 5-14 lists common bitmap file types. You can save an image to another bitmap format using image-editing software or apps.

Bitmap Formats and File Extensions

Format	File Extension
Windows Bitmap	.bmp
Graphics Interchange Format	.gif
JPEG File Interchange Format	.jpg or .jpeg
Portable Network Graphics	.png
Google WebP Image File	.webp
Tagged Image File Format	.tiff
Adobe Photoshop	.psd

Figure 5-14 Bitmap images are referenced by their file extensions.

Vector images, or **vector graphics**, consist of a group of separate drawing objects, such as shapes, curves, and lines, combined to create a single image. Vector images are **resolution independent**. You can resize a vector image with no loss of image quality. With illustration software, as shown in Figure 5-11, you can draw vector images.

To use a vector image on the web, you must rasterize it by saving it in a bitmap file format. Some illustration and image-editing software contain features for working with both vector and bitmap images.

DESIGN TIP The images you choose for your website likely will be in the GIF, JPEG, or PNG bitmap formats. Most web browsers and mobile devices support these formats.

Graphics Interchange Format (GIF)

The **Graphics Interchange Format (GIF)** bitmap image file format was the original image format used on the web. CompuServe created the GIF format in the late 1980s. GIFs contain a compression algorithm that reduces file size. GIF images are 8-bit color images, meaning they have a maximum of 256 colors. This color limitation makes the GIF format inappropriate for complex images, such as photographs. GIFs are optimal for basic, solid-color images, such as cartoons (Figure 5-15), diagrams, and navigation buttons. Different types of GIF images include interlaced, transparent, and animated.

Figure 5-15 GIFs are most suitable for basic, solid-color images, such as cartoons, diagrams, or navigation buttons.

An **interlaced GIF** image appears on the screen in a sequence of passes. Each pass displays the whole image at a higher resolution as the image changes from blurry to distinct. An interlaced GIF gives a preview of the image to come without extensively affecting file size. To create a **transparent GIF**, you can specify that the webpage remove a specific color. The absence of that color allows the webpage background to show through from behind the image. Animated GIFs consist of a series of frames that repeat to simulate movement. You will learn about animated GIFs in Chapter 6.

> You should use interlacing only for large images that might require more time and bandwidth to download completely, unlike smaller images that typically can be displayed in one pass. You can use image-editing software to create both interlaced and transparent GIFs.

JPEG File Interchange Format (JFIF)

The **Joint Photographic Experts Group (JPEG)**, an international committee sponsored by the International Organization for Standardization (ISO), published the **JPEG File Interchange Format (JFIF)** image compression format standard. Most people refer to JFIF images as JPEGs. Web designers use the JPEG image format for digital photographs, photo-like paintings, watercolors, and complex illustrations requiring more than 256 colors. JPEG image files, containing millions of colors, are compressed. The compression creates smaller files, which results in some loss of quality, usually undetectable. Because of smaller file sizes, JPEG images are a good choice for photographs and other high-quality digital images used on webpages.

Portable Network Graphics (PNG) Format

The **Portable Network Graphics (PNG)** image format is a free open-source image format developed to replace the GIF format. The PNG format has two primary advantages over the GIF format: the PNG format supports more than 16 million colors, giving it a greater range of colors than the GIF format; the PNG format also has superior transparency capabilities compared to other formats.

Q&A

Why was the PNG format developed? At one point, the companies that developed the technology used to compress GIFs required anyone using GIFs pay a license fee. Although you no longer need a license fee to use GIFs, PNGs remain a popular alternative.

> Use the GIF image format for basic, solid-color images that do not require more than 256 colors, such as cartoons, diagrams, and navigation buttons. Use the JPEG image format for photographs or art-like images.

Q&A

What is a progressive JPEG?
A **progressive JPEG** is similar to an interlaced GIF and appears on the screen in a sequence of passes. The progressively improved image quality allows the viewer a preview of the image while it downloads. Progressive JPEGs and interlaced GIFs are not in common use today because more people have access to high-speed Internet, which improves download speed more than the use of these two file formats would.

Web-Ready Images

Creating **web-ready images** involves using image-editing software to refine and enhance the images as necessary, selecting the right format for the type of image, and then optimizing the images or providing multiple options for different screen sizes to find the balance between the smallest possible image size and the highest possible quality.

If you include images without optimizing them for file size, visitors using mobile devices might experience excessive webpage download times and become frustrated. Additionally, using image file sizes that are larger than necessary wastes server storage space. You can use image-editing software to optimize your images by achieving a balance between compressing your image files into a smaller size and maintaining the best possible image quality.

Refining Images

Image-editing software can help you refine your images to improve their quality. For example, if an image contains more detail than you want to include, you can crop the image using image-editing software. When you **crop** an image, you select the part of the image you want to keep and remove the unwanted portion. Another benefit of cropping an image is reduced file size. Figure 5-16 illustrates cropping an image in Microsoft Paint.

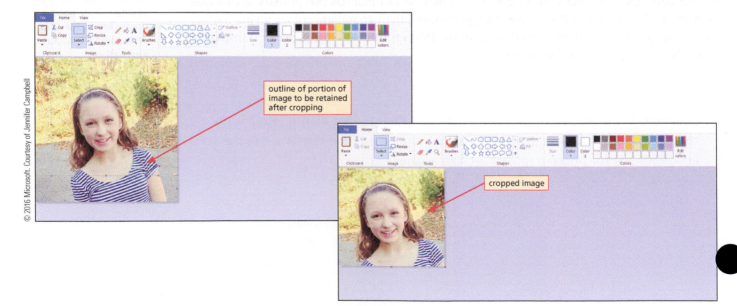

outline of portion of image to be retained after cropping

cropped image

Figure 5-16 Cropping an image creates a focal point and reduces the file size.

Cropping an image eliminates distracting background elements, establishes a focal point, and results in a smaller file size. Failure to focus or resize images will give your website an unprofessional appearance and detract from your website's message.

DESIGN TIP

Image-editing software has image-enhancement features ranging from predetermined, automatic settings to very precise, sophisticated, customizable adjustments. For example, you can manipulate the levels of shadows and highlights in an image. Additionally, you can use image-editing software to correct an image that is too dark, blurry, or has unwanted spots or markings.

Optimizing Images for Size and Quality

The three most popular image file formats for webpages—GIF, JPEG, and PNG—all contain a compression feature that reduces the size of an image file during saving. The GIF and PNG formats offer **lossless compression**, which retains all the image data during compression. Image data retention maintains the quality of the image. As you have learned, the GIF format is not suitable for photographs or images containing more than 256 colors. The PNG format supports millions of colors, but creates files that might be too large for efficient webpage downloading. Some designers suggest using the PNG format for editing photographs or other images containing millions of colors, but then saving the images in the JPEG format to reduce the file size.

The JPEG format provides **lossy compression**, meaning that some image data is lost permanently during compression. Using a low level of compression results in a loss of data that is undetectable by the human eye; there is no apparent deterioration in the image quality. You can control the level of JPEG compression with digital camera settings or by using the optimizing feature in image-editing software.

JPEG compression values and the resultant image quality have an inverse relationship: a greater compression value yields a smaller file size, but also leads to poorer image quality. If you are selecting a JPEG image compression value for your webpage images and your primary concern is image quality, a lower compression value will result in a higher image quality, but at the cost of a larger file size. If you need smaller, faster-loading image files, use a higher compression value. Higher compression values lead to a greater loss of image data, called image degradation or **compression artifacting**. Compression artifacting can result in areas of an image that appear blurred or distorted. Note that each time you reopen, edit, and resave a JPEG image, the loss of data due to compression artifacting increases and becomes more visible in the image.

To protect image quality in an image that requires multiple edits, some designers suggest saving the image in a lossless compression format, such as PNG, until editing is complete. You then can save the image in the JPEG format to reduce its file size. Although it is important to keep a backup copy of all your original unedited images, it is critical to do so for a JPEG image. Because of the progressive compression artifacting that takes place each time you save a JPEG, you should make a copy of the original unedited JPEG file to maintain it.

DESIGN TIP

Image-editing software provides the capability to refine and optimize any image—whether from a digital camera, created with illustration software, or purchased from a website that sells predesigned images. Most popular image-editing software contains features for manually or automatically optimizing images for use on webpages. You can use these optimization features to help find the best balance between image file size and image quality. Image-editing software offers a variety of quality settings of the same JPEG image. Typically, the quality settings range from very high quality to low quality. For most webpage usage, medium-quality JPEGs are sufficient.

Chapter Review

Webpage text is most effective when you follow the rules of good typography—the appearance and arrangement of the characters that make up text. The features that define type include typeface, type style, and type size. Combined, these three features are known as a font. As a web designer, you should evaluate potential fonts for webpage content text based on the readability, accessibility, and availability of the font along with the mood you want website visitors to experience. Use embedded, proprietary, or unusual fonts only for headings. Include font stacks to ensure that all computers, mobile devices, and browsers can read your website content, even if they do not include your preferred font. If you are creating your own images, you can use a digital camera (standalone or part of a smartphone), screen capture software, and illustration software. You also can purchase or locate free predesigned images online.

When you choose images, be sure to select quality and relevant images that add value to your website, match or complement your website's color scheme, support the website's message, and contribute to the overall mood you want to set for visitors. Consider responsive web design practices, and include options for adjusting or replacing images depending on screen size. Choose GIF, JPEG, or PNG compression file formats in which to save your images and, if using image-editing software, take advantage of the built-in file optimization features. Creating a web-ready image involves refining the image, selecting the right format for the type of image, and then optimizing the image for both image size and image quality.

After reading the chapter, you should know each of these Key Terms.

absolute font size (131)
antialiasing (140)
background image (134)
backup font (131)
bitmap (139)
bounding box (133)
compression artifacting (143)
content text (128)
crop (142)
digital camera (134)
em unit (131)
embedded font (131)
file extension (139)
font (129)
font family (131)
font stack (131)
Graphics Interchange Format (GIF) (140)
heading (128)
hero image (134)
illustration software (137)
image-editing software (133)
interlaced GIF (141)
Joint Photographic Experts Group
    (JPEG) (141)
JPEG File Interchange Format (JFIF) (141)
kerning (128)
leading (128)
lossless compression (143)
lossy compression (143)
megapixel (137)

OpenType (131)
photo sharing website (135)
Portable Network Graphics (PNG) (141)
PostScript (131)
progressive JPEG (142)
proprietary font (133)
raster image (139)
rasterizing (139)
relative font size (131)
rem (131)
resolution dependent (139)
resolution independent (140)
sans serif (129)
scanner (137)
screen capture software (136)
screen shots (136)
serif (129)
tracking (128)
transparent GIF (141)
TrueType (131)
type (128)
type size (128)
type style (128)
typeface (128)
typography (128)
vector graphics (140)
vector image (140)
Web Open Font Format (WOFF) (131)
web-ready image (142)
web-safe font (130)

Complete the Test Your Knowledge exercises to solidify what you have learned
in the chapter.

Matching Terms

Match each term with the best description.

_____ 1. bitmap

_____ 2. crop

_____ 3. embedded font

_____ 4. font stack

_____ 5. hero image

_____ 6. JPEG

_____ 7. kerning

_____ 8. leading

_____ 9. PNG

_____ 10. proprietary font

_____ 11. relative font size

_____ 12. rem

_____ 13. vector image

_____ 14. serif

_____ 15. WOFF

a. CSS specification that includes a default font and backup font types.

b. A font standard that includes compression.

c. A font designed especially for a brand.

d. Images created pixel by pixel; also known as raster images.

e. Adds or removes space between two individual characters.

f. You can resize a(n) _____ image with no negative effect on image quality.

g. A short line extending from the top or bottom of a character.

h. A font that must first download in order to allow the webpage text to display.

i. A large, banner-type image used primarily as the center image on a website's home page.

j. To remove portions of an image to emphasize certain parts of the image.

k. The font size specified as a percentage in relation to the font size of surrounding text.

l. The image file format most suited for photographs.

m. An image file format originally designed to replace the GIF file format.

n. Line spacing, or the amount of vertical space between lines of text.

o. Unit used in CSS to determine font size relative to that specified in the HTML document's root, or top-level heading.

Short Answer Questions

Write a brief answer to each question.

1. Describe the characteristics that define type. How do web designers use typography?

2. Compare the terms *type style* and *font* as used in web design.

3. Describe the five generic typeface or font families and when to use each.

4. Discuss the role of font stacks when specifying website fonts.

5. Discuss responsive web design guidelines for determining website font sizes.

6. What should you consider when selecting images for webpages?

7. Describe tools you can use to create your own webpage images.

8. Identify methods for transferring image files from a digital camera to a computer or the Internet.

9. Compare and contrast lossless and lossy compression methods for image files. Which image file types provide lossless compression and which provide lossy compression?

10. Describe how to optimize your images to create web-ready images.

Investigate current web design developments with the Trends exercises.   **TRENDS**

Write a brief essay about each of the following trends, using the web as your research tool. For each trend, identify at least one webpage URL used as a research source. Be prepared to discuss your findings in class.

1 | Smartphone Digital Camera Attachments

Research digital camera attachments for smartphones. List types of attachments you can purchase, and choose one to research further, such as lenses or flashes. Find three top-rated options to compare. Create a table listing the price, available devices, quality, and features. Find reviews from professional and amateur photographers. Which would you choose? Why?

2 | Typography, Images, and Visual Identity

As you learned in Chapters 2 and 3, using design to establish a visual identity or brand for a corporation or organization can contribute to widespread recognition of the corporation's or organization's products and/or services. Locate a real-world website of your choice that has a very well-known visual identity (for example, a recognizable logo, such as the Nike swoosh, or proprietary font, such as Disney). Discuss how typography and image selection contribute to the website publisher's visual identity and brand.

@ISSUE

Challenge your perspective of the web and web design technology with the @Issue exercises.

Write a brief essay in response to the following issues, using the web as your research tool. For each issue, identify at least one webpage URL used as a research source. Be prepared to discuss your findings in class.

1 | A Question of Integrity

Image-editing software and apps are evolving constantly, increasing web designers' capabilities to apply highly sophisticated techniques. Cloning, editing, blending, and image-correction tools can reconfigure an image, so even experts have difficulty perceiving whether the image is an original or an altered version. The negative aspect to these evolving capabilities is the potential to misrepresent reality. For example, it is possible to place an individual in a photo to suggest he or she was present when the photo was taken. This capability to alter images raises the question of integrity. Identify one or two legal and moral issues surrounding misrepresentation using altered images. In addition, discuss the responsibility of web designers to protect against misrepresentation using altered images.

2 | Readability

Find three current articles discussing web design trends, such as low contrast or background images, and their impact on website readability. If possible, locate examples of websites that use the trend. Are the websites readable? If not, how might you improve readability? If possible, view the websites on different devices, and adjust the brightness of your device display. What impact do these changes have on readability? As a web designer, would you recommend incorporating this trend? Why or why not?

HANDS ON

Use the World Wide Web to obtain more information about the concepts in the chapter with the Hands On exercises.

1 | Explore and Evaluate: Cloud-based Photo Storage Websites

Create a table or other comparison tool in which you list three types of photo storage websites or services. Use a search engine to include the following information about each.

a. For which devices or platforms is the photo storage website available?

b. Is the photo website owned or under the control of any company or organization? If so, are there any restrictions upon its use? Is there a storage fee?

c. Find reviews about the photo storage website. Would you use the service? Why or why not?

d. What features does the photo storage website offer? How might you use the service as a web designer?

2 | Search and Discover: Images in the Public Domain

Use a search engine to identify sources of images in the public domain. Create a list of public domain image sources, including the website name, URL, type of images, and required credit information, if any. List factors you should consider when using public domain images. Explain how an image becomes part of the public domain.

Work collaboratively to reinforce the concepts in the chapter with the Team Approach exercises.

1 | Using Font Stacks

Use a search engine to find a list of fonts and font stacks considered to be web safe. Join with another student to research how to use CSS to create font stacks. Include discussion about techniques, tools, and commonly used font stacks. Explore the use of generic fonts. Explain why or why not you might use embedded fonts in your website. Discuss why including similar backup and generic fonts can meet the website's design goals, and why it is important to include them in your website.

2 | Create Vector Images

Join with another student to create or describe a vector image you would add to an existing website of your choice, such as a personal website you have created, or your school's website. If available, use image-editing software to create a vector image that you could use on the website. If you do not have access to image-editing tools, sketch an image by hand. Discuss the website for which you would use the image, and explain how your image's colors, lines, and size meet the needs and support the goals of your website.

Apply the chapter concepts to the ongoing development process in web design with the Case Study.

The Case Study is an ongoing development process using the concepts, techniques, and Design Tips presented in each chapter.

Background Information

In this Case Study assignment, you begin to create, gather, and prepare some of the content that you have determined in your website plan will help achieve your website's goals and objectives. First, you need to review guidelines and principles presented in this chapter and previous chapters. Specific sections for review are detailed in the assignment.

Chapter 5 Assignment

1. Review the guidelines in Chapter 2 for writing for the web. Then, use word-processing software to create the text for your webpages. Remember to check the text's spelling and grammar. If possible, wait at least one day after creating your text before proofing your pages and have at least one other qualified person proofread your pages.

2. Select the fonts you will use for your webpage text. Determine the backup fonts you will use in your font stack.

3. Gather or create value-added images for your website. Ensure that your images are free of copyright or usage restrictions.

4. Prepare your web-ready images by using image-editing software to refine the images and then optimize them for size and quality.

5. Save your text and images in the appropriate folders in the directory structure you have created for your website.

6. Save a backup copy of your files to an external storage device.

6 | Multimedia and Interactivity

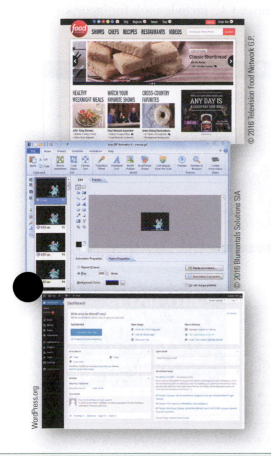

© 2016 Television Food Network G.P.

© 2016 Blumentals Solutions SIA

WordPress.org

Introduction

Now that you know how to develop a website plan, understand the rules of good typography, and are familiar with the methods to prepare and optimize images for your website, the next step is to learn how to enhance your webpages by using multimedia to add animated and interactive elements. As you learned in Chapter 3, multimedia can combine text, images, movement, audio, or video, and frequently involves interactivity. Animated elements create excitement and interactivity, and interactive elements allow you to connect with your target audience. Strategic use of animated and interactive elements can provide a means for entertaining, educating, and collecting feedback from your website visitors. Interactive elements enable you to place calls-to-action on your webpages and allow visitors to act on or react to the calls-to-action. Calls-to-action are methods of gathering feedback or contact information from visitors, enabling the creation of user accounts, and more.

You can download or link to ready-made animated and interactive elements available for purchase or for free on e-commerce and sharing websites. With the proper tools and expertise, you can create your own animated and interactive elements. As with any website element, you should consider the value it adds to your website and ensure it helps you meet your website goals before adding it.

Objectives

After completing this chapter, you will be able to:

1. Explain webpage multimedia and animation issues

2. Discuss adding and editing webpage audio and video elements

3. Describe types of webpage animation

4. Identify ways to effectively use interactive elements

Multimedia and Animation Issues

In Chapter 3, you learned that multimedia and animated elements typically are some combination of text, images, animation, audio, and video used to produce stimulating and engaging webpage content, as shown in the Food Network website in Figure 6-1. Animated elements can inform and educate website visitors in an entertaining way. You can add a video clip of an interview that supports a news story, an animation that shows how to use a product correctly, or audio to teach the proper pronunciation of a foreign language. Web design tools, such as Adobe Dreamweaver CC, include tools for incorporating animated elements into your webpages.

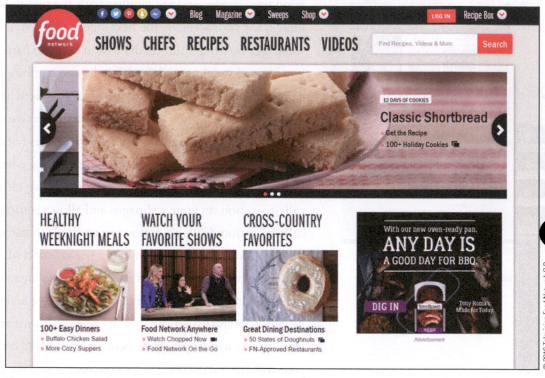

Figure 6-1 The Food Network website effectively incorporates animated and multimedia elements.

DESIGN TIP   When adding an animated element, ensure that its placement on the webpage is appropriate and that you add proper credit and captioning.

Although animated elements can add value and interest to your website, they are not essential. Many well-designed websites achieve their objectives without it. Drawbacks associated with adding multimedia components include longer download time, the possible need for browser plug-ins, and the substantial use of storage space on your website's host server. Lastly, creating professional quality animated elements often exceeds the expertise and budget of many designers. A poorly executed element can detract from your website's message and make you look unprofessional.

Instead of including source media on your website, you might consider embedding it. For example, embedding a YouTube video or playlist enables you to show the video or playlist while maintaining a link to its original source. This not only keeps a connection to the video's credit information (author and copyrights) but also enables the video to play without any additional programming or support from you. Playing a video within your webpage also keeps the visitor engaged with your website. Figure 6-2 shows a Cisco employee's blog post with links to embedded YouTube videos. Other websites such as Flickr (photography) and Spotify (music) enable you to incorporate media content by adding a link to the media they host onto your webpage or blog.

Q&A

What are the Web Accessibility Initiative (WAI) guidelines for multimedia?
Within your webpages, you should provide a text equivalent or descriptive text for every nontext element, including all multimedia elements. For more information, use a search engine to search for *WAI guidelines animation video audio*.

Figure 6-2 Embedding a YouTube video plays the video within the webpage using the YouTube video player.

> Use multimedia and animated elements only when their use supports your website goals. Ensure that it adds value and satisfies target audience expectations for content at your website.
>
> **DESIGN TIP**

You will learn about optimizing multimedia for efficient web delivery later in this chapter. However, consider the following general guidelines:

- Allow your website to adapt the content to show a low- or high-bandwidth version depending on the visitor's speed or device.
- Instruct the website to inform the visitor of any necessary plug-ins and provide links to any downloads if necessary.
- If possible, provide options for full-screen viewing of videos or animations.
- Provide text equivalents or descriptive text for all multimedia elements to meet accessibility standards.
- When developing original elements, break audio or video files into short segments to create smaller files.

Q&A

How can I add streaming audio and video to my website?
A variety of sources exist online to help you add your own streaming media, or link or embed existing streaming media that plays within its source program and gives proper credit to the source. For more information, use a search engine to search for *audio and video streaming hosts*.

Audio and Video Elements

You can include audio and video on your website as either downloadable or streaming media. HTML5 uses the *<audio>* and *<video>* tags to enable multimedia content to stream, or run within a webpage. **Streaming audio** begins playing as the server delivers the audio file to the computer or device. Visitors must have a compatible browser, or a plug-in or app installed, such as Spotify or Last.fm to listen to audio. To stream audio, your webpage files must be stored on a server that also has streaming software to deliver the audio stream when requested by the browser. Figure 6-3 lists common audio file formats.

Web Audio Formats

File Format	Description
.aac	Advanced Audio Coding format used by Apple Music streaming service
.aiff	Apple's standard audio file format
.Au	Audio file format used by Sun, Unix, and Java
.m4a	Format used by Apple for iTunes music downloads
.mp3	Most common file format
.ogg	Free, open source audio format type similar to mp3, used by Spotify streaming service
.ra, .rm	Online streaming audio format developed by RealAudio
.wav	Audio file format commonly used by Windows PCs
.wma	Microsoft-created Windows Media Audio Format

Figure 6-3 Common web audio file formats.

Q&A

Why is it called pseudo streaming?
The term *pseudo* means fake or simulated. Because the media plays as it downloads, it appears to be streaming. Once downloaded, it resides on the computer or device and can be played in its entirety without interacting with the host server.

As you learned in an earlier chapter, the website visitor's browser must store downloadable media in its entirety before the device can begin playing it. In contrast, streaming media begins to play as soon as the data starts to *stream*, or transfer from the server to the browser. **Progressive downloading**, or **pseudo streaming**, allows the media to play while it downloads. Because the entire media file does not download before playback starts, there may be delays in playback. Each media type has specific advantages and disadvantages, as illustrated in Figure 6-4.

Downloadable versus Streaming Media

Media Type	Advantages	Disadvantages
Downloadable	User can access downloaded files again and again; utilizes the HTTP protocol to transfer the data and, therefore, does not require a specific media server.	Files typically are extremely large, resulting in a long download time and taking up considerable storage space on the user's computer or device.
Streaming	Users can choose the file portion they want to play using the player's control buttons; consumes RAM only while being played.	Very high bandwidth requirements; frequently requires a specific media server to transfer the data.
Pseudo streaming	Users can access the content as it downloads, without waiting for the entire file to begin playback; users can access the files offline once the download is complete.	Once downloaded, files typically are extremely large, resulting in a long download time and taking up considerable storage space on the user's computer or device. Playback during download may be interrupted if the speed at which the media plays exceeds the download speed.

Figure 6-4 Advantages and disadvantages of downloadable and streaming media.

Many website visitors dislike background audio or sound effects. Ensure that website visitors can turn off sound and give them a warning before sound plays. Avoid repeating or looping audio.

DESIGN TIP

Audio Elements

Adding audio files to your webpages enables you to add sound effects, entertain visitors with background music, deliver a personal message, or promote a product or service with testimonial statements. You can provide a webpage link to download an audio file, or embed the audio file in the page's HTML coding. Sources of web-deliverable audio include websites that offer royalty-free and copyright-protected audio files, as well as services you can purchase from vendors that allow you to create and edit your own audio files.

Avoid copyright infringement when incorporating media at your website by researching public domain media or securing permission from the artist or copyright holder. Always give proper credit and citation, even for free or public domain materials.

DESIGN TIP

Most computers or devices have a sound card or capability, a microphone, and speakers. With these tools, you can create your own audio easily and inexpensively. You also will need to use audio-recording and editing software, such as Adobe Audition® CC and WavePad to save, edit, and publish your audio files.

A **podcast** is digital audio or video available to listen to remotely. Originally called webcasts, they more commonly are known as podcasts due to the popularity of the Apple® iPod® player. Examples of podcasts include radio shows, interviews, and classroom lectures. NPR offers a library of podcasts available to download or stream to a remote device or computer (Figure 6-5).

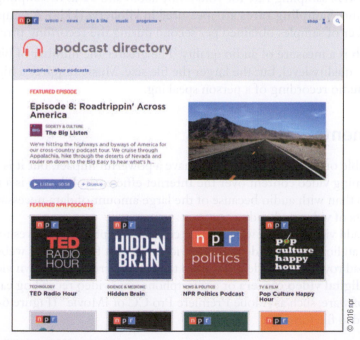

Figure 6-5 NPR offers a variety of podcasts.

Exploring Audio Products and Services

1. Use a search engine to research vendors that provide audio recording, mixing, and/or editing software.
2. Compare and contrast the products or services offered by at least three vendors. Find reviews of the products or services. Examine costs, file quality, and features of each product or service. List any known incompatibilities with devices or platforms.
3. Explore the sound recording capabilities of your computer or device. Evaluate your computer or device's file quality and formats.
4. Submit your findings in the format requested by your instructor.

Q&A

How can I eliminate background noise from my sound files?
Using sound-editing software, such as WaveLab®, you can edit digital audio files by focusing on foreground sounds to eliminate other sounds that distract listeners or detract from the message.

Q&A

Why should I worry about the audio channel?
Selecting a mono audio channel reduces the file size approximately by half over a stereo audio channel. A mono audio channel also is the best choice for an audio message. Whether to choose mono or stereo for a music file depends in part on the desired sound quality and the type of file compression.

EDITING AUDIO FILES   Although you might never need to edit audio files, understanding certain aspects of audio file editing can help you make better choices when selecting audio files for your website. Web audio must be in digital format. Keep in mind the following guidelines for creating and editing audio files for the web:

- Keep recorded audio messages or music clips short, such as 15 seconds, and only include necessary content in the audio message. Shorter audio messages equal smaller files.
- Consider the audio channel type when editing an audio file. **Mono (one-channel)** and **stereo (two-channel)** are the two more well-known audio channels. A mono audio channel has a smaller file size, but might not provide the best listening experience for your website visitors. Sound-editing software enables you to change the audio channel of an audio file.
- Use an 8 kHz sampling rate for voice-only audio and 22 kHz sampling rate for music audio. **Sampling rates** are measured in kilohertz (kHz). A sampling rate is the number of samples obtained per second during the recording process.
- **Bit depth** is a measure of audio quality. The greater the number of bits, the higher the audio quality level, but the larger the file size. Music requires a higher bit depth than an audio recording of a person speaking.

Video Elements

Downloadable or **streaming video** can have a powerful impact, but it is a challenge to deliver streaming video content over the Internet efficiently. File size is a much greater issue with video than with audio because of the large amount of data necessary to play the dual components of video and audio.

Before you add video to your website, first consider simpler alternatives to video, such as animation or audio. If you decide that only video will best further your website's purpose, you can download royalty-free video files from the web, or create your own video files with a good-quality **digital video camera** or a smartphone with video recording capabilities, and video-editing software, such as Adobe Premiere Pro CC or iMovie® (Figure 6-6). Figure 6-7 lists common video file formats.

© 2016 Apple Inc.

Figure 6-6 iMovie is video-editing software that enables you to create and optimize videos.

Web Video Formats

File Format	Description
.avi	Name comes from audio/video interleaved; common format used by digital video cameras
.mov	Originally designed for Apple systems, now usable with the free QuickTime player on most devices and platforms
.mpeg	Platform-independent file format created by the Motion Pictures Expert Group
.rm	One of the first streaming media formats, used with the Real Player
.wmv	Windows Media Video format, available for streaming or download

Figure 6-7 Common web video file formats.

Exploring Video-Editing Software

1. Use a search engine to search for video-editing software. Research at least three video-editing software programs. Compare the features and cost for each. Does each software program have features for creating videos optimized for the web?
2. Review the procedures and capabilities each has for sharing your edited web videos using social media or uploading directly to your blog or website.
3. Based on your research, which video-editing software program would you purchase or download? Submit your findings in the format requested by your instructor.

Q&A

What is a screencast?
A **screencast** is a video of a computer screen's changing content over time. You can use software such as Camtasia Studio to create screencasts for web-based training videos and demonstrations.

EDITING VIDEO FILES   You can manipulate certain aspects of video—frame size, frame rate, bit depth, compression scheme, and overall video quality—to optimize web videos. Although you might never edit video yourself, understanding these aspects can help you make informed choices about including video on your website. For web-based videos, consider the following:

- **Frame size** is the number of pixels for the width and height of the video display.
- The **frame rate** is the number of times per second that the picture within the video changes. Web video frame rate ranges from 10 to 15 frames per second (fps). A higher frame rate means smoother playback.
- As with audio, the greater the number of bits or bit depth, the bigger the file size. If you decrease a video segment from 16-bit to 8-bit, the file size will decrease significantly, as will the quality. Experiment with different settings to find a balance that produces quality videos optimized for playback on various computers, download speeds, and devices.
- You can adjust the general quality level of your video by changing the compression. Similar to editing photographic images, video compression is lossy or lossless. A lossy compression reduces the file size of your video by removing data, but the quality of the video may decrease noticeably. A video with compression between low and medium typically is suitable quality for the web.

Animation

Webpage animation can catch a visitor's attention, demonstrate a simple process, or illustrate change over time, such as the metamorphosis of a butterfly. Animations—whether simple buttons, short animated GIFs, or complex animated movies—can entertain, educate, and engage the visitor. They also can help the user understand how to interact with the website. You will learn more about UX-driven interactive animations later in this chapter.

Animated Elements

TOOLKIT

Appendix A: HTML5
To learn more about HTML5 and animations, see Appendix A.

Animations use a fast-paced presentation of changing static images to simulate motion. During creation, animation software records the changing images in a series of frames along a timeline. With **frame-by-frame animation**, the designer must change the image manually, such as by erasing a portion or increasing the size of the image. With **animation with tweening**, the beginning and ending frames identify the original and final location and/or appearance of an image. The software automatically creates the necessary frames within the changing image in between (or "tween") the beginning and ending frames. Animation with tweening is a more expedient, less-intensive method than frame-by-frame animation.

Animation software programs provide a range of animation creation, editing, and optimization tools for web designers of all levels, from basic tools such as HTML5Maker for novice users to more advanced tools such as Adobe Animate CC or GreenSock Animation Platform. More experienced web programmers might use a scripting language, such as JavaScript, or a combination of scripting plus HTML5 and CSS to create high-quality animations.

Web designers increasingly rely on JavaScript, HTML5, and CSS3 standards to create browser- and device-independent animations. They produce animations with an open format, which do not need proprietary viewing or creation tools. Screen readers and adaptive devices can interpret the content without using a separate plug-in.

When deciding whether to incorporate animations or animated movies at your website, consider whether you have the necessary expertise and resources. Depending on your level of experience, you may wish to purchase ready-to-use animated elements or hire a skilled developer to create custom animations.

You can purchase ready-to-use animated elements from countless websites, such as Animation Factory. Once purchased, you then can download the file and embed it in your webpage. Costs for animated elements vary, as do restrictions on usage. For example, some animation developers allow unrestricted personal use, but place restrictions on use in commercial websites. Before purchasing an element, read the terms of use to ensure that your intended usage meets with the developer's guidelines. Ensure that the developer does not require you to renew your purchase after a certain amount of time has passed. Select only those ready-to-use animations that fall within your budget and satisfy your target audience's expectation for content at your website.

Q&A

What are Flash and Silverlight? Historically, web designers relied on Adobe Flash® and Microsoft Silverlight® to generate web animations and movies. To view these animations, visitors must have the appropriate plug-ins installed. Because of developments with HTML5, both Flash and Silverlight are not used widely today.

DESIGN TIP

Use animations and animated movies on your website only if they add value to the visitor's experience or enhance page content.

Exploring Animation Tools

YOUR TURN

1. Use a search engine to find examples of four programs you can use to create animations. List the capabilities of the programs. What types of animations would you create with each program? How might you incorporate them into a website?
2. Find online tutorials or videos for each program that show the animation creation process. What skills do you need?

Which program(s) might be a good fit for you?
3. Find reviews in the form of articles or blog posts for at least two of the animation programs. What are the strengths and weaknesses of the programs?
4. Explain which program you might use and why. Submit your findings in the format requested by your instructor.

Animated GIFs

Chapter 3 introduced you to animated GIFs. Animated GIFs are popular and prevalent web elements. An animated GIF is a single file that stores separate images within multiple **animation frames**. Displaying these animation frames in sequence over a specified time interval, usually stated in **frames-per-second** (**fps**), gives the illusion of movement or animation. An individual animated GIF file also contains the instructions and timings to display the image in the browser. Websites such as Tumblr and Giphy (Figure 6-8) provide platforms for posting user-created animated GIFs.

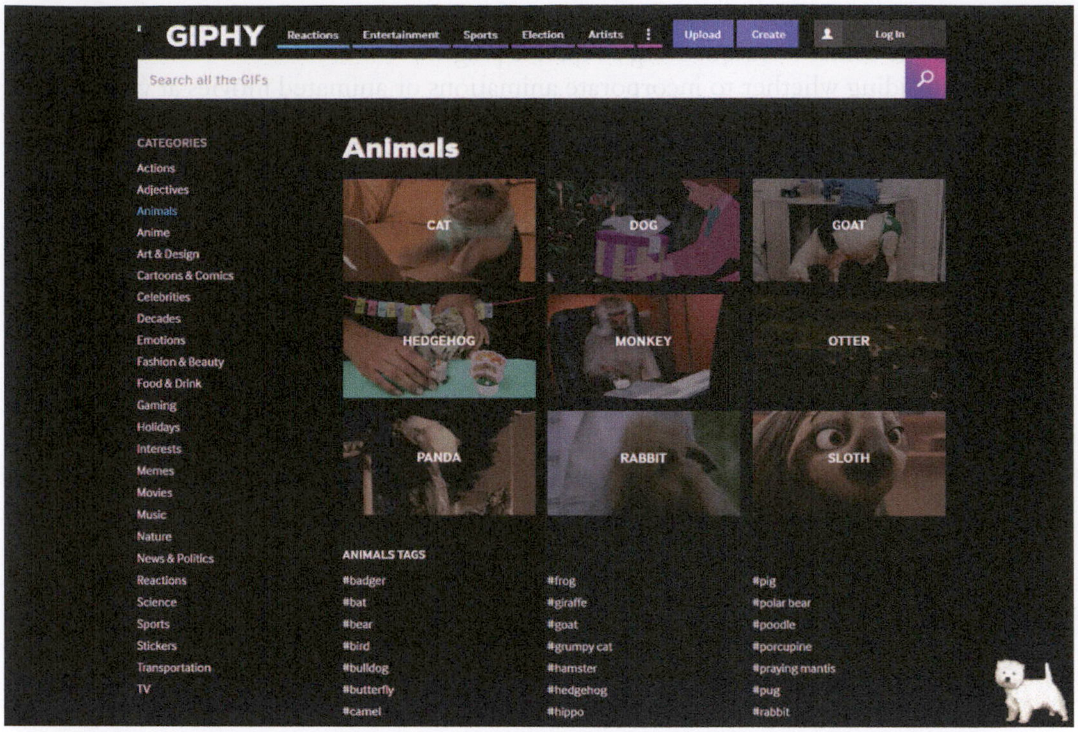

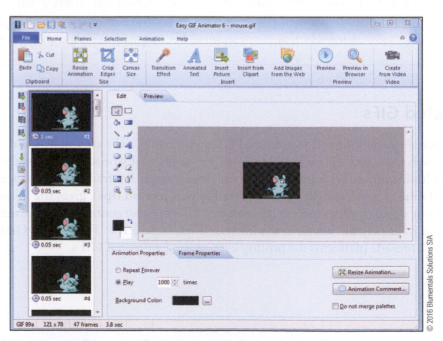

Figure 6-8 Users post animated GIFs to websites such as Giphy.

Q&A

What are the copyright guidelines for creating animated GIFs?

Sometimes animated GIFs use images from TV shows or movies for which the GIF creator does not own the copyright. To learn more, use a search engine to search for *animated GIF copyright restrictions*.

You can download inexpensive software specifically designed to create animated GIFs, such as Easy GIF Animator and ScreenToGif. You also can use high-end image-editing software, such as Adobe Photoshop CC, to create animated GIFs. Some animated GIF software allows **tweening**, in which you only create a beginning and an ending animation frame. With tweening, the software creates all the animation frames in between. Figure 6-9 illustrates the frame-by-frame preview of an animated GIF button created with a wizard in the Easy GIF Animator software.

Figure 6-9 You can use software specifically designed to create animated GIFs.

In general, when creating animated GIFs, you perform the following steps:

1. Identify the sequence of the images you want to animate. Use predesigned GIF images, photos, or videos for which you own the copyright, or create original images using illustration or image-editing software.
2. Specify the time interval between frames, typically in seconds or fractions of a second.
3. Specify whether the animation should **loop**, or repeat.
4. Set background transparency, and add a layer of text, or a caption, if desired.
5. Test the animation and make color, transparency, timing, and looping adjustments as necessary.

DESIGN TIP

Follow good design practice when creating and adding GIFs to your website. Restrict the number of animated GIFs per webpage, and limit the number of loops per GIF. An endlessly looping animated GIF can distract and annoy visitors.

To optimize your animated GIFs for size and quality, apply the following guidelines:

- Plan ahead to determine the essential animation effects that you want to achieve to limit the number of animation frames.
- Limit image colors for each frame to the same or similar palette of colors selected.
- Crop unwanted pixels from the image.
- Use GIF animation or image-editing software to optimize the file for size and quality when saving or exporting it.

Exploring Animation Optimization Tools

YOUR TURN

1. Use a search engine to search for *animated gif optimization tools* or similar keywords. Locate and read three recent blog posts or articles that discuss optimization.
2. List reasons why web designers should optimize animations. Describe how web designers optimize animations (and other content) for the web. List any tools or skills needed.
3. Explain how, as a web designer, you would optimize animations on your website.
4. Submit your findings in the format requested by your instructor.

Interactivity

In Chapter 2, you learned that a well-designed website should include elements that enable the website publisher and website visitors to engage in interactive, two-way communication. You also learned about a variety of elements you can use to promote interactivity, such as contact pages, social media integration, and web-based forms. Interactive elements also can serve as calls-to-action.

In addition to videos and animated GIFs, animations also can be small, UX-driven interactive elements such as buttons or hidden menus. Many UX-driven animations are calls-to-action that encourage interactivity by telling the visitor what he or she can do on the website. Others have the goal of gathering user information, such as through a form or creation of an account.

Q&A

What is a micro-interaction?
A **micro-interaction** is a small detail that gives feedback to the website visitor based on his or her actions. Social media sharing prompts; autocomplete or autoformat in comments or forms; and pop-up notifications, sounds, or button changes to indicate progress or an incorrect action are examples of micro-interactions.

Web-based forms allow visitors to submit information to a website publisher using email or directly to a database or spreadsheet. Scripting languages play a role in creating interactive content elements, such as quizzes or polls, for webpages. Enabling your visitors to post comments to an article, or share it using social media, provides you with feedback about users' reactions and interest in a topic. Some e-commerce websites encourage communication and promote interactivity by using avatars or live chat. All of these are examples of how web designers incorporate calls-to-action.

UX-Driven Interactivity

Few things have impacted web design in recent years more than the focus on UX. As you have learned, UX considerations put the website visitor's needs first. UX-driven interactivity includes adding buttons, menus, animations, forms, and more to engage and instruct the user. As discussed in Chapter 4, examples of UX-driven interactivity trends include sidebar and off-canvas navigation links to provide context-specific navigation, and galleries and slideshows to instruct or entertain. Many trends have the added benefit of saving screen space, which is of special importance to the high number of mobile web users. Because space is limited, and current web design trends value sparse design, animations and other interactive features that accomplish multiple goals and serve as calls-to-action become even more important. Touch screen users also need interactive features, such as buttons that change color or shape after being clicked, to indicate change in status, or that an action is pending (such as a new page loading). Other UX-driven interactive features include animations that respond to the website visitor's actions, such as scrolling, or movements and gestures, such as shaking or rotating the device as in the Hunger Crunch game (Figure 6-10).

monster moves as the device moves

© 2014 Rice Bowls, Inc.

Figure 6-10 Animations that change when the device moves are one example of UX-driven interactivity.

TOOLKIT

Appendix A: HTML5
JotForm and Formidable are web development tools that use HTML5 to assist you in creating web-based forms. HTML5 form features include autocomplete, placeholders, and specifying the input type (such as email). To learn more, see Appendix A.

Web-Based Form Guidelines

Web designers include forms to obtain comments and feedback or to enable customers to order products or services. In Chapter 2, you learned that web-based forms are structured web documents in which a website visitor can enter information or select options. Common form elements include text boxes, check boxes, option buttons, drop-down list boxes, and a Send or Submit button. Each form element is called a **field**.

Breaking your form into multiple form pages can help by chunking the information into smaller, screen-sized forms. One benefit is that if a visitor makes an error on one part of the form, he or she only has to go back to that page to find and fix the error. An example of multiple, sequential form pages is an e-commerce website shopping cart. A series of shopping cart form pages allows an online shopper to review purchases, enter shipping information (name, address, and phone number), enter billing information (third-party payment service or credit card number), and, finally, verify entered information and submit the form. To further simplify forms for your visitors, enable autocomplete or autofill.

Q&A

What fields should be required in my forms?
Consider the most important information you need to collect from a form. For example, in a contact form, required information might include name, address, telephone number, and email address. Optional information might include position title, income, or marital status.

> Follow a logical, predictable sequence for the order of form fields. Most forms require you to enter basic information, such as name and address, before more specific information, such as your credit card number. Group related information together: addresses with phone numbers, and billing with payment information.

DESIGN TIP

To create forms that follow UX principles, you should:

- Require visitors to complete fields containing essential information before submitting the form. Prompt visitors to provide the missing information, and enable users to confirm data before submitting.

- Let users indicate values that should be copied to other fields, such as indicating that the billing and shipping addresses are the same. Include a reset button so that the user can clear the form quickly and reenter the information if necessary.

- Make text boxes large enough to hold the approximate number of characters for a typical response, and to adjust as necessary.

- Use an **input mask**, where appropriate, to limit the number and type of characters, and provide parentheses, hyphens, or other characters to guide the user to properly format, for example, a phone number or Social Security number.

- Send an email or text confirmation notice informing the user that the server received the form data.

- Use check boxes to allow users to submit more than one response to a query, and provide space for additional comments or requests for further information.

TOOLKIT

Appendix A: HTML5
You can use HTML5 tags such as *<fieldset>* (the box for a form element) and *<legend>* (the title or label for that box) to generate forms that adhere to accessibility guidelines. To learn more, see Appendix A.

When creating a form, you also must plan how you will collect, store, analyze, and use the data. For example, an e-commerce form should connect to the inventory and sales database to ensure that the product is available, and then update the inventory. A form that collects website visitor information to create or add to a mailing list should feed the information into a spreadsheet or database that enables you to sort and filter the data, as well as create custom mailings. Google Forms (Figure 6-11) is one example of a web-based tool that assists you in creating a web-based form, and provides data storage in the Google Drive spreadsheet program.

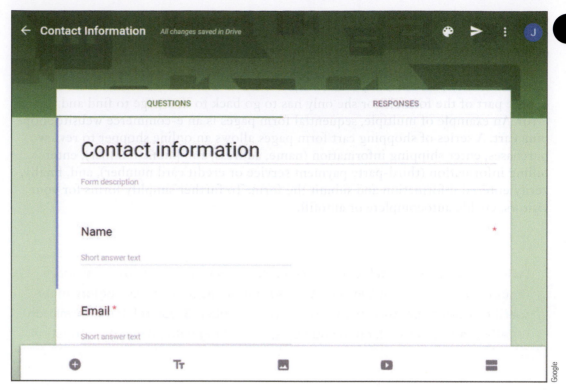

Figure 6-11 Web-based tools can assist you in creating forms.

YOUR TURN

Exploring Web-Based Forms

1. Locate a web-based form at an e-commerce website that enables you to create a user account.

2. Read the website's privacy and security statement for user accounts. Does the statement meet your security needs? What concerns, if any, do you have?

3. Fill out several fields of the form, but do not submit the form. Skip required information, such as your name or email address. Does the form generate a notification when you skip these fields? Make a note of any input masks you come across. Note any examples of UX principles, such as autofill.

4. Take note of any other observations you have about the form, its setup, and ease-of-use. Submit your findings in the format requested by your instructor.

Interactive Content Elements

JavaScript, PHP, and CoffeeScript are all examples of scripting languages that web designers use to create interactive content elements. Web designers use programming tools to create customized interactive webpages, verify form information, and to create rollover buttons, advertising banners, and pop-up windows. Programmers insert scripts directly into a page's HTML code.

Scripts also can be packaged together into a format that web designers without programming experience can insert into webpages to add functionality. Website **widgets**, also called **gadgets**, are small code objects that provide dynamic web content, including clocks, weather reports, breaking news headlines, and more. On a personal webpage or a blog, you might add a widget to display the current weather or to launch a slide show to add interest or enhance your visitors' website experiences. To add a widget, you can copy and paste the script or code directly into the HTML file of your webpage from a source such as AccuWeather (Figure 6-12).

Figure 6-12 You can copy the HTML code for a widget and paste it into your website.

© 2016 AccuWeather, Inc.

Blogs

Millions of personal and professional blogs exist. Businesses use blogs to promote their products and services and provide valuable information to their customers. Personal bloggers publish anecdotes or observations about their lives, or on topics such as food, entertainment, parenting, or special interests. Some bloggers manage to turn a profit from a blog by soliciting advertisements or providing links to purchase products mentioned on the blog. To gauge the success of any website, including blogs, you can use **analytics** to track website statistics such as page views, page clicks, social media shares, time spent on a page, and more.

Sites such as Blogger, Medium, and WordPress are CMS (content management system) platforms that provide tools you can use to create a blog hosted on your own server or on the tool provider's server. Creating a blog using one of these tools can be as simple as entering an email address and password, selecting a layout template for your blog, and specifying where to host the blog. These tools all include a **dashboard**, which is the blog's (or website's) control panel. Dashboards offer tools to create and publish posts, as well as present analytics, and add social media sharing options, as shown in the WordPress dashboard in Figure 6-13.

Q&A How can I protect myself from malware when using JavaScript?
Many websites offer free JavaScript scripts for rollover buttons and banners. You should use caution before downloading any type of free dynamic content from an unknown source to prevent downloading malware to your computer. To learn more, use a search engine to search for *JavaScript malware concerns.*

Q&A What is a sandbox?
A sandbox is a browser feature that restricts a script from running on the computer or device to protect the device from malware risks. To learn more, use a search engine to search for *sandbox security.*

TOOLKIT Appendix D: SEO
To learn about how SEO affects analytics, see Appendix D.

Q&A Where can I find blogs on a specific topic?
Blog hosting services, such as WordPress, enable you to search for blogs by area of interest, keyword, and other criteria. You can follow and read blogs and blog posts directly from within the host website, add a blog to your RSS feed, or sign up to receive email alerts when an author submits a new blog post.

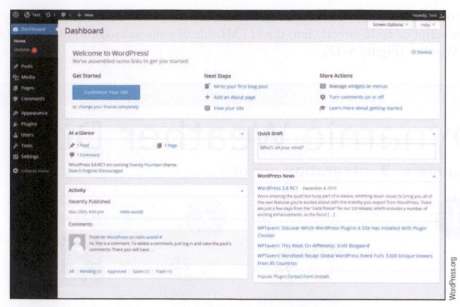

Figure 6-13 A dashboard is a website or blog's control panel in a CMS.

Comments

Adding a comments feature to your website enhances interactivity by enabling visitors to comment on articles and by creating a sense of community. News websites allow visitors to comment on a specific article and to respond to others' comments. Entertainment news websites that regularly feature recaps or information about a specific television show use the comments feature as a venue in which viewers can discuss characters, story lines, and other aspects of the show. Blogs use comments features extensively to promote interactivity. Comments help the website's creators gauge interest in each post or article. To add a comments feature to a website or specific website content, you can add a premade script available from many online sources to your website code. You also can use a service such as Disqus (Figure 6-14) to incorporate and manage comments and other interactive tools.

Figure 6-14 Disqus offers comment management tools.

It is important to monitor comments posted to your website. Many websites have a disclaimer stating that the website owner will remove anything offensive. Some websites permit visitors to rate the comments made by other visitors. Spam often appears in comments as well. Having someone monitor comments before or as they post gives you control over any postings that might be offensive or that may contain links to malware or phishing websites. Consider requiring users to create an account before posting comments. Doing so helps you keep track of and block users who violate the code of conduct by introducing spam or using inappropriate language.

Exploring Comment Features

YOUR TURN

1. In separate tabs in a browser, open the following websites:
   a. Entertainment Weekly
   b. NBC News
   c. TechCrunch
2. On each website, find a post or article that allows comments. Review the comments. What restrictions or disclaimers regarding comments does each website have?

3. For each website, answer the following questions: In what way do comment postings promote interactivity between the website publishers and the visitors who read and post comments to the blog? How would a website creator find these postings helpful? How do the comment features of the three websites differ and how are they similar?
4. Submit your findings in the format requested by your instructor.

Avatars

In Chapter 1, you learned that millions of gamers interact with each other by playing massively multiplayer online games (MMOGs) or by participating in 3D virtual worlds. These gamers create **avatars**, which are alternative personas, sometimes called **virtual identities**, for MMOGs or 3D virtual worlds. You also might find avatars used in email marketing campaigns, on business or personal blogs, or at e-commerce websites. Depending on your intended usage, you may find that adding an avatar does not fit within your budget. Companies such as SitePal™ provide web designers with low-cost tools to create an avatar quickly. You can create a custom avatar and then can copy and paste the HTML code for the avatar to your website's pages.

Some e-commerce websites use avatars as virtual models. Customers can use a **virtual model** to "try on" clothing before purchasing it, such as at MyStyleRules.com (Figure 6-15). Other e-commerce websites use avatars to welcome website visitors,

Figure 6-15 Website avatars are alternate virtual identities that can be used as virtual models.

provide a virtual salesperson to promote products and services, personalize customer support responses, direct visitors to specific website pages, provide instructions for webpage tutorials, and more. Avatars have other uses, such as in social media and e-learning platforms. You can create an avatar for use in multiple websites, social media sites, and apps, using services available from a number of companies.

DESIGN TIP   E-commerce avatars can add interest to a website. By including an avatar for a company mascot, or by dressing the avatar in company colors, you can use avatars to help establish or reinforce brand identity. Use avatars only to further the website's message and purpose and enrich the target audience's experience at the website.

Live Chat

Q&A

What software or apps can I use to include live chat on my website?
LiveChat, WebsiteAlive, and LiveEngage are a few of the many chat tools available. To learn more, use a search engine to locate the website of any of these tools, or search for *live chat software*.

Live chat allows visitors to ask questions and receive answers in real time using text, voice, or video. Web designers include live chat features to enable website visitors to query product information, ask for customer service, or troubleshoot problems with a computer or device. Websites either offer **reactive** or **broadcast live chat**, in which visitors initiate the chat, or **proactive live chat**, where a chat window opens automatically. Live chat uses a browser window in which a visitor exchanges messages with a **chat agent**, a customer service representative who handles the visitor's query. Chat agents can be in-house or they might be outsourced chat agents located in a call center. Figure 6-16 illustrates the live chat window at the Lands' End e-commerce website.

Figure 6-16 Live chat allows website visitors to interact with chat agents in real time.

DESIGN TIP   Blogs and live chat are two useful content elements that add interactivity to a website. If you do not operate your own servers, you can purchase hosted blog or hosted live chat software or services. You also can purchase outsourced chat agent services.

Chapter Review

Animated and interactive elements can serve as calls-to-action on a website. Multimedia generally is defined as some combination of text, images, animation, audio, and video. Interactive elements promote communication between a website publisher and website visitors. A combination of animated and interactive elements can generate exciting, entertaining, and more useful webpages. Multimedia and interactive elements are not essential for the success of a website. Only include them on a website to add value, further the website's message and purpose, and meet the target audience's expectation for content.

Web audio and video can be either downloadable or streaming, or use pseudo streaming to combine the two technologies. Each has distinct advantages and disadvantages. Designers should consider alternatives to video that would circumvent issues related to delivering video on the web.

Effective uses of animation can include catching a visitor's attention, demonstrating a simple process, or illustrating change over time, such as the metamorphosis of a butterfly. HTML5 and CSS include capabilities to create and add animations and movies that entertain and inform visitors. You can use software specially designed for creating web graphics to create animations, animated movies, and animated GIFs. Animated GIFs are a widely used form of animation on the web. Popular interactive elements include UX-driven elements, web-based forms, widgets, blogs, comments, avatars, and live chat.

TERMS TO KNOW

After reading the chapter, you should know each of these Key Terms.

analytics (165)
animation frame (159)
animation with tweening (158)
avatar (167)
bit depth (156)
broadcast live chat (168)
chat agent (168)
dashboard (165)
digital video camera (156)
field (163)
frame rate (158)
frame size (158)
frame-by-frame animation (158)
frames-per-second (fps) (159)
gadget (164)
input mask (163)
live chat (168)

loop (161)
micro-interaction (162)
mono (one-channel) (156)
podcast (155)
proactive live chat (168)
progressive downloading (154)
pseudo streaming (154)
reactive live chat (168)
sampling rate (156)
screencast (158)
stereo (two-channel) (156)
streaming audio (153)
streaming video (156)
tweening (160)
virtual identities (167)
virtual model (167)
widget (164)

TEST YOUR KNOWLEDGE

Complete the Test Your Knowledge exercises to solidify what you have learned in the chapter.

Matching Terms

Match each term with the best description.

_____ 1. analytics

_____ 2. animated GIF

_____ 3. avatar

_____ 4. comments

_____ 5. dashboard

_____ 6. podcast

_____ 7. proactive live chat

_____ 8. pseudo streaming

_____ 9. reactive live chat

_____ 10. widget

a. Digital audio or video available to listen to remotely.

b. Live chat where a chat window opens automatically.

c. A small code object that provides dynamic web content.

d. Live chat in which visitors initiate the chat.

e. Technology that allows media to play while it downloads.

f. A virtual identity.

g. A feature that enables website creators to gauge visitors' reactions to content.

h. A blog or website's control panel, which offers tools to create and publish posts, as well as present analytics, and add social media sharing options.

i. A single file in which separate images in multiple animation frames are stored.

j. Used to track website statistics such as page views, page clicks, social media shares, and time spent on a page.

Short Answer Questions

Write a brief answer to each question.

1. List the general guidelines for adding animated elements to a website.

2. Differentiate between downloading and streaming media.

3. Discuss the guidelines for creating and editing audio for the web.

4. Describe how to optimize video for the web in terms of frame size, frame rate, bit depth, compression scheme, and overall video quality.

5. Define tweening and how it is used to create objects. What type of software enables tweening?

6. List steps for creating and optimizing animated GIFs.

7. Describe UX-driven interactivity. Why is it important to add to your websites?

8. Explain the design guidelines for creating attractive and UX-friendly web-based forms.

9. Discuss guidelines for adding and monitoring comments for a website.

10. Describe how an e-commerce website would use avatars and live chat. What is the difference between proactive and reactive live chat?

Investigate current web design developments with the Trends exercises.

TRENDS

Write a brief essay about each of the following trends, using the web as your research tool. For each trend, identify at least one webpage URL used as a research source. Be prepared to discuss your findings in class.

1 | Micro-Interactions

Find two blogs or articles that discuss micro-interactions. List types of micro-interactions. Have you encountered these? Describe how web designers use micro-interactions to increase UX. What negatives or limitations, if any, are mentioned about micro-interactions? Choose one type of micro-interaction to research further. What technologies might you need to implement it? Describe how, as a web designer, you would use this on a website.

2 | Widgets

Research the types of widgets website designers can add to their website. Find two sources for reputable, safe gadgets or widgets. List the concerns website designers and website visitors have with making website content accessible to users of all devices and platforms, and address any restrictions or guidelines for including widgets. Discuss the advantages of including this type of content on a website.

@ISSUE

Challenge your perspective of the web and web design technology with the @Issue exercises.

Write a brief essay in response to the following issues, using the web as your research tool. For each issue, identify at least one webpage URL used as a research source. Be prepared to discuss your findings in class.

1 | Website Analytics

As you have learned, analytics report on website usage data, including views, sharing, and more. Find at least two articles discussing what a web designer or website manager needs to track using analytic tools. Research CMS platforms' analytic capabilities. Are any CMS platforms more robust than others? If so, how? Describe, as a web designer, what tools you would use to provide your client or company with website analytics, what data you would track, and how you would measure the website's success.

2 | Streaming versus Downloadable Multimedia

Describe the differences between streaming, downloadable, and pseudo streaming media. List the advantages and disadvantages of each. Use a search engine to find websites, forums, or blogs where web professionals discuss which method is best. Describe any experience you have with watching or listening to media on the web, and what type of delivery was used. If possible, discuss your experiences with accessing media on different device types with varying bandwidths and screen sizes.

HANDS ON

Use the World Wide Web to obtain more information about the concepts in the chapter with the Hands On exercises.

1 | Explore and Evaluate: Embedding Video or Audio Content from Other Sources

Browse the web and locate three websites that effectively include links to video, audio, or images from YouTube or other original sources.

a. Describe the animated or multimedia element and explain how the element is used by a visitor.

b. Describe the advantages and disadvantages of including this type of content on your website.

c. Which of the three websites does the best job of incorporating animation and multimedia?

d. What might you change about how any of the websites link to external animation or multimedia sources?

2 | Search and Discover: HTML5 and Forms

Research how web designers use HTML5 to create forms for websites. List specific tags and techniques that HTML5 offers, and how each is used. Find articles that discuss the benefits of using HTML5 to create forms. If possible, list and describe any emerging technologies that might replace or add to HTML5's capabilities.

Work collaboratively to reinforce the concepts in the chapter with the Team Approach exercises.

1 | Evaluate Avatars

Join with another student to evaluate avatar-creation websites.

a. Locate two reputable avatar creation websites.

b. Describe terms of use and costs for using the services.

c. Describe the steps needed to create an avatar.

d. If possible, create an avatar of your own.

Report on your experiences.

2 | Apply Your Knowledge

Join with two other students to form a team to identify a list of interactive elements that you should add to the Fit4U sample website discussed in previous chapters. Have each team member come up with a list of five elements. As a team, discuss the benefits of each, and come up with a final list of five elements to add.

a. As a team, write a report for your instructor that lists the interactive elements in the order of priority (from most to least effective).

b. For each element, describe what its purpose would be as part of your website, and how adding it meets your website goals. Which elements are calls-to-action?

c. For each element, briefly describe the technical skills you would need to employ to add the element.

CASE STUDY

Apply the chapter concepts to the ongoing development process in web design with the Case Study.

The Case Study is an ongoing development process using the concepts, techniques, and Design Tips presented in each chapter.

Background Information

In the Case Study assignments in the previous five chapters, you have created your website plan, generated the text content for your webpages, and created or gathered and optimized the images for your website.

Chapter 6 Assignment

In this chapter's Case Study, you will create your website. In the final part of the process, you will apply the concepts presented in this chapter and gather or create any animated and/or interactive elements that will help achieve your website's purpose. Remember that animated and/or interactive elements are not required elements for a successful website. Using the website plan you created in Chapters 3 and 4, and the guidelines in Chapters 2, 5, and 6, complete the following steps to create your website.

1. Decide whether you will generate your pages with HTML code and a text editor such as Notepad, with web design software, such as Dreamweaver, a web template, or a CMS.

2. Begin to create your webpages. As you add your text and position your optimized images, review your design plan and keep the following guidelines in mind:

   a. Use responsive web design techniques to ensure your website will be effective on multiple devices and screen sizes.

   b. Apply the rules of good typography.

   c. Include alternative text descriptions for images and follow other WAI accessibility guidelines.

   d. Develop your home page and subsidiary pages according to your chosen website structure.

   e. To achieve unity, establish and apply a consistent page layout and color scheme for all pages at your website. Limit the color scheme to no more than three colors.

3. Download from the web, purchase, link to, or create any animated elements you want to include on your webpages. Insert the elements into your pages and give proper credit where necessary.

4. Develop any web-based forms you want to include on your webpages following this chapter's guidelines for creating usable forms.

5. Download from the web, purchase, or create interactive elements. Incorporate the interactive element(s) into your website.

6. Save your completed website files. Submit your work in the format requested by your instructor.

7 | Promoting and Maintaining a Website

© 2016 SmartSoft Ltd.

© 2016 British Gas

© 2005–2016 KickFire

Introduction

Chapter 1 introduced you to Internet and web fundamentals and how businesses and individuals use the web for communication, e-commerce, and more. In Chapters 2 through 6, you learned about essential design guidelines for creating a website's structure and adding page content such as text, links, images, and multimedia. You also read about how to use color and layout effectively to promote branding and visual identity at your website. You learned about UX and RWD principles, and how and why to incorporate them. Along the way, you created a website plan. At the end of Chapter 6, you used your website plan to create pages for your website.

Once your website structure and content are complete, you must test your website to make certain that all elements work as intended, that your website accomplishes the website plan's stated goals and objectives, and that the content satisfies your target audience's needs and expectations. After thorough testing, you are ready to publish your website to a web server to make it available to your audience. Once you publish your website, you then start the ongoing processes of maintaining and promoting it.

Objectives

After completing this chapter, you will be able to:

1. Explain how to test a website before it is published

2. Describe how to publish a website to a web server

3. Identify ways to promote a published website

4. Discuss the importance of maintaining and evaluating a published website

Website Testing

In Chapter 4, you learned why it is important to perform usability testing during website development to ensure that your website's navigation system is both user-based and user-controlled. Before publishing your website to a web server, you must test the website thoroughly to identify and fix any undetected problems with navigation. Testing also identifies any structural problems or content issues. Failure to test your website thoroughly might lead to loss of credibility with your website's visitors, which could lead to your website's failure. In addition, you should incorporate the following questions into your testing plans:

- Does my website meet its goals and objectives?
- Does the design and functionality incorporate UX principles?
- Have I met all accessibility standards?
- Have I successfully incorporated RWD guidelines?

Beta testing involves using a prepublication version of your website, not available to the general public, called a **beta website**. Beta testing helps you ensure that the website's pages look and function as designed and confirm that you have satisfied all aspects of the design plan. Some beta websites are online but are password protected or not visible to search engines. Only those with passwords or the direct link can access the website for testing. Some organizations and businesses publish beta websites to a temporary web server, called a staging server. A **staging server** enables testing in an environment similar to that of a live web server. Beta testing a website incorporates self-testing or internal testing, and testing by interested parties not involved with the website's design and development. As part of beta testing, sometimes testing occurs on two (or more) versions of a website simultaneously, to test how different features of each might provide a better user experience.

Self- and Internal Testing

The first phases of prepublication website testing are **self-testing** or **internal testing,** where testing is limited to those involved in web design. During this phase, you (self) or your web development team (internal) test and evaluate your website's structure and page layout, color scheme, and other elements. If you are using a web design tool or CMS, use the available tools to test links, accessibility, spelling, and responsiveness.

As part of this process, you and your team should do the following:

1. Ensure that all images and animated elements work as intended. Verify that the page code does not contain misspellings of the image or multimedia file names and does not link to an invalid folder location or external webpage.

2. Test the navigation and search tools and examine the website's structure to determine whether visitors can find all pages easily.

3. Test all links to make certain they work properly and none are broken. A **broken link** is one that does not work. Verify that the link text clearly identifies its target and that the correct page opens when clicked. If relevant, make sure that the new page opens in the same browser window, a new tab, or a new window as specified.

4. Confirm that there is a text equivalent for all nontext elements to satisfy WAI guidelines for images and multimedia.

5. Use any optimization tools provided by your web design tool or CMS, such as HTML validation and cleanup, accessibility testing, and website speed testing.

6. Ensure RWD compliance by using different browsers, devices, and screen sizes to perform Steps 1 to 5. You can expect a reasonable range of variances as long as the page appears legible and looks well laid out in each instance.

7. Correct any problems uncovered by testing and fully retest to verify whether your corrections solved the issues and did not create any new issues.

Target Audience Testing

The second testing phase involves recruiting a small group of people to act as testers. Using an outside group of testers to evaluate your website can help provide insight about how potential visitors will respond to your website and use its pages. Although you should perform usability testing during development, this phase of testing ensures your website is navigable. As verification of RWD compliance, testers should use a variety of devices and screen sizes. Additionally, the testers might find problems that you, as the designer, could not identify because you were too close to the process.

Include colleagues not involved in the website development, people who represent your target audience, and other interested parties. The testers should review your website and test its navigation, links, and other features. For an e-commerce website, target audience testers might be employees, vendors, and other business partners.

Observe the testers or use analytic tools to determine the following:

- Which pages appear to appeal to them?
- Which pages appear to disinterest them?
- How much time do they spend on various pages?
- Which links do they visit or ignore?
- How easily do they navigate the website?
- Do they at any time demonstrate any confusion or frustration?

Ask testers to complete a survey in which they can express their candid opinions. In addition to identifying specific settings (such as browser version, screen resolution and size, and device type) the tester is using, your survey should include questions that answer the following UX guidelines:

- Did the website's content satisfy your needs, wants, and expectations for content at the website?
- Was the website's content interesting and valuable?
- Was it easy or difficult to navigate the website?

Exploring How to Organize a Test Group

YOUR TURN

1. Review the audience profile you developed for your website. The profile should include age range, gender, educational background, geographic location, careers, income levels, and interests and activities. Review the identified target audience needs, wants, and expectations for website content.

2. Identify individuals you know who match your target audience's profile. Ask the identified individuals and other interested parties, such as friends, family members, and fellow students, to participate in the testing of your website.

3. Develop questions for the testers in which they can express their opinions about their experiences at your website. Does the testing reveal changes you need to make? How will you address these changes?

After testing, seriously consider all comments, both negative and positive. Implement suggestions that will further the original purpose, goals, and objectives; meet the audience's needs; and generally improve the website's value, functionality, and usability.

DESIGN TIP   Consider a second round of testing if the comments led you to make considerable changes. File away any suggestions that you cannot implement at this time for valid reasons, such as time or cost limitations, for future consideration.

Website Publishing

Once you have tested your website thoroughly and corrected any problems, you can make it available to your audience by publishing it to a live web server. Publishing your website to a live web server involves acquiring a domain name, allotting server space, and uploading all of your website files—HTML and CSS documents, images, multimedia, and other related files—to the web server. Select a domain name that clearly identifies your website's purpose, such as your business name. If you are using a CMS that includes website hosting, you should explore the hosting requirements, costs, and services before starting work on your website. Before you begin your research into web server and hosting options, you should know the approximate amount of server space you will need and how frequently you will update content. Also ensure that you have access to any tools, scripts, or other technologies necessary to display your content or support your website's interactive and multimedia features.

Domain Name

In Chapter 1, you learned about selecting and registering a domain name for your website. Selecting a domain name is one of the most important decisions you will make. If possible, use your business or organization name. Avoid abbreviations and hyphens, or other modifications that will make your website difficult to find. If your website name does not easily correspond to a unique domain name, consider changing it or adding words that further specify your website purpose. For example, a hardware supply company named Cunningham's might find that the domain name *CunninghamsTools* would be a unique name and distinguish the website further than *Cunninghams* alone would. In addition, purchase your domain name with as many TLD (top-level domains) as you reasonably can afford to avoid other companies purchasing your domain name with *.biz* while you use *.com*. You can go to an accredited registrar's website, identify an available name, and register it at the website for a fee. Accredited registrars include register.com and GoDaddy (Figure 7-1). Alternatively, some web hosting services might assist with acquiring a domain name for an additional fee or as part of the original setup fee for the hosting services.

Q&A

How can I find reputable domain name registrars?
Just like any online shopping you might do, when purchasing a domain name, it is best to review ratings and look where the experts go. Domain name sellers exist online that do not have the proper accreditation and might engage in unscrupulous practices, such as acquiring domain names based on your search terms in order to resell them to you at a high cost. To learn more, search for *top accredited domain name registrars*.

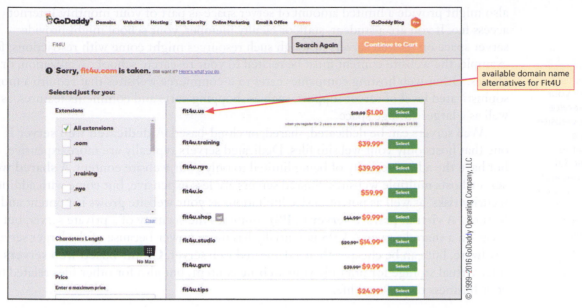

Figure 7-1 Domain name registrars enable you to purchase and reserve several domain names at once.

> Your domain name will follow you across all social media platforms. Search Facebook, Twitter, and other platforms you intend to use for marketing or other purposes to check availability of your domain (or a variation).

DESIGN TIP

Server Space

In Chapter 1, you learned that a web server is an Internet-connected computer used to store webpages. A web server runs **server software** that displays webpages and their related files upon request from a browser. Thousands of **web hosting companies**, such as iPage (Figure 7-2), offer server space for a monthly fee. Your Internet service provider (ISP)

TOOLKIT

Appendix D: SEO
Your domain name choice also might affect your SEO rankings. To learn more, see Appendix D.

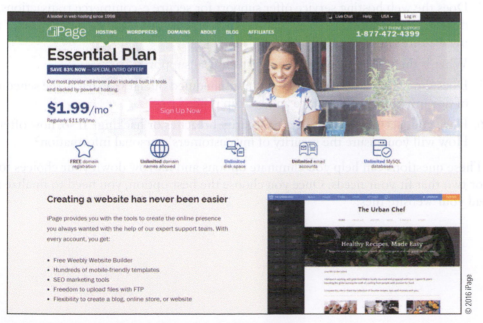

Figure 7-2 Web hosting companies offer server space for a fee.

also might provide a limited amount of server space as part of your monthly Internet access fee. If you are a student, staff, or faculty member, your school might provide server space on its web server, although such resources might come with restrictions; for example, the website content must be related to your research, school organization, or classes. Other web hosting companies cater to e-commerce websites that require a more sophisticated level of server support, such as shopping carts and comments features, as well as a larger storage space.

Web servers can be dedicated, shared, or cloud-based. A **dedicated web server** is one that hosts only your website files. Dedicated servers typically are more expensive, but have the added security of being limited to only your website content. A **shared web server** hosts multiple websites. Shared servers are less expensive, but come with additional security risks, as well as potential size limitations as your website grows in content and features. A **virtual private server (VPS)** combines the security of a private server, but exists on a shared server. A VPS potentially has more power because of the larger server hardware, but can be cheaper than a dedicated web server. **Cloud-based web servers** offer virtual storage for not only your website content, but also for other files related to your business or personal life.

Q&A

What type of server should I request? You should ask your web hosting service whether your website will reside on a dedicated, shared, or cloud server. All have advantages and disadvantages related to cost, security, and reliability. To learn more, use a search engine to search for *dedicated, shared, VPS, cloud-based web server*.

DESIGN TIP To find the right web hosting service, seek recommendations from business associates. Ask them which hosting service they use, and how they would rate the customer support quality. You also can research the web to find reviews of web hosting service options.

Evaluate potential web hosting services by learning about the server type, cost, customer support, and technical requirements. In addition, you should get answers to the following questions:

1. How much available server space will I have for my website? Does the web hosting service limit the number, size, or type of files that I can upload?

2. What is the procedure for updating and republishing pages to my website?

3. Does the web hosting service offer support for secure e-commerce transactions, multimedia, scripting languages, interactive features, or other elements related to my website and its pages?

4. What is the typical response time for technical support?

5. Does the server experience frequent nonscheduled outages? What is the schedule of downtime for maintenance and backup procedures?

6. Have your servers been subject to security breaches or hacking? If so, how often? How will you ensure the security of my customers' personal information?

These questions can help you eliminate options and narrow down your choices to one or two that fit your needs. Once you choose the best option, you need to finalize and upload your website files.

Uploading Website Folders and Files

To publish your website, you must upload all of the website files to a dedicated folder on the server. For the initial website publication, you upload the contents (HTML and CSS documents, images, multimedia files, and so forth) for all pages at your website. To make updates to your website, you only need to add the new files or replace any changed files.

You must know the name and URL of the web server. Your web hosting company will provide you with a username and password in order to access the web server. If you are using a CMS, you will save files to the host company's web server as you create them. The pages simply need your go-ahead to publish. If you are working with a web design tool, your files reside on your own computer. To upload your files, you can use FTP, or the publishing feature included with your web design tool. **File Transfer Protocol (FTP)** is the standard for uploading or downloading files over the Internet, such as webpage files to a web server.

DESIGN TIP

Before uploading, review the contents of your website folders. Move any unnecessary files, such as original image or word-processing files or backup files, to another location to save space on the server and to limit any extra time in loading pages in your website.

CONTENT MANAGEMENT SYSTEM   A CMS offers publication tools, hosting services, server space, and more. If you are using a CMS, such as WordPress (Figure 7-3), your files already exist on the server but are not on the web until you publish them.

Figure 7-3 A CMS offers publication tools for your website.

FILE TRANSFER PROTOCOL   You can upload your website files directly from your computer's hard disk to your host's web server using FTP. An **FTP client** is a software program that provides a user interface for transferring files using the FTP protocol, such as SmartFTP (Figure 7-4), or FileZilla. Typically, the FTP client user interface provides a split view of the folders and files on a local computer or device, such as the user's hard drive, and on a remote computer, such as the web server. You can use menus or buttons to

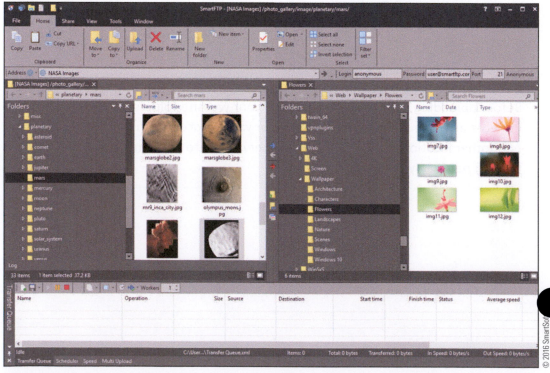

Figure 7-4 An FTP client transfers files between a computer or device and a web server.

initiate publication, or drag and drop files from the local computer or device to the web server location to begin copying the files from a local computer to a remote computer or vice versa. After you publish the website, you can **sync** the files, which makes sure that any changed files are the same on both servers.

WEB DESIGN TOOL   If you are using a web design tool, such as Adobe Dreamweaver CC (Figure 7-5), you can publish and update your website from within the program. As with other uploading methods, you need to arrange for server space and provide access information—the name and URL of the remote server and your assigned username and password—before uploading your web folders and files.

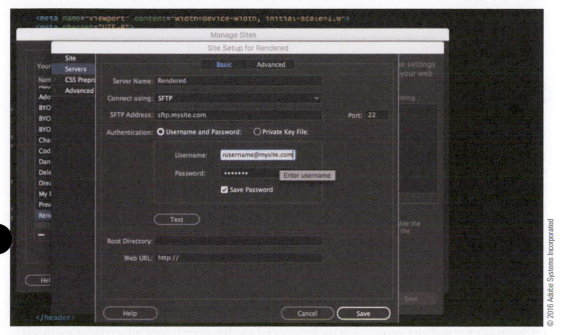

© 2016 Adobe Systems Incorporated

Figure 7-5 A web design tool provides tools for uploading or publishing web folders and files to a web server.

Retesting Published Pages

After publication, you must monitor your website continually to ensure that it functions correctly and contains current information. Conduct periodic testing similar to your prepublishing testing, using self- or internal testing, or by using features of your CMS or web design tool, or tools specific to concerns such as SEO. Check the following:

- Confirm that all images are displayed properly.
- Make certain that no broken links exist.
- Ensure all interactive elements, such as forms, function properly.
- Correct or update page file(s) on your local computer as needed, and upload the corrected page file(s) to the server.
- Skim the content, especially when it contains schedule or date information that may be time sensitive.

TOOLKIT

Appendix D: SEO
Use SEO tools such as Google Webmaster's Search Console to perform SEO testing. To learn more, see Appendix D.

Use widgets or other tools to update time-sensitive content automatically, such as calendars, weather, and more.

Website Promotion

Once you publish your website, you need to promote it in order to reach the target audience. The amount of traffic you want or need to generate depends on your goals and the type of website you have.

DESIGN TIP   Attracting numerous visitors might or might not be a top-level concern for a personal website or blog. For an organizational/topical or e-commerce website, having a large number of visitors affects the website's success or failure.

Q&A

What are web industry awards?
Many award websites recognize characteristics related to design, creativity, usability, and functionality. Some award websites focus on a specific industry or type of business. If you decide to compete for an award, ensure that the award is relevant to your website's content and objectives.

Q&A

What is geotargeting?
Geotargeting determines the user's location by the ISP, IP address, Global Positioning System (GPS), or user-provided location information, such as ZIP code, and provides ad content relevant to the user's location.

To generate a high volume of traffic to your website, use both online and offline promotional techniques. Take advantage of social media to establish an online community of subscribers and direct them to your website. To maximize your promotion budget, consider using manual search tool submission, search tool optimization techniques, and free link exchanges. For an e-commerce website, you should consider increasing your promotion budget to add other online promotional tools: paid or sponsored placement on a search engine, a search tool submission service, in-app advertising, an affiliate program, and email advertising. Offline promotional techniques such as postcards can extend your audience beyond those who might find you using social media or search engines.

Online Promotional Techniques

The Internet offers a variety of ways to announce your website, drive visitors to it, and keep them engaged and returning. For example, in previous chapters you learned about the increasing importance of business blogs in promoting e-commerce websites. Other online tools for website promotion include social media, search tool advertising methods (search engine optimization and search tool indexing), online advertising, in-app ads, affiliate programs and advertising networks, and opt-in advertising.

SOCIAL MEDIA   Establishing a basic social media presence is easy and free. You can use social media to share updates, invite customers to an event, ask for feedback, and more. You also can use social media platforms' paid tools to create advertisements, promotional posts, and more. One advantage of social media is that you can create **targeted ads** that reach a specific audience based on information in the users' profiles, as well as the users' social media activity.

DESIGN TIP   Most websites have social media buttons that provide website visitors with tools for following the website's social media profiles and sharing website content to visitors' own social media profiles.

Figure 7-6 shows Knowem, a website that helps establish a social media presence with domain name registration, branding, and more. Figure 7-7 describes several popular social media tools and how you can use them.

Figure 7-6 Establish your social media presence while determining your domain name.

© 2016 knowem

Social Media Websites

Platform	Uses
Facebook	Create a page for your website, business, or organization. Post status updates, photos, and links to webpage content. Build a community of users. Buy and sell targeted ad space.
Google+	Manage your online and business profiles using the many expanding tools Google offers. Integrates with the Google search engine. Allows you to create events, groups, and hangouts.
Instagram	Post pictures or short videos that your followers can see, share, and comment on.
LinkedIn	Create a business profile for your website, organization, or company. Post links to articles of interest, and share updates regarding content postings, job openings, and more.
Pinterest	Create boards of "pins," images that link to webpages, to share information about your products or related topics of interest.
Twitter	Attract followers to your profile. Post short messages or links to web and multimedia content. Share others' tweets and use hashtags to create and participate in trending topics.
YouTube	Create a channel for your website, organization, or business. Upload product demonstrations, speeches or lectures from employees, advertisements, and more.

Figure 7-7 Social media platforms offer both free services and fee-based targeted ads.

YOUR TURN

Exploring Social Media Promotion Tools

1. Select three companies or organizations with which you do business or whose online presence you follow.

2. Visit each company's website. Make a note of how the website promotes its social media presence.

3. Visit at least two of the social media profiles. What content does the website promote using social media? Did the social media presence enhance the website content?

4. List three specific ways you could use social media to promote the Fit4U website.

TOOLKIT

Appendix D: SEO
Keyword stuffing is adding or repeating commonly used search terms in a website to increase a website's search rankings. Web designers recommend learning about proper use of keywords to ensure your website reaches its target audience. To learn more, see Appendix D.

SEARCH ENGINE OPTIMIZATION   As you learned in Chapter 1, search engine optimization (SEO) refers to applying design and development techniques to your webpages to increase the possibility that they will appear near the top of a search results list for specific keywords. For example, you can increase the possibility of your webpages appearing in some search results lists by including meta tags and carefully crafting each page's title. Clearly worded webpage text, the density of specific keywords in your page text, and an impressive number of incoming links to your webpages are also elements of SEO. For medium to large e-commerce websites, it might be helpful to hire an SEO consultant to help direct SEO efforts.

SEARCH TOOL INDEXING   In Chapter 1, you learned about search engines and search directories and how these tools build their webpage databases or indexes. When your website appears in search engines' indexes, users can find your relevant webpages using specific keywords. You can wait for search engines' spiders to find your pages and add them to their indexes, which might take days or weeks. Alternatively, you can take the initiative and register your website's URL with major search engines and directories such as Bing and Google. Some search engines require a fee to expedite your submission, while others are free.

A **search tool submission service** registers websites with multiple search tools. Using a search tool submission service is an alternative to waiting for search engines to find and index your website or spending your own time registering your webpages with multiple search tools. SEO consultants often offer submission services. To use a submission service, you typically provide information about your website, such as its URL, a brief description of the website, and keywords to associate with the website.

DESIGN TIP

If you use a submission service, select one that registers your website with the most frequently used search tools.

ONLINE ADVERTISING   In Chapter 1, you also learned about paid or sponsored search results placement as an online advertising tool. Search engine advertising programs, such as Google AdWords (Figure 7-8), and Bing Ads, as well as many social media platforms, blogs, and more, allow you to add a paid placement or sponsored listing for specific keywords to a search results page. You often pay for the advertising on a **pay-per-click** basis: if a user clicks on your ad, you pay a small fee or share of any revenue generated.

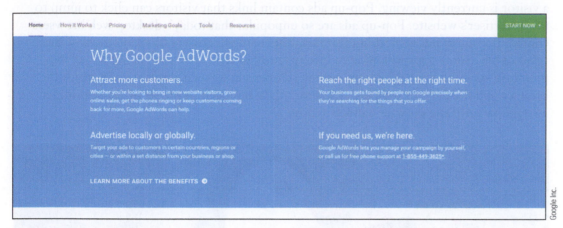

Figure 7-8 Search tool paid placements allow website owners to purchase advertisements based on keyword searches.

The types of website and in-app ads typically offered by an online advertising network include banner ads, pop-up and pop-under ads, and rich media ads. A **banner ad** is a rectangular webpage advertisement that links to the advertiser's website. Figure 7-9 illustrates banner ads on the SportsDay home page. Banner ads often are horizontal.

Figure 7-9 Banner ads link to the advertiser's website.

When a banner ad is a vertical rectangle, it sometimes is called a **sidebar ad**. The purpose of a banner or sidebar ad is to motivate visitors to click the ad, thereby driving traffic to the advertiser's website, in a process called a **click-through**.

Rich media ads contain multimedia elements, such as the British Gas ad shown in Figure 7-10. This category of online ads includes **floating ads** that seem to float across the screen for a few seconds, **expandable banner ads** that grow larger when clicked, and **multimedia ads**. A **pop-up ad** opens in its own window on top of the webpage or app a visitor is currently viewing. Pop-up ads contain links that visitors can click to jump to the advertiser's website. Pop-up ads are so unpopular that today's desktop web browsers contain pop-up window blocking features, which are effective at blocking most of these types of ads. Some apps will offer an incentive to block ads, such as paying to get the premium version of an app. A **pop-under ad** opens in its own window underneath the browser and the current webpage. A visitor might not even be aware of the pop-under ad window until the browser window closes.

interactive button

Figure 7-10 A rich media ad uses multimedia and allows for interactivity.

© 2016 British Gas

Publishers base the amount of money they charge advertisers for an ad on **impressions** (the number of views of an ad), or on the number of click-throughs to the advertiser's website. Your website hosting service likely will offer analytical tools that help you measure the success of your ads.

YOUR TURN

Exploring Paid or Sponsored Placement Online Advertising

1. Use a search engine to find the online advertising webpages on the following websites:
   a. Google AdWords
   b. Bing Ads
   c. Facebook
2. You want to explore using online promotion for the Fit4U website. Determine the types of promotions you want to use and what budget you might need.

3. Use your research to make a recommendation based on price, services offered, and other significant program features. Submit your findings in the format requested by your instructor.

MOBILE AND IN-APP ADVERTISING　The number of mobile users continues to increase, making these users a prime market for advertising. **Mobile web advertising** is simply the placement of ads on a mobile version of a webpage. A user sees the ad when looking at another webpage and can click the ad to view more information. Mobile web ads can include cookies, which can gather and send information back to the host. **In-app advertising** refers to ads that appear periodically while using an app. Figure 7-11 shows

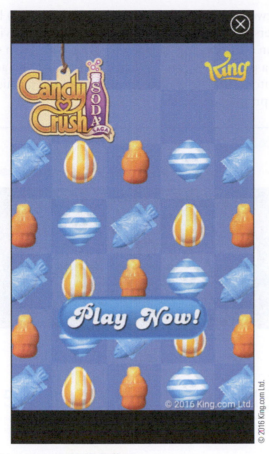

© 2016 King.com Ltd.

Figure 7-11 In-app advertising is expensive but effective.

a gaming ad that appears between rounds of play in another gaming app. Gaming ads during a gaming app is an example of how marketers target in-app advertising. In-app ads can further target ads, and can access geolocation and preferences indicated by the app choice or usage. In-app advertising is more expensive than mobile web ads.

Q&A

What are in-video ads?
Similar to in-app ads, **in-video ads** are targeted advertisements that appear at the start of a video, such as on YouTube. Users must watch the ad, or a portion of the ad, before the playback of the video begins.

Exploring In-App Advertising

YOUR TURN

1. Search the web using the search tool of your choice and the keywords *in-app ad services* or similar keywords to research companies or services that manage in-app ads, such as Google AdMob.

2. What are the fees for in-app advertising? How do the fees and compensations differ from other forms of website advertising?

3. Discuss the advantages and disadvantages of in-app advertisements. What sort of return-on-investment is guaranteed? How does the service target ads?

4. What service or type of in-app advertisement would you recommend for the Fit4U website?

5. Summarize your research. Submit your findings in the format requested by your instructor.

ADVERTISING NETWORKS AND AFFILIATE PROGRAMS The primary players in website advertising are merchant companies, called **advertisers**, that want to purchase online or in-app advertising, and companies, known as **publishers**, that want to sell ads on their websites or in their apps.

An **advertising network** such as Advertising.com (Figure 7-12) brings together advertisers and publishers to complete ad sale transactions. Ads provided by an advertising network are stored on an ad server and "served up" when added to a search results page or when a visitor requests a publisher's pages. When a visitor clicks an ad from a publisher's webpage or app, the visitor's browser goes to the ad's link target, which usually is a landing page for the advertised product or service.

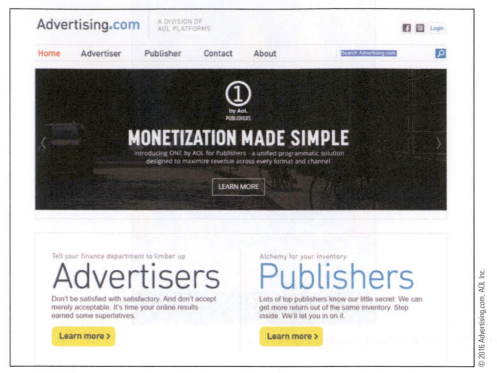

Figure 7-12 Advertising networks connect advertisers with businesses selling ad space.

An **affiliate program** is an e-commerce performance-based online advertising program in which the advertiser pays a fee or commission on sales generated by links on the publishers' websites. Affiliate program publishers place specially formatted links to advertisers' websites on their webpages, mobile web pages, or within apps. When a visitor clicks an affiliate link on the publisher's webpage, the advertiser's website (often a landing page) opens. If the visitor makes a purchase at the advertiser's website after arriving there from the publisher's website, the publisher receives a commission on the sale or a flat fee, depending on the affiliate agreement. An **affiliate management network**, such as Google Affiliate Network, helps affiliate programs by helping to establish the relationship between advertisers and publishers, by monitoring visitors' click-throughs, and by processing commission or fee payments.

DESIGN TIP   Joining an online advertising network as an advertiser is a good way to ensure that your online advertising appears on a variety of appropriate websites; joining as a publisher is a way to generate revenue at your website.

OPT-IN ADVERTISING   Email and text messages can be a cost-effective way to promote a website's content, products, and services. **Opt-in advertising**, also called **permission-based advertising**, requires that the message recipient "opt-in" or formally agree to receive the email or text advertising. Opt-in advertising begins with a visitor submitting his or her email address and/or cell phone number and other required information, and then agreeing to receive messages. This arrangement is doubly beneficial—the recipient gets information he or she wants, and the advertiser can send a targeted message to a receptive audience.

Q&A

What are the benefits of an affiliate program?
Beyond the financial benefits, affiliate programs help build your website audience by targeting users who fit your audience profile. For more information, use a search engine to search for *affiliate program benefits*.

Q&A

What is a link exchange program?
A **reciprocal link** is a link between two website owners who agree informally to put a respective link to the other's website on their webpages. Reciprocal links work well when the companies are in related fields but are not direct competitors. Some websites provide **link exchange programs** that offer reciprocal links free or at a cost to members. Members of a link exchange program can choose other member websites with which to exchange reciprocal links.

Creating a list of opt-in subscribers often is a focus of a website's calls-to-action, with a widget that enables a visitor to subscribe appearing on all or most webpages. Although you hate to lose subscribers, you must always provide an option to unsubscribe. Many people dislike receiving email or texts, even from websites they visit frequently. Allowing customers to choose the frequency or type of advertisement you send them prevents you from losing them as customers, even if they choose to opt out as a subscriber. Figure 7-13 illustrates an opt-in email advertising message from Amazon.

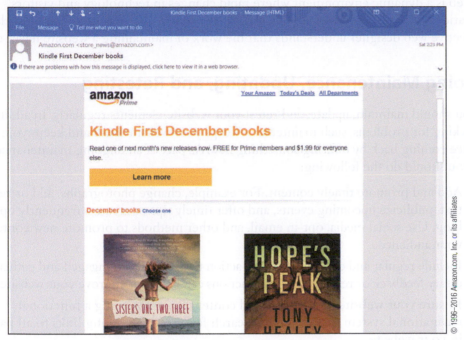

© 1996–2016 Amazon.com, Inc. or its affiliates

Figure 7-13 Opt-in advertising requires that the recipient agree to receive messages from the advertiser.

Exploring Opt-In Advertising

YOUR TURN

1. Use a search engine to search for *opt-in email advertising* or similar keywords. Find two recent articles or industry blog posts that describe how these messages should be used to promote your business.
2. Use a search engine to locate messaging advertising services or consultants. Compare costs, services, and features of each.
3. Do any services offer widgets for adding calls-to-action to your website? What types of ads do they send? What return-on-investment do they offer?
4. Summarize your research and list five things that you learned that would help you come up with an opt-in advertising strategy for a small business.

Always provide a way for recipients to unsubscribe from opt-in email and text advertising messages and newsletters.

DESIGN TIP

Offline Promotional Techniques

You can use offline techniques to promote your website. **Word-of-mouth**, or simply telling people about your website, is an easy, free way to market your website. Your website's URL should appear prominently on all **printed material** you use, including stationery, business cards, brochures, reports, print media ads, signage, and magazines. **Promotional giveaways** include items such as magnets, coffee mugs, coasters, t-shirts, caps, pens, memo pads, and calendars. Include your website information on all promotional giveaways. Hand out promotional giveaways when meeting new customers or distribute them at trade shows, conferences, or other events.

Website Maintenance and Evaluation

The web is a dynamic environment where rapid changes in technology and visitors' expectations can cause websites' design and functionality to become out of date quickly. An effective web designer understands that the work of maintaining a website never ends.

Ongoing Maintenance, Updating, and Retesting

You should maintain, update, and retest your website elements regularly. In addition to checking for problems, such maintenance keeps your website fresh and keeps your audience coming back by offering something new. As part of an ongoing maintenance plan, you should do the following:

- Add and promote timely content. For example, change photographs, add or replace text, publicize upcoming events, and offer timely tips or create a frequently updated blog. Use social media, opt-in email, and other methods to promote new content to your audience.

- Include regular and changing calls-to-action to keep visitors engaged and gather necessary feedback or results. Visitors' reactions can help you improve your website.

- Ensure your website visitors can find content by maintaining a functional navigational system that includes a search feature and working links to all pages in your website.

- Use analytics to track webpage views, sharing of your content using social media, and trending content. Make content or functionality changes as necessary to meet your website goals.

- Evaluate and implement new technologies that further your website's objectives and increase its accessibility and usability.

 DESIGN TIP   To update the web design, be sure to work within the CSS style sheets to make global changes to all associated webpages at once. To ensure the integrity of your global design, do not make style, design, or layout changes from within individual HTML webpages.

Most web design tools and CMS platforms include the capability to update page content by editing individual HTML files. Updating live pages carries the risk that your audience will see incomplete or undesired changes. Follow these steps for maintaining and updating your website content:

1. Ensure you have the most current HTML file of the webpage through your CMS, or download the desired file from the web server to your computer work offline. Back up the original files before you start work in case you decide to revert to the old content or layout.

2. Edit the webpage using the CMS or your web design tool.

3. Preview the webpage in a browser and verify the changes that appear as you want.

4. Upload or republish the page to the server, replacing the existing page.

Evaluating Website Performance

When you created your original design plan, you first created a purpose statement and listed your website's primary and secondary goals and the necessary objectives. After publishing your website, you then begin the ongoing process of evaluating your website's performance toward achieving its goals and purpose.

Website performance evaluation for large, complex organizational or commercial websites with multiple goals and broadly defined purposes rely heavily on analytics. Analytics can determine how much a website can charge for advertisements, for example. Typically, large websites follow a formal evaluation plan that includes analytics, benchmarking, and web server log transaction analysis. Many large organizations and e-commerce companies contract with professional marketers that focus on website performance evaluation. Professional marketers, such as KickFire (Figure 7-14), often provide a complete analytic package that combines a variety of data-gathering techniques, including web server log transaction analysis, with software that measures and reports on website performance.

Figure 7-14 Professional marketers that focus on website performance offer analytic services and more.

Large websites might have an entire department devoted to evaluation, or hire marketing professionals to gauge the website's success against its goals.

DESIGN TIP

ANALYTICS   Developing **web analytics**, sometimes called **web metrics**, involves combining various types of visitor data—server log analysis, geolocation, device type, social media sharing, tracking cookies, page tagging, sales data, and so forth—to discover information about who visitors are and how they interact with your website. Typical web analytics reports contain a variety of measurements, such as unique visitors, repeat visitors, page views, click-stream analysis, and, for e-commerce websites, conversion rate.

A **unique visitor** is an individual visitor to a website. Counting unique visitors can determine the success of your website promotional efforts. A **repeat visitor** is a unique visitor who visits your website more than one time during a specific time period. A small number of repeat visitors might indicate those who are visiting your website are not finding useful information or helpful features. **Page views** determine page popularity.

For example, if you have a page that receives few views, you might consider evaluating the page's content and retesting links to the page to see if there is a problem with the page. A **click-stream analysis** identifies how a visitor moves through your website by clicking from link to link and might also indicate how long the visitor stayed at each page. Finally, an important measurement for an e-commerce website is the **conversion rate**—the rate at which a visitor shopping at the website becomes a buyer of the website's products or services. To calculate the conversion rate, divide the number of completed shopping cart transactions by the number of unique visitors.

One factor in an e-commerce website's success is **monetization**, the overall profit generated from sales or products and advertisements. However, it is also important to measure the number of visitors, the percentage of visitors who initiate a transaction, and the percentage of visitors who complete a transaction. Having a large number of visitors who do not initiate a purchase could mean that your advertising dollars attract the wrong audience or that there is something wrong with either the products themselves or the way they appear on the webpage.

DESIGN TIP It is normal to experience a percentage of visitors who initiate but do not complete a transaction. If many customers abandon the website in the middle of a purchase, it could indicate usability issues. You must address, test, determine the cause of, and solve any usability problems.

BENCHMARKING **Benchmarking** involves using a defined standard to measure overall performance, or to evaluate a specific aspect of a website. For example, a benchmark goal for an organizational or e-commerce website might be to increase the number of visitors by 10 percent per month over the next 12 months. Comparing the goal with the actual growth in the number of website visitors each month can help a website's owner determine what, if any, changes to make at the website. After evaluation against actual performance, you might need to adjust a benchmark goal to make it more realistic.

WEB SERVER LOG ANALYSIS In Chapter 2, you learned that each time a browser requests a webpage from a web server, that request for a page is recorded in the server's transaction log. Web server log transactions provide a wealth of information, such as the following:

Q&A

What are tracking cookies?
Tracking cookies are small text files stored on a webpage visitor's hard drive, usually without the visitor's knowledge. Web marketers use tracking cookies to monitor which websites the visitor visits and other visitor behaviors. Many visitors consider tracking cookies an invasion of privacy and most popular computer security software packages, such as Norton, locate and remove tracking cookies.

- The requesting computer's IP address
- The browser making the request
- The type of device used to make the request
- The date and time of the request
- The URL of a referring link (the link the visitor clicked to jump to the website's page)
- The path a visitor takes from page to page through a website

From the raw data contained in a web server transaction log, additional measures of visitors' behaviors can be evaluated using **web server log analysis software**. You can install web server log analysis software on your own servers or use tools provided by your hosting company.

By combining benchmarking, web server log analysis, and other web analytics with management expertise, the owners and managers of a complex organizational or e-commerce website can better understand the website's overall performance and take steps, if needed, to correct any problems or make necessary improvements.

Chapter Review

This chapter introduced you to testing, publishing, promoting, maintaining, and evaluating a website. You learned that beta testing is an important step that web designers must take before publishing a website to a live server. To publish your website, you first must purchase a domain name and acquire server space. Then, you are ready to upload all your website files to a server using a CMS, web design tool, or FTP. After publishing your website to a live server, you should continue to test your pages for usability, functionality, and currency on an ongoing basis.

You can use both online and offline promotional techniques to make your target audience aware of your website. Online promotional techniques include social media, search engine optimization and indexing, online advertisements, in-app or web advertisement, participating in an advertising network or affiliate program, and sending opt-in advertising. Offline methods include word-of-mouth, and inclusion of your website's name and URL on all printed materials and promotional giveaways.

After you publish your website, the work continues as you update your website with current content, check for broken links, and implement new functionality and technologies. You also must continue to evaluate your website's ongoing performance against your stated goals and purpose using techniques such as analytics, benchmarking, or web server log analysis. You can contract with third-party marketing professionals to develop your website's web analytics.

TERMS TO KNOW

After reading the chapter, you should know each of these Key Terms.

advertiser (189)
advertising network (190)
affiliate management network (190)
affiliate program (190)
banner ad (187)
benchmarking (194)
beta testing (176)
beta website (176)
broken link (176)
click-stream analysis (194)
click-through (188)
cloud-based web server (180)
conversion rate (194)
dedicated web server (180)
expandable banner ads (188)
File Transfer Protocol (FTP) (181)
floating ad (188)
FTP client (182)
geotargeting (184)
impression (188)
in-app advertising (188)
internal testing (176)
in-video ads (189)
keyword stuffing (186)
link exchange program (190)
mobile web advertising (188)
monetization (194)
multimedia ad (188)
opt-in advertising (190)

page views (193)
pay-per-click (187)
permission-based advertising (190)
pop-under ad (188)
pop-up ad (188)
printed material (191)
promotional giveaways (192)
publisher (189)
QR code (192)
reciprocal link (190)
repeat visitor (193)
rich media ad (188)
search tool submission service (186)
self-testing (176)
server software (179)
shared web server (180)
sidebar ad (188)
spam (191)
staging server (176)
sync (183)
targeted ads (184)
tracking cookies (194)
unique visitor (193)
virtual private server (VPS) (180)
web analytics (193)
web hosting companies (179)
web metrics (193)
web server log analysis software (194)
word-of-mouth (191)

TEST YOUR KNOWLEDGE

Complete the Test Your Knowledge exercises to solidify what you have learned in the chapter.

Matching Terms

Match each term with the best description.

_____ 1. tracking cookie

_____ 2. monetization

_____ 3. click-stream analysis

_____ 4. impression

_____ 5. beta testing

_____ 6. benchmarking

_____ 7. pay-per-click

a. A vertical banner ad.

b. The overall profit generated from sales or products and advertisements on a website.

c. An e-commerce online advertising program in which a website, called the advertiser, pays a fee or commission on sales generated by visitors driven to the website by links on other websites.

d. Identifies how a visitor moves through your website by clicking from link to link and might also indicate how long the visitor stayed at each page.

_____ 8. affiliate program

_____ 9. opt-in advertising

_____ 10. sidebar ad

e. Using a defined standard to measure overall performance, or to evaluate a specific aspect of a website.

f. Small text files stored on a webpage visitor's hard drive, usually without the visitor's knowledge.

g. Requires that the message recipient agree to receive the advertising.

h. A measure of the number of times an online ad is viewed.

i. A payment method for online advertising in which the advertiser pays a small fee each time a visitor clicks on an ad from the publisher's webpage.

j. Testing using a prepublication version of your website to ensure the website's pages look and function as designed and confirm that you have satisfied all aspects of the design plan.

Short Answer Questions

Write a brief answer to each question.

1. Discuss the processes of self- and internal testing and target audience testing for a beta website. What should you determine during each testing phase?

2. Identify at least three options for acquiring web server space.

3. Describe methods for uploading and publishing pages to a web server.

4. Briefly discuss why it is necessary to retest the pages at a published website and how to perform retesting.

5. Discuss how you can use social media tools to promote your website. What are the benefits of social media promotion and advertising?

6. Explain how to use affiliate programs and advertising networks.

7. Define the following terms as they relate to website promotion: geotargeting, spam, and keyword stuffing.

8. Describe different types of online and in-app advertising techniques.

9. Define opt-in advertising and explain why unsolicited advertising is an inappropriate method for promoting a website.

10. Explain the purpose of benchmarking and web analytics in evaluating website performance.

Investigate current web design developments with the Trends exercises.

Write a brief essay about each of the following trends, using the web as your research tool. For each trend, identify at least one webpage URL used as a research source. Be prepared to discuss your findings in class.

1 | In-App Advertising

As a website designer, you can use in-app advertising to monetize, or earn money to support your website. Research costs, methods, and effectiveness of in-app advertising. Find services that help you create messages and reach your target audience. How do these companies match user profiles with a company's products or goals? How would you use this approach as a website designer?

2 | Third-Party Analytic Services

Research companies that offer web analytic services. Choose three to research further. Compare the companies to determine what services they each offer and the costs of those services, and obtain client reviews. What type of reporting do they offer? As a web designer, would you find this type of reporting helpful?

Challenge your perspective of the web and web design technology with the @Issue exercises.

Write a brief essay in response to the following issues, using the web as your research tool. For each issue, identify at least one webpage URL used as a research source. Be prepared to discuss your findings in class.

1 | Data Gathering

Web marketers use a variety of advertising techniques, some of which enable the web marketer to identify website visitors' actions and then analyze these actions to develop the web metrics or analytics necessary to evaluate website performance. Some of these data-gathering techniques might be considered an invasion of privacy by website visitors. Research the ways in which web analytics data is gathered and analyzed. Create a presentation for your class that describes data-gathering and analysis methods and related privacy concerns. Discuss the effect of data gathering from two perspectives: as a website visitor and as a website owner.

2 | Security Issues

Search the Internet for articles that deal with security issues surrounding rich media ads and other online ads. Find recommendations for your browser settings. Check the settings in your browser. Summarize what you have learned about security concerns and recommendations. List the steps you took, if any, to protect yourself.

Use the World Wide Web to obtain more information about the concepts in the chapter with the Hands On exercises.

1 | Explore and Evaluate: SEO Careers

Use an employment search engine such as monster.com to locate SEO jobs in your area. Choose three jobs to compare. List the skills and requirements needed for each job. What qualifications might you need to be considered for the positions? Compare the duties listed. Based on your research, create a job description related to SEO that you feel would be of value to a small business such as the Fit4U website. List the education and work experience you would find valuable, as well as the tasks required of this position.

2 | Search and Discover: Affiliate Programs

Use a search engine to identify at least three affiliate programs. List the services and costs for each program. If possible, find user reviews of each program. Explain how you might use the program to market an e-commerce website.

Work collaboratively to reinforce the concepts in the chapter with the Team Approach exercises.

1 | Recommend Promotional Techniques for a New Informational Website

Join with two other students to create a team. Assume the team is charged with the responsibility of identifying free or low-cost online promotional techniques for a new informational website whose audience will be parents with young children interested in finding information on online educational programs and apps. Create a presentation for the website's owner that summarizes at least three online techniques the team recommends. Give reasons for your recommendations.

2 | Website Evaluation

Create three teams of students according to the type of website they designed: personal, organizational/topical, or commercial. Within each team, each member should present his or her website to the team for evaluation, explaining how he or she developed and implemented his or her website plan. Each team then chooses the top two websites in their group according to overall design and the degree to which each website achieves its stated goals and purpose. Next, have the entire class evaluate the top two websites from each team and select the one website whose design and implementation best fits its stated goals and purpose.

CASE STUDY

Apply the chapter concepts to the ongoing development process in web design with the Case Study.

The Case Study is an ongoing development process using the concepts, techniques, and Design Tips presented in each chapter.

Background Information

You are now ready to test, publish, and promote your own website. You will apply what you have learned about self-testing, target audience testing, online and traditional promotion techniques, and ongoing website maintenance and evaluation.

Chapter 7 Assignment

Create an outline that describes exactly how you will complete the following steps. If possible, actually test and publish your website.

1. Self-test your prepublished website. Create a team of testers that simulate target audience members and have them test your website.

2. Select an appropriate web hosting service or CMS. Determine how you will upload your files to the hosting service's web server. If possible, actually upload your website files to a web server using information provided by your instructor.

3. Identify the promotional techniques you will use to promote your website. Create a mock-up of at least one method—a social media promotion, an online or in-app ad, or an opt-in advertising message.

4. Develop a regular schedule for website maintenance, updating, and, when necessary, retesting.

5. Identify the methods you will use to analyze your website's performance against its stated goals and purpose.

Introduction

Hypertext Markup Language (HTML) is the original language used for publishing webpages. It is a nonproprietary format, originally based on Standard Generalized Markup Language (SGML). HTML code instructs web browsers how to display webpage content. Since 1990, HTML has been the standard technology for creating webpages. The World Wide Web Consortium (W3C) adopted HTML5 in 2014. This appendix covers HTML uses, HTML documents, HTML syntax, HTML tools, HTML5, and HTML tags and attributes.

HTML Uses

Q&A

What is the relationship between CSS and HTML?
An HTML document contains the structure and content of a webpage, whereas a CSS document specifies the formatting of the webpage content.

HTML is a markup language that uses rules to specify the structure of webpage content. It is not actually a programming language because its purpose is not to create programs or apps. An HTML document contains not only the content of the webpage, but also instructions for presenting that content. HTML uses tags such as *<h1>* and *<p>* to differentiate content into headings, paragraphs, lists, hyperlinks, images, and so on. While HTML still includes some formatting tags, web developers increasingly rely on CSS to apply formatting to the content types specified in an HTML document.

HTML Documents

HTML documents consist of a header and a body. The body contains the webpage content and structural information.

The header contains **meta data**, which is information about the document itself, such as the title, description, and keywords. Header information appears between the *<head>…</head>* tags. Information in the header is not visible on the webpage. The browser uses meta data to display the webpage's title and description in the browser title bar and in search engine results. Title, description, and keyword meta data factor into a webpage's SEO rankings. The following list identifies important header information to include:

- **Title**—The webpage's title appears in the browser's title bar and can provide a description of the page's contents. Place the title between the *<title>…</title>* tags.
- **Language**—You must not only specify the document language (HTML), but also which human language you are using. Screen readers and other adaptive devices use this information to ensure proper pronunciation and interpretation of webpage content. For example, you would use the following syntax for an HTML document written using British English: *<html lang="en-GB">…</html>*. Users of translation services rely on identifying the source language in order to translate webpage content into the user's preferred language.

- **Description**—The page description appears under the webpage title when a search engine lists search results. The description should be one or two full sentences that give a complete webpage description. Both the description and keywords use the *<meta name>* tag. For example, a webpage description for a summer camp's home page might be: *<meta name="description" content="Camp Blue Ridge provides boys and girls ages 8 to 15 a summer wilderness experience. Activities include swimming, boating, hiking, horseback riding, archery, and more.">*.

- **Keywords**—Keywords are a list of words that describe the page content. Search engines use a webpage's keywords to locate results based on a user's search and to determine SEO rankings. Keywords for the summer camp could be: *<meta name="keywords" content="summer camp, blue ridge, boys camp, girls camp, wilderness, swimming, boating, hiking, horseback riding, archery">*.

- **External style sheet**—You specify any external CSS documents (style sheets) in the document head. For example: *<link rel="stylesheet" type="text/css" href="mystylesheet.css">*. You can specify separate style sheets for different device types as part of your RWD strategy.

HTML Syntax

Most HTML tags follow the same basic structure *<name attribute=value>…</name>*. An example of an HTML tag is *<ol type=A>…</ol>*. As described below, this tag indicates an ordered list that uses capital letters (A., B., etc.) to numerate the list items.

- **Start tag**—The start tag introduces the element by name. For example, *<ol>* is the start tag for an ordered list.

- **Attribute**—Many HTML tags have modifiers called **attributes** that you can use to specify additional structural or formatting requirements. Tags can have several associated required, standard, and optional attributes. Many tags also use **event attributes**, which occur based on an action, such as *onkeypress* or *onclick*. An ordered list attribute example is *type*, which refers to the type of ordered list.

- **Value**—Values define the attribute. Not all elements require a value. Values appear after an attribute, and start with an equal sign. Ordered list type values include *=A* (capital letters), *=i* (lowercase roman numerals), and *=1* (numbers).

- **End tag**—The end tag follows the completed element. For example, *</ol>* is the end tag for a paragraph. Not all elements require an end tag. **Void elements** or **empty elements**, for example *<meta>*, *<embed>*, *
*, and *<link>*, are elements that do not need an end tag.

HTML Tools

You can create HTML documents using a variety of tools: simple text editors, web design tools, developer toolkits, and tools for specific purposes, such as forms.

- **Text editors**—Text editors are simple programs that enable you to write HTML code as text. Using a text editor requires knowledge of HTML codes and syntax. Notepad (Windows) and SimpleText (Mac) are default programs installed with your operating system. Komodo Edit, TextMate, and Bluefish are other text editing tools.

- **Web design tools and CMS platforms**—With the web design tool Adobe Dreamweaver CC or a CMS such as WordPress, you can create complete and professional-looking websites without knowing or learning HTML code. These tools offer website and CSS templates, web preview tools, accessibility and other checking tools, and more.

- **Form tools**—JotForm and Formsite assist you in the process of creating UX-driven web-based forms. HTML5 includes support of features that assist the user when completing forms, including autocomplete and the inclusion of placeholder or default data. Tags such as *<fieldset>…</fieldset>* specify the layout, structure, and order of the form fields.

HTML5 Development

HTML5 made many changes to the existing standards from HTML 4.01 and XHMTL 1.1 (extensible HTML) to combine them into one single markup language. One of the goals for HTML5 was to remove support of some formatting tags that CSS typically addresses, including font type. Removing formatting instruction removes potential for conflicts with CSS documents and results in smaller HTML files.

Another focus for developers of HTML5 was to include standards that would optimize HTML files for multiple devices, including those with less power than PCs or laptops, such as smartphones. New tags such as *<video>* and *<audio>* remove the need for plug-ins, such as Adobe Flash, to view and play animations, multimedia, or gaming graphics. Other changes include the addition of *<details>* and *<summary>* tags, enabling developers to provide extended information for users who want to read more.

HTML5 Tags and Attributes

The W3C constantly updates the HTML specifications by adding, deleting, and replacing tags. In the list below and on the following pages, italicized terms indicate where specific values, names, or elements are used. **Deprecated elements**—tags replaced with newer elements—do not appear. Most browsers still support many deprecated elements. A deprecated element is one that widely is replaced with another method of completing the same task, such as using CSS. As a web designer, you should keep up to date with current standards and trends.

The table on the following pages lists HTML tags and associated attributes.

Q&A

Where can I learn more about HTML tags and attributes?
This appendix includes a table with many HTML tags and associated attributes. For a comprehensive list, more thorough descriptions, and examples of all HTML tags, visit the W3C website at www.w3.org.

Q&A

What is an obsolete element?
Obsolete elements are ones that web designers no longer use and current browsers do not support. This appendix does not list currently obsolete elements. As specifications change rapidly to keep up with new technology, web designers use resources to keep track of obsolete elements. For more information, use your browser to visit the website www.caniuse.com.

HTML Tag and Attributes	Description
Page Structure	
<body>...</body>	Defines the start and end of the visible part of a webpage
** **	Inserts a line break
<div>...</div>	Defines block-level structure or division in the HTML document
<!DOCTYPE html>	Defines the document type; required

HTML Tag and Attributes	Description
Page Structure *(continued)*	
\<footer>…\</footer>	Defines a footer for a document or section (e.g., copyright, policy, and contact information)
\<header>…\</header>	Specifies a header for a document or section
\<html>…\</html>	Indicates the start and the end of the HTML document
lang=*language_code*	Defines the language for the content
manifest=*URL*	Specifies the address of the document's cache for offline browsing
\<meta>	Provides additional data (metadata) about an HTML document; also used to set width for devices
content=*text*	Specifies the value for the \<meta> information; required
name=*text*	Provides a name for the \<meta> information supplied in the content attribute
\<title>…\</title>	Defines the title for the HTML document; always should be used
Page Elements	
\<a>…\</a>	Creates a hyperlink
\<details>…\</details>	Specifies additional details that the user can view or hide
open	Specifies that the details should be visible (open) to the user
\<embed>	Defines a container for an external application or interactive content (a plug-in)
height=*pixels*; width=*pixels*	Specifies the dimensions of the embedded content
src=*URL*	Specifies the URL of the external application
\<h*n*>…\</h*n*>	Defines a header level *n*, from the largest (h1) to the smallest (h6)
\<li>…\</li>	Defines the enclosed text as a list item in a list
\<link>	Establishes a link between the HTML document and another document, such as an external style sheet
href=*URL*	Defines the URL of the linked document
media=*media_query*	Specifies on what device type the linked document will be displayed (e.g., "print" for a print preview or "aural" for speech synthesizers)
rel=*relationship*	Indicates the relationship going from the current page to the target
type=*media_type*	Indicates the data or media type of the linked document (e.g., "text/CSS" for linked style sheets)
\<object>…\</object>	Includes an external object in the HTML document such as an image, a Java applet, or other external object

HTML Tag and Attributes	Description
Page Elements *(continued)*	
data=*URL*	Identifies the location of the object's data
type=*media_type*	Specifies the content or media type of the object
<ol>...</ol>	Defines an ordered list that contains numbered list item elements (<li>)
type=*option*	Sets or resets the numbering format for the list; options include: =A (capital letters), =a (lowercase letters), =I (capital Roman numerals), =i (lowercase Roman numerals), or =1 (numbers)
<p>...</p>	Delimits a paragraph; automatically inserts a blank line between paragraphs
<script>...</script>	Inserts a client-side script into an HTML document
src=*URL*	Identifies the location of an external script
type=*media_type*	Indicates the data or media type of the script language (e.g., "text/javascript" for JavaScript commands)
<section>...</section>	Defines sections in a document, such as chapters, headers, footers
<ul>...</ul>	Defines an unordered list that contains bulleted list item elements (<li>)
Media and Graphics	
<audio>...</audio>; **<video>...</video>**	Defines an audio or video file
autoplay	Specifies that the audio or video will start playing as soon as the browser or playback app has the necessary data to start. Note: may not work on all mobile devices
controls	Specifies that audio or video controls should display, such as a play or pause button
loop	Specifies that the audio or video will start over again every time it finishes
src=*URL*	Specifies the URL of the audio or video file
<canvas>...</canvas>	Used to specify container for graphics and other media elements created using scripts
height=*pixels*	Specifies the height of the canvas
width=*pixels*	Specifies the width of the canvas
<figcaption>...</figcaption>	Defines a caption for a <figure> element
<figure>...</figure>	Specifies self-contained content, like illustrations, diagrams, photos, etc.
<img>...</img>	Inserts an image into the current webpage
alt=*text*	Provides a text description of an image if the browser cannot display the image; always should be used

HTML Tag and Attributes	Description
Forms	
height=*pixels*; width=*pixels*	Sets the dimensions of the image in pixels; always should be used
src=*URL*	Specifies the URL of the image to be displayed; required
<source>...</source>	Used with the <audio> and <video> elements to identify the source of media files; multiple sources can be identified for a variety of devices and playback capabilities
type=*media_type*	Specifies format of audio or video file (e.g., type="audio/ogg")
<form>...</form>	Marks the start and end of a webpage form; a form can contain one or more of the following elements: <button>, <fieldset>, <input>, <label>, <option>, <optgroup>, <select>, <textarea>
action=*URL*	Specifies the URL of the application that will process the form; required attribute
autocomplete=*on* or =*off*	Specifies whether a form should have AutoComplete on or off
<button>...</button>	Defines a clickable button
<fieldset>...</fieldset>	Groups related form controls and labels; the <legend> tag is used within the <fieldset> element to provide a caption (used by screen readers)
<input>	Defines controls used in forms
autocomplete=*on* or =*off*	Specifies whether an <input> element should have AutoComplete on or off
disabled	Disables an <input> element
form=*form_id*	Specifies one or more forms to which the <input> element belongs
formaction=*URL*	Specifies the URL of the file that will process the input control when the form is submitted (for type="submit" and type="image")
max=*number* or =*date*	Specifies the maximum value or latest acceptable date for an <input> element
maxlength=*number*	Sets a value for the maximum number of characters allowed as input
min=*number* or =*date*	Specifies the minimum value or earliest acceptable date for an <input> element
multiple	Sets an <input> element to allow multiple selections
name=*text*	Assigns a name to the control
placeholder=*text*	Specifies a short hint that describes the expected value of an <input> element
readonly	Prevents changes to the control
required	Specifies that the user is required to select a value before submitting the form
type=*typename*	Specifies the type of <input> element, such a radio button, check box, date, or range
value=*data*	Sets the initial value of the <input> element

HTML Tag and Attributes	Description
Forms	
\<label>...\</label>	Creates a label for a form control
for=*element_id*	Indicates the name or ID of the element to which the label is applied
form=*form_id*	Specifies one or more forms to which the label belongs
\<optgroup>...\</optgroup>	Groups related options in a drop-down list
\<option>...\</option>	Defines individual options in a selection list, as defined by the \<select> element
\<select>...\</select>	Defines a form control to create a multiple-choice menu or scrolling list; encloses a set of \<option> tags to define one or more options
\<textarea>...\</textarea>	Creates a multiline text input area within a form

B Cascading Style Sheets (CSS)

Introduction

Cascading Style Sheets (CSS) is a formatting specification used with any documents in HTML or any other XML-based markup language. The W3C recommends using CSS standards to format webpages. CSS is also the Web Accessibility Initiative's (WAI) standard for webpage element formatting and page layout. This appendix covers CSS uses, syntax, style sheets, addressing conflicts, CSS tools, and developments in CSS.

CSS Uses

CSS separates the formatting and appearance instructions from the structure and content found in HTML documents. Using CSS to determine the presentation of the content allows a web designer to change a document's appearance without impacting the document's structure. CSS enables web designers to control typography and page layout by allowing the specification of the following:

- Font formatting, including for headings
- Leading (space between lines)
- Tracking (space between words)
- Kerning (space between letters)
- Margins, indents, and element positioning
- Font color and background color

Q&A

How widely used is CSS?
All browsers today offer support for CSS. Most professional web designers use CSS when developing webpages to promote accessibility and usability and to comply with industry standards.

With CSS, you can control the appearance of hundreds of webpages using a single style sheet. A primary benefit of CSS is the ability to make global changes to a website by modifying or replacing the CSS document associated with the pages at a website. Editing the style sheet allows you to make changes to all the pages in a website quickly and consistently. This allows for flexibility in web design. Applying a new or edited CSS document enables you to make changes to a website's appearance to meet new accessibility standards or to apply the latest RWD techniques. In addition, websites that use CSS for formatting can reduce overall storage space because multiple webpages share the same formatting document.

Style Rule Syntax, Properties, and Values

CSS defines the appearance of webpage elements in the associated HTML documents, such as headings, lists, and paragraphs. You apply formatting instructions to page elements in the HTML document by assigning styles within the CSS document. The elements are identified with tags in the HTML document, such as *<h2>…</h2>* for level 2 headings.

CSS formatting uses style rules to define the appearance or location of webpage elements. A style rule consists of a **selector**, the element affected by the rule, and a **declaration**, the property and value that provide the actual formatting instructions. Figure B-1 illustrates two style rule examples.

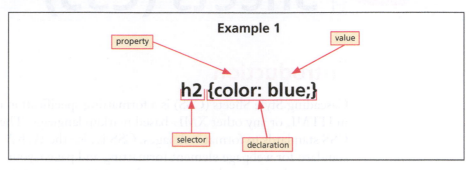

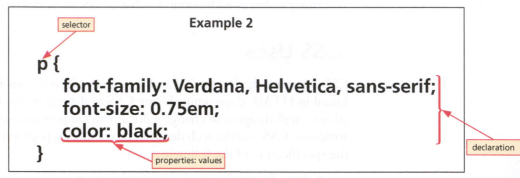

Figure B-1 A style rule consists of a selector and a declaration containing properties and associated values.

In style rule Example 1, the *selector* is the *h2* heading style element, corresponding to the *<h2>…</h2>* tags in the HTML document. The declaration contains the *color* property and the *blue* value. The property and value appear within brackets ({ }) and are separated by a colon (:). The semicolon (;) after the value indicates the end of the value specification. The style rule in Example 1 specifies that all level 2 heading text will be blue.

The style rule in Example 2 is more complex and uses a line-by-line arrangement of the style rule elements to improve readability and facilitate editing. The selector is the *p* element (paragraph text) and the declaration contains multiple property:value pairs. CSS syntax requires you to separate multiple values by a comma, as shown in the font-family property line in Example 2, and end all property:value pairs using a semicolon. The first property, *font-family*, specifies three values indicating three font choices for paragraph text:

- The Verdana web font—The web designer's preferred choice
- The Helvetica sans-serif font—An alternate choice if the user's computer or device does not have the Verdana web font
- An available sans-serif font—A default choice if the computer or device does not have access to either the preferred or alternate font choice

The second property, *font-size*, specifies the paragraph text font size as 0.75em. The third property, *color*, specifies the paragraph text font color as black.

Each CSS property has its own rule about acceptable values, such as colors, numbers, percentages, predefined values, and so forth. For example, the *font-size* property in Example 2 could have an absolute size value stated in the number of points, inches, or centimeters; a size value stated in pixels, which is relative to the screen; a size value stated as a percentage of the base font size; or a size value stated as an em value.

Pseudo-classes enable you to create special effects by specifying different properties for the same element (selector), depending on the user's action or other criteria. The syntax for pseudo-class is *selector:pseudo-class {property:value;}*. For example, you can provide instructions to change the color of a navigation button or a link depending on whether the user already has clicked a link in the browsing session, or when the user points to it, hovers the mouse over it, or selects it.

Styles and Style Sheets

You apply CSS style rules to a webpage in one of three ways:

- As part of an **external style sheet** saved in the folder with the website's pages. The webpages are linked to the style sheet with an HTML tag.
- As part of an **internal style sheet** inserted using the *<style>* element within a page's HTML heading tags.
- As an **inline style** inserted using the *style* attribute within the individual HTML tags on a page.

An external style sheet, sometimes called a linked style sheet, is a separate text document that contains style rules. You can apply the style rules in an external style sheet to one or more webpages by linking the pages to the external style sheet. External style sheets are a powerful tool for changing the formatting or layout of multiple pages at a site at one time simply by editing the style sheet. Figure B-2 illustrates the link to an external style sheet within a webpage's heading tags.

```
<head>
<title>My Document</title>
<link rel="stylesheet" type="text/css"
href="fundamental.css">
</head>
```

link relationship and document type information

external style sheet URL for style sheet saved with the related webpages

Figure B-2 An external style sheet can be applied to multiple webpages by linking the pages to the external style sheet.

Internal style sheets, or embedded style sheets, appear within a page's HTML *<head>…</head>* tags along with other heading information, such as a page's title. Unlike an external style sheet that can affect several webpages, style rules in an internal style sheet only modify elements on the webpage that includes the rules. Using internal style sheets increases the load time for webpages as the file size of the page is larger. Figure B-3 illustrates an internal style sheet.

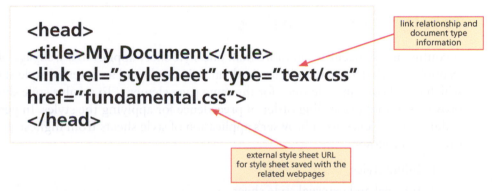

```
<head>
<style>
    h2 {color: blue;}
    p {font-family: Verdana, Helvetica, sans-serif; font-size: 0.75em; color: black;}
</style>
<title>Applying Styles</title>
</head>
```

<style>…</style> tag pair define the style sheet boundaries

style rules

Figure B-3 Style rules in an internal style sheet only affect elements on the webpage in which the rules exist.

Inline styles involve inserting the style rule within an element's HTML tag. You should use this method sparingly because inline styles have a number of disadvantages, including failure to separate content from design (which is the primary goal of CSS), increased webpage maintenance issues, and accessibility issues. Figure B-4 provides an example of an inline style as part of the *<h2>...</h2>* tag pair.

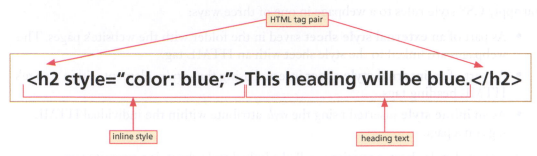

HTML tag pair

<h2 style="color: blue;">This heading will be blue.</h2>

inline style   heading text

Figure B-4 Definitions for inline styles exist within an element's HTML level 2 heading tag.

Q&A

When is it appropriate to use inline styles or internal style sheets?
Although external style sheets are the most flexible CSS option, inline styles and internal style sheets enable you to make exceptions to specific instances of an element. To learn more, use a search engine to search for *using inline styles and internal style sheets*.

External style sheets are the most flexible of the three methods because you can use them to apply formatting rules to multiple site pages.

Style Sheet Conflicts

A conflict might occur when more than one style sheet applies to a webpage element. For example, a web designer could use both an inline style and an external style sheet, both of which could contain style rules for the same page element. To resolve style sheet conflicts, browsers follow a cascading order of precedence for applying the styles. In general, the order of precedence for a browser's application of style sheets from highest to lowest order is as follows:

1. Inline styles
2. Internal and external style sheet
3. Default browser styles set by the user

Q&A

Are all properties inherited by child elements in CSS?
No. Fonts are an example of an inherited property. Borders are an example of a property that does not automatically apply to a child element. To learn more, use a search engine to search for *inherited properties CSS*.

In addition to the location of the style sheet, two other factors play a role in resolving style rule conflicts: inheritance and specificity. You can nest some HTML code elements by placing them within other code elements. In CSS, nested elements have a parent–child type of relationship in which nested child elements *inherit* certain parent element properties, such as the color property, when no separate style rule exists for the child elements. In general, when style sheets conflict, the more *specific* style rule takes precedence. For example, because an inline style modifies a specific HTML tag, the inline style overrides a conflicting style rule in an internal or external style sheet. Another determination when style sheet conflicts exist is that the style rule that the browser reads last takes priority. For example, if a browser starts "reading" the styles that appear at the top of an HTML page and comes across a conflicting rule farther down on the page, the browser will apply the second rule.

Style Sheet Tools

To create or acquire a style sheet, you can use a word processing tool such as Notepad to manually enter all style rules. Tools exist that assist you in the style sheet creation process. Stylizer and Rapid CSS are examples of tools you can use to create and apply CSS documents. These tools provide templates, code that you can insert or modify, autocomplete, and error messages if you misuse syntax. You also can use these tools to test and debug style sheets. Numerous sources enable you to download and apply, or modify, a predefined CSS style sheet, or a style sheet template. Before downloading a CSS style sheet, review any restrictions on its use, pay any associated fees, and give proper credit to the source. Make sure to find reviews of the vendor or provider to ensure that the CSS document is safe to use and does not include any unwanted or potentially harmful code.

The Evolution of CSS

CSS is an evolving set of standards, constantly evaluated to ensure its relevance as new technologies develop. The W3C approves and regulates CSS standards. Updates to version CSS3 do not revise the entire CSS standards at once, but rather release updated standards in context-specific *modules*, such as the use of color. Another important update is the implementation of media queries, which web designers use to determine changes in display based on the device type upon which the user is viewing the webpage. CSS3 is backwards compatible to previous versions of CSS, meaning that it uses the same syntax as previous versions, and therefore does not cause problems with devices or technologies that use earlier versions.

Figure B-5 provides a quick reference for CSS properties.

Property		Description
Background		
	background-color	Specifies the background color in hex or word codes
	background-image	Specifies the background image
Font		
	font-family	Specifies typeface
	font-size	Specifies the size of the text as absolute, relative, a percentage, or by em unit
	font-style	Specifies the style, such as normal or italic
Text		
	color	Specifies text color
	text-align	Aligns text horizontally
	text-decoration	Adds or removes underline, line-through, or other text decoration
	text-indent	Specifies the amount of the first-line indent from a paragraph's left margin

Figure B-5 CSS Properties Quick Reference

Responsive Web Design

Introduction

As you learned in earlier chapters, the goal of responsive web design (RWD) is to optimize your website for multiple device types and screen sizes. When designing a website, your primary focus should be to optimize the user experience (UX) of your website visitors. Website visitors dislike websites that are text heavy, require the user to zoom in and out, include difficult-to-use navigation, and take a long time to load. RWD techniques help you create device-independent websites that deliver the best possible UX. In this appendix you will learn about RWD guidelines, how to employ a mobile-first strategy, and RWD tools.

RWD Techniques

Creating a website that is optimized for a range of screen sizes ensures that your audience can access relevant web content on their mobile device (such as a tablet or smartphone) or computer (desktop or laptop). These strategies also take into consideration autorotation of screens, as well as the ability to zoom in and out. RWD strategies include adjusting content, white space, and navigation depending on the device.

RWD not only addresses differing screen sizes, but also differences in device capabilities. When designing a website, keep in mind the following examples of current guidelines and techniques:

- *Use a fluid grid-based layout for your webpages.* You can use grids to move and resize webpage items to adapt to different screen sizes or devices using breakpoints.
- *Use CSS for formatting.* Define flexible formatting specifications to adapt to the device and screen size.
- *Use flexible image sizing.* Instead of a fixed size (such as inches), set the image width to a percentage of the device **viewport**, or screen area. In addition, compress image file sizes as much as you can without sacrificing display quality to ensure your webpage loads quickly in lower-bandwidth mobile devices, or provide smaller images for those with smaller screens.
- *Consider mobile devices' differing navigation needs and restrictions.* Most mobile devices use touch screens, which make using small drop-down menus difficult or, in some cases, impossible to use. Minimizing the navigation increases the amount of web content a user can see on a smaller screen. Examples of mobile-friendly navigation include off-canvas or sidebar menus. A user clicks the icon to display off-canvas navigation options, which appear to the side of the screen.
- *Carousels and slide shows enable you to maximize screen real estate.* Use touch-friendly navigation for your carousel or slide show, apply transition effects if desired, and consider providing thumbnails in addition to navigation so that users can click a thumbnail to move directly to that content.

How does a web server detect screen size?
Web designers use media queries in CSS to determine factors such as screen size. A **media query** provides instructions to adjust formatting depending on screen size or other factors. For example, a media query could provide a specific formatting rule for screen widths under 500 pixels. Media queries use **breakpoints**, which are screen sizes measured in pixels to determine which style rules to apply. Media queries are one method web designers use to provide the best UX.

Besides UX, why should I focus on RWD?
Studies have shown that search engines rank RWD websites higher in search results. Google's SEO algorithm update, called Mobilegeddon, is one example. To learn more, search for *Google Mobilegeddon SEO*.

In addition to differences in screen size and bandwidth, mobile devices and some newer laptops have introduced other considerations that affect web design:

- **Auto rotation**—Most newer tablets and smartphones, and even some laptop or desktop monitors, automatically switch screen orientation depending on the angle of the screen. Auto rotation enables users to make the screen wider than it is long (landscape) or longer than it is wide (portrait) in order to best view the content.

- **Touch screens**—As previously mentioned, touch screens affect web navigation. Because there is no mouse or other pointing device, adding extra space around icons improves users' accuracy when tapping screen items with their fingers. In addition, most users are right-handed, so consider placing elements on the right side of the screen. In addition to selecting items, other gestures enable users to affect the screen, such as swiping (moving the view), pinching (to zoom in and out), and more. Recognized touch screen gestures differ between devices and even within apps running on the same device.

It is important to test your website on multiple devices, screen sizes, screen orientations, and bandwidths. RWD is not an exact science, but the goal is to maximize UX by addressing obvious, known issues to the best of your ability.

Mobile-First Strategies

As you have learned, RWD techniques exist to adapt content and layout depending on the screen size. With RWD, you might instruct the browser to hide certain images or content, or provide shortened content or a simpler image, when a webpage displays on a small screen size. When adopting a mobile-first strategy, the designer focuses on the type of content and visual imagery that will display best on smaller mobile screens, and applies RWD techniques to add images or content on larger screen sizes. Web designers whose target audience tends to view websites on mobile devices might adopt a mobile-first strategy from the beginning phases of web design. Mobile-first decisions often lead to less text, streamlined imagery, and a priority on faster page loading.

RWD Tools

Many tools exist that help you develop, optimize, and test your websites for RWD. The following are some current examples:

- **Foundation for Sites**—Free front-end framework software for developing responsive web design. Features include grid management, flexible navigation, user-interface elements, and the ability to incorporate CSS, JavaScript, and other web technologies.

- **Bootstrap**—An open source web design framework for developing responsive, mobile-first websites that supports JavaScript, HTML, and CSS. Bootstrap includes templates and modules to create and manage forms, buttons, navigation, and typography.

Q&A

What other RWD tools exist?
As new technologies and devices become popular, RWD must adapt to meet new standards. New downloadable or cloud-based software and apps, as well as plug-ins, attempt to address these changes. To learn more, use a search engine to search for *RWD tools* and filter or sort to see the most recent results.

Q&A

What else can I do to make my content mobile friendly?
Many companies and organizations, especially large e-commerce companies such as CVS create apps that users can download and use. One advantage to a mobile app includes increased user interaction because an app can include coupons or other features that users can access directly from the app, in-app purchasing, and text or other notifications. Native mobile apps are expensive to develop and maintain because they require different content and features than a website, and they must be developed separately for different devices.

Search Engine Optimization (SEO)

Introduction

As you learned in Chapter 1, the basic goal of search engine optimization (SEO) is to write content, add meta data, and design webpages that will appear high in search engine rankings. The higher your search ranking, the more likely a website visitor is to click the link to your content in the search results. As a website owner or promoter, you should always keep in mind that SEO is also about providing accessible content to your target audience, helping you reach your website goals. This appendix introduces you to how search engines rank websites, SEO techniques, SEO tools, and careers in SEO.

How Search Engines Work

Search engines use complicated, patented, ever-changing algorithms to create search rankings. **Search engine algorithms** instruct the search engine to locate and rank search results based on keywords, summary text, headings, meta data, and a variety of other factors. In addition to using programs called web crawlers or spiders to locate webpages, search engines determine relevancy of search results based on page rankings, frequency of content updates, RWD, and number of inbound and outbound hyperlinks. In addition, search engines may use analytical tools to rank search results based on factors such as number of website visitors, trending topics, and more.

Google, Bing, and other search engines keep their search engine algorithms private to prevent SEO marketers from manipulating web content to improve search rankings. Google updates its search algorithm approximately 500 times each year, requiring SEO marketers to follow best web content-writing practices rather than focusing exclusively on search engine rankings. Other trends and developments in search engine algorithms include the following:

- Personalized searches based on a user's previous search history.
- Geolocal searches that provide results targeted to a user's geographic location.
- Analysis of what terms people search for in order to improve the algorithms.
- Increased focus on social sharing, by analyzing trending and commonly shared web content on social media platforms such as Facebook and Twitter.
- Focus on natural language searches that use phrases or questions rather than keywords. For example, a keyword search might be: *SEO search engine rankings*. A natural language search for the same topic might be: *How can I use SEO to improve my search engine rankings?*
- Banning or removing webpages from the search index if they use manipulative or unethical SEO practices, such as keyword stuffing, ensuring the best search results for the users.

Q&A

What is the difference between paid search results and SEO?

The goal of SEO is to affect the visibility and accessibility of your content in unpaid search rankings. Many search engines offer opportunities to pay to sponsor, or promote, your website by matching your content with search keywords. Most search engines distinguish between search results and sponsored results.

SEO Techniques

SEO techniques constantly evolve to accommodate new search engine algorithm practices and new web technologies and tools. Just as you do not want to publish websites that no one visits, you are also not meeting your website goals if your website is high in search rankings where your content is not relevant to visitors. Make sure to focus on creating and promoting your web content in a meaningful way that increases your website's chances of meetings its goals. Common SEO techniques include the following:

- Using relevant meta data in the HTML document, such as keywords (meta tags), page descriptions, and page titles, to provide the most accurate depiction of your web content.

- Editing webpage content to include common search terms that will lead website visitors to your webpage, and placing that content in headings or at or near the top of the page.

- Adding links to and from pages within your website and to other webpages.

- Integrating your social media presence with your website by providing links to and from your profiles on different social media platforms.

- Use RWD and other mobile-first strategies to ensure your content meets the latest standards.

- Add captions, relevant filenames, alt text, and figure titles to your images to ensure that the images contribute to your SEO rankings.

SEO Tools

Many tools exist to help you prepare your websites for the highest SEO results. Some tools are free, while others require payment for their services. Popular SEO tools include Google Webmasters resources, Bing Webmaster Tools, and Open Site Explorer.
Features of SEO tools include the following:

- **Keyword and meta tag generators**—Provide suggested relevant keywords and meta tags based on your content. Some generators include common misspellings of your keywords and meta tags to ensure spelling does not keep your visitors from finding you.

- **Webpage audits**—Review your website content to ensure your keywords, content, heading, and placement will yield the highest rankings.

- **Link analysis**—Suggest additional relevant links to add to your webpages to increase your rankings.

- **Competitive research**—Take a look at your closest competitors' websites to compare your webpages and SEO results.

- **Analytics**—Provide analysis of search terms used to find your website and other measures to suggest improvements.

In addition to using a tool, you can hire SEO experts to help you with your SEO strategy and ongoing SEO marketing.

SEO Careers

SEO careers require you to have knowledge of general marketing practices and web design, as well as to keep current with web marketing trends, search engines, and social media. Most SEO jobs require a bachelor's degree and some experience with either marketing or web design or both.

A related SEO career is **search engine marketing (SEM)**. SEM uses paid and sponsored links to increase website traffic. Another area of expertise is **social media marketing (SMM)**. SMM experts use social media platforms to expand a website's audience, such as by providing valuable, relevant content on its Facebook page or using platforms such as Pinterest to entice followers to link to new products on the website.

An SEO job opportunity may require you to combine all of these skills, or have knowledge of how they all relate. Many SEO consultants and consulting companies exist to help small and large businesses with optimizing web content. In addition, many large companies who rely on web traffic to increase profits hire internal SEO experts. Some responsibilities of SEO, SEM, and SMM experts include the following:

- Creating and maintaining SEO guidelines for the website, including providing templates for web content and other digital assets.
- Using web analytics and monitoring tools to evaluate success of the website's current SEO practices, and making recommendations for improvements in content, layout, or meta data. Creating reports and providing analysis for web analytics.
- Keeping up-to-date with SEO, search engine, social media, and Internet marketing trends.
- Managing and maintaining relationships with other websites to provide mutual linking to website content.
- Evaluating search results and search performance across the major search channels, including any differences in mobile search engine algorithms.
- Comparing the success of the website with that of your competition by determining search rankings of competitive websites on different search engines.

Q&A

What are white hat and black hat SEO? White hat SEO techniques focus on creating content that will be helpful to the user. Black hat SEO includes hidden text, keyword stuffing, and other methods to manipulate search rankings. For more information, use a search engine to search for *white hat black hat SEO*.

Index

and final location and/or appearance of an image while the in-between frames are created by software. **158**

antialiasing: A technique for smoothing jagged edges by adding shaded pixels that make the image appear to have smooth lines and curves. **140**

app: Typically refers to programs that run on mobile devices (mobile apps) or the web (web apps). Apps are an integral part of Internet technology. **188**

application: Typically refers to programs that run on mobile devices (mobile apps) or the web (web apps). Apps are an integral part of Internet technology. **5**

ASP.NET Core, 29

asymmetrical: An off-balance arrangement of webpage elements that creates an energetic mood. **11**

asymmetrical digital subscriber line (ADSL): A type of DSL that supports faster transmission when receiving data than when sending data. **11**

attributes: HTML tag modifiers. **23, APP 2**

audience
  design tips, 76
  identifying website's target, 74–77

audio: Sound used to persuade, inspire, personalize, motivate, or soothe. **85**
  design tips, 85–86, 155
  editing files, 158
  streaming, 154–156
  using on webpages, 85–86

auto-rotate: Feature that changes the screen orientation from landscape (wider) or portrait (higher) depending on the angle of the screen or device. **59**

autocomplete: A website search feature that suggests terms to users as they type. **108**

avatars: An animated alternative persona or virtual identity used for MMOGs or 3D virtual worlds or who provides welcome messages, sales support, or customer support at an e-commerce site. **167, 168.** *See also* virtual identities

B

back-end web developer: An individual responsible for behind-the-scenes web technologies, such as databases, programming, and security. **30**

background audio, 155

background image: A large, banner-type image used primarily as the center image on a website's home page. **134.** *See also* hero image

backup font: Replacement font used when the browser cannot locate the font used on a webpage. Backup font in the stack ensures that all browsers can display the webpage content. **131**

balance: The harmonious arrangement of webpage elements. **47**

bandwidth: The quantity of data that can be transmitted in a specific time frame, measured in bits per second (bps). **58**

banner ad: A horizontal, rectangular webpage advertisement that links to the advertiser's website. **187**

B2B, 10

B2C, 10

benchmarking: Using a defined standard to measure overall performance, or to evaluate a specific aspect of a website. **194**

Berners-Lee, Tim, 3

beta testing: Using a prepublication version of your website, not available to the general public. **176**

beta website: A prepublication version of your website. **176**

big data: Large and complex collections of information from a variety of sources, including website statistics, e-commerce transactions, social media profiles, databases, and other personally identifiable information about a person available through public records and other sources. **63**

bit depth: A measure of audio quality; the greater the number of bits, the higher the audio quality level, but the larger the file. **156**

bitmaps: Images that are created pixel by pixel. **139.** *See also* raster images
  formats and file extensions (table), 139

blog: An online diary or journal to which readers can add their own commentary. **6**
  creating, 165–166
  design tips, 168

blogging: Hosting and participating in blogs. **6**

Bluetooth: A popular, short-range wireless connection that uses a radio frequency to transmit data between two electronic devices, such as a smartphone and an earpiece. **11**

bookmark: A saved link to a webpage. **4.** *See also* favorite